**Praise for**
**INDEPENDENT VI**

"Go out immediately and buy a copy of *Independent Visions*. Donald Lyons and his book are informative, illuminating, and entertaining."
—Fran Lebowitz
Author of *Metropolitan Life*

"*Independent Visions* is a valuable reference—a who's who of today's independent filmmaking, filled with illuminating information and a few surprises. Donald Lyons writes with the zeal of a true film lover."
—Mason Wiley
Co-author of *Inside Oscar*

"Donald Lyons is a great critic. *The* cultural polymath, he is incomparable in cinematic discourse."
—James McCourt
Author of *Time Remaining*

"If, like me, you don't usually read this kind of book (a survey), read this one. It's different. There's no academic jargon here—and on the other hand, no fan magazine trivia. If you are interested in Mr. Lyons' subject, you will enjoy his crisp, witty, perceptive writing and learn something too—I did."
—Eric Bentley
Author of *What Is Theatre?* and *Are You Now or Have You Ever Been?*

# *I*ndependent *V*isions

## A Critical Introduction to Recent Independent American Film

## Donald Lyons

BALLANTINE BOOKS • NEW YORK

All rights reserved under International and Pan-American
Copyright Conventions. Published in the United States by Ballantine
Books, a division of Random House, Inc., New York, and
simultaneously in Canada by Random House of Canada
Limited, Toronto.

Grateful acknowledgment is made to Random House, Inc. for
permission to reprint an excerpt from "Orpheus, Eurydice,
Hermes" from *Selected Poetry of Rainer Maria Rilke,* edited and
translated by Stephen Mitchell. Copyright © 1982 by Stephen Mitchell.

Library of Congress Catalog Card Number: 93-90471

ISBN: 0-345-38249-8

Cover design by Christina Rannacher
Designed by Ann Gold

Manufactured in the United States of America

10 9 8 7 6 5 4 3 2

PARENTIBUS OPTIMIS

"It was that windless hour of dawn when madness wakes and strange plants open to the light and the moth flies forth silently."

—James Joyce
*A Portrait of the Artist as a Young Man*

# Contents

# Preface

*I*t is much easier to agree that this is a rich and productive moment for American independent filmmaking than it is to demarcate the boundaries of that field. What constitutes independent filmmaking?

On the one hand, the "independence" that it boasts is independence of the Hollywood studio system. That system is in even deeper crisis than usual both in the *way* it makes movies and in *what* it makes. The expensive and increasingly agent-driven prepackaging of material is succeeded by executive and marketing interference with that material as it is made and, not infrequently, after it is finished. To an extent, it was ever thus in Hollywood, but in the studios' salad years artists managed to make space within, and even to flourish under, the prevailing economic and structural conditions. But the content of contemporary studio product is now so infantile—at best adolescent—as to leave little room for any creativity beyond that of toy technology. So embarrassing is the crisis in self-confidence in the industry that, when a good Hollywood movie like Clint Eastwood's *Unforgiven* appears, pains are taken to assert that it is *really* an independent movie.

At the same time, good—and innovatively good—films are being made all over the country. And they are of all species, so to speak. What this book examines is fiction features. This is not to deny the importance of shorts, for most of today's long-form filmmakers were yesterday's makers of shorts, or of documentaries, which are today experiencing a period of metamorphic growth, or of what used to be called the avant-garde—purely formal experimenters. These are no longer completely separate entities; there is much cross-fertilization between, say, feature and documentary and avant-garde. But they are separable for the purposes of a study like this.

The selection of filmmakers within these parameters is not exhaustive or encyclopedic, but a serious attempt has been made to be thorough and representative.

One of the most evident realities of vital filmmaking today is its decentralized, its regional, nature. And so the rough—sometimes very rough—organizing dynamic of the study was geographical, beginning with Northeastern filmmakers, going on to the Midwest and thence to California and thence to the Northwest and to Canada. A chapter at the end gathers some eccentric films in special "dialects," but in truth very many of the films throughout the book are eccentric and employ a unique dialect. This may, indeed, be the place to remark on the consistent brilliance of the dialogue and the wording in these films, very often, but far from always, the product of the film-

maker herself or himself and sometimes the result of
collaborative freedom accorded intelligent performers. At
any rate, the book, like more than one of the movies it
looks at, is on the road, but with many detours and diver-
sions.

The backgrounds of the filmmakers are as varied as
life. Some went to film school; some, defiantly, did not.
A number studied something other than film—often art—
in school. And the lived lives—female, male; African-
American, Hispanic, Asian; gay, straight—are present in
the made art. Most directors have had to scrabble together
the financing—for their early projects, anyway—from
family or friends or savings or a mosaic of grants. Some
have gone on not so much to *be* co-opted by the studios
as to themselves co-opt studios (think of *Malcolm X*);
some remain aggressively marginal.

The variety of these artistic sensibilities is amazing;
one of the few things they mostly share is a visual and
verbal sureness—amounting to audacity—in seizing the
screen. There is often a modernist awareness of the
screen as screen, and a willingness to bring the resources
of poetic play to the narrative enterprise. These are the
grandchildren of the Golden Age filmmakers and the
children of the independent pioneers; they can draw on
Golden Age film easily, unlike some Seventies directors
who seemed oedipally compelled to remake Golden Age
work, but these filmmakers have, too, the guts of their
parents.

*T*here is included a full roster of winners of the Independent Spirit Awards (very roughly, the independent Os-

cars) from their inception in 1985 through 1992. And there are filmographies of the directors treated.

*I*t is a pleasure to thank two editors who have encouraged me to write about film. Annie Flanders, founder and editor of *Details,* made room for writing in a fashion magazine. But then Annie's was an innovative concept of fashion in the first place.

Richard Jameson, editor of *Film Comment,* approaches the platonic ideal of an editor. Scholar, appreciator, savorer of what is lovely or juicy in film, he has a sharp eye for any nonsense that might be uttered about film. All the more fun to make him laugh. He and his brilliant wife, Kathleen Murphy, embody, in themselves and in their hospitable warmth, a community irradiated by love of film.

A small part of the material herein appeared in an earlier form in *Film Comment.*

There is nothing like an editor with unfailing good humor and a deep knowledge of the material to actually get an author to write a book. There is nothing like Joe Blades at Ballantine Books. He liked the idea from the start.

I also want to thank Alexander Krieckhaus for making clean copy out of a messy manuscript.

For taking a little time to talk, I am grateful to Stacy Cochran, Gus Van Sant, Christopher Münch, John O'Brien, Roger Hedden, Tony Chan, Nick Gomez, James LeGros, and River Phoenix.

# Independent
# Visions

# CHAPTER ONE

# *A*round New York

There is an America out there full of what John Dryden called the "sad variety" of life—the funny variety, too, one must add. And it is this America that is being represented in the jerry-built, my-uncle-lent-me-the-money crazy quilt of independent film. Hollywood is most comfortable as a factory of technical effects *(Jurassic Park, Batman, Under Siege, Lethal Weapon, Bram Stoker's Dracula, Beauty and the Beast)* that are self-contained and self-referential and do not touch life. And when the studio films do grope toward life, as in the sentimental *Driving Miss Daisy* or the earnest *Grand Canyon,* or toward sex, as in designer porn like *Basic Instinct* or *Indecent Proposal,* there still remains the feeling that, as James Agee once remarked of a Hollywood film, one is allowed to see "just so much of the Id as could be safely displayed in a Bergdorf Goodman window."

Filmmaking and film distribution and film recognition are increasingly decentralized and democratized in

America. It is a good time for independents with a vision of, and a knowledge of, some corner of life and art. Art is not, of course, sociology—still less geography—but a way into this burgeoning filmmaking field is to look at some cinematic poets of life in, first, the New York area. It is, after all, an area rich in filmic tradition.

D. W. Griffith got things going in the decade before World War I—at Biograph Studios on Fourteenth Street. There was a large underground scene in the 1950s and 1960s, as witness Andy Warhol and Paul Morrissey—and John Cassavetes, in the discussion of whose work the subtle shift from the term *underground* to the more respectable *independent* can be observed.

John Cassavetes was the quintessential pioneer in independent cinema. His mode was set in *Shadows* (1959), which was about a light-skinned African-American woman in Manhattan discovering racism in her white lover when she stops "passing," and in *Faces* (1968), which chronicled the drunken and maudlin adulteries of salesmen and business types and their wives. In black-and-white, with rough camera technique and improvisatory, let-it-all-hang-out acting by a regular troupe that included Peter Falk, Seymour Cassel, and Gena Rowlands, Cassavetes' films were unmistakable for anyone else's. He used long, relentless, blowsy, improvised takes as a tool to expose the shakiness of middle-class life. He counterpointed what he saw as extremes of concealment with extremes of exposure. A later exercise in diagnostic improvisation like Abel Ferrara's *Bad Lieutenant* owes a debt to Cassavetes. *Overlong* and *self-indulgent* are words don, Spike is thrown out of his home and his gym and migrates from the manicured Italian lawns of Benson-hurst to the inferno of Red Hook, depicted here as a Puerto Rican ghetto terrorized by cracklords.

It is here that Spike comes into his own, allying himself with a decent Puerto Rican family (mother a schoolteacher, son an honest boxer, daughter a beauty named India) in a blazing, Guardian Angel–style campaign to reform the 'hood. He reforms the family diet with gentle words ("Lay off the fried foods"), he reforms a crack den with a baseball bat, he reforms public school education by taking kids out of the toilet (literally, a toilet) in which they are forced to attend classes to a huge, dry, pastel-painted pool nearby, he reforms the curriculum (which has consisted entirely of fashionable subjects such as sex hygiene and ethnic history) by substituting patriotic chestnuts like Emma Lazarus's Statue of Liberty poem, "The New Colossus," and the pledge of allegiance. A hilarious and irresponsible mix of Allan Bloom and Julia Child, Spike brings his reactionary nostrums to bear upon the cancers of anarchic hedonism.

Our last glimpse of Spike sees him settled down in Red Hook a few years later, playing with his two half-Spanish kids (he has married India) and wearing a cop's uniform. That a figure like Spike should find a vocation in the police force is both a comic paradox and a tiny sign of hope. The humdrumly happy domesticity of Spike echoes the similarly bittersweet coda of Elia Kazan's *Splendor in the Grass*. Talisa Soto as the sultry India and Sasha Mitchell as Spike, with his gangly walk and his one-way-ticket-

frequently used to describe Cassavetes' films, and there is justice in those characterizations. But he never indulges in excess for greed's sake, only for honesty's sake.

Andy Warhol's innovatory function in cinema was to create a space for the marginal types of New York in the late 1960s. Literally, he rented a series of spaces, decorated in silver foil and collectively dubbed The Factory, where his crowd might assemble and be passively photographed. It remained for his collaborator, Paul Morrissey, to bring to Warhol's inert observations of things (e.g., *Empire,* a day in the life of the Empire State Building) and behavior (e.g., *Blow Job*) a degree of visual sophistication and narrative order.

In the early Sixties Morrissey, born in 1938 and a graduate of Fordham University, had made experimental silent shorts on the Lower East Side; he was then a card-carrying member of the downtown avant-garde that showed its work in storefronts or at Jonas Mekas's Ciné-mathèque on Avenue B. The films were sharp little street stories. One, called *Mary Martin Does It,* after the legend on a celebrity antilitter poster, had a scowling youth scouring the East Village for bums to shovel into the back of garbage trucks. His longest early work, *Civilization and Its Discontents,* takes its title from Freud and shows a panorama of anecdotes such as a heroically handsome horseman kicking a cripple in Central Park, a pea-jacketed thug strangling a fat retarded albino in Cooper Square, a willowy youth with a flower in his hand watching without emotion as a girl jumps into the Hudson River. The remote, mocking, Nietzschean wit of these images is oddly counterpointed by the dreamy lyricism of the photography.

Morrissey then spent some seven years at the Warhol Court, emerging to make feature-length, lower-depth farces on his own in *Flesh* (1968) and *Trash* (1970). On one level, they were Hogarthian looks at the life of the Lower East Side, calmly taking place in a milieu of prostitution and addiction. On another, they were traditional bourgeois comedies in the vein of Michael Curtiz's *Four Daughters*.

What is funny in them is funny precisely because this isn't the way people, and families especially, are supposed to behave. Morrissey has an Irish feel for the centrality and normality of the old-fashioned nuclear family. When the wife (Geraldine Smith), in *Flesh*, tells her male-hustler husband (Joe Dallesandro) to get out and hustle to raise money for her girlfriend's abortion, we laugh at this crazy new mix of ethical standards. This outré nonsense can coexist with a pretty vignette of Joe feeding crumbs to his baby.

The idea of family is equally key in *Trash:* when the transvestite (brilliantly played by Holly Woodlawn) collects garbage and uses beer bottles for sex, it is with a dream of family and normalcy in her mind. She wants to get back on welfare and live like a family with her junkie boyfriend, who has been rendered impotent by dope (Dallesandro in another superbly cinematic, minimalist performance). In parodying family, Morrissey had affirmed its importance; Holly's ratty home was in fact an island of affection and human feeling amid a carnival of cold,

rich uptowners, acid-head nymphos, and drugged go-go girls.

*Spike of Bensonhurst* (1988) marked Morrissey's return to local comedy after two films in Italy *(Andy Warhol's Dracula* and *Andy Warhol's Frankenstein),* one in Vienna (the underrated *Beethoven's Nephew*), and two noncomic films made about New York's lower depths: the filmed play *Forty Deuce* about desperate hustlers looking to get rid of a corpse, and *Mixed Blood,* about, characteristically, a family of drug dealers ruled with an iron fist by a matriarch (the superb Marilia Pera). *Spike* presents a society as destructive, chaotic, and hellish as—but bigger than—the sordid pockets of *Trash.* In deepest Brooklyn, the only surviving social mechanism is the Mafia, but it is riddled with corruption—that is, it is attempting to go legit, to launder its crack money into real estate, the pockets of liberal politicians, and videocassette stores. (Morrissey cowrote *Spike* with *Forty Deuce* playwright Alan Bowne.)

A Mafia don (Ernest Borgnine) is a man of the old crooked school at heart, but he has forced himself to accommodate the latest yuppie look in Mafiosi by engaging his daughter to a bland preppie. The true tribal code lives in Spike, a handsome neighborhood kid who wants nothing more than to live by the old goombah values such as taking dives in the ring when ordered to do so and stealing a bit from his numbers route and marrying the don's daughter. But history has passed Spike by—boxing is no longer an Italian game, the don's daughter is a slut, his own mother is savagely unfeeling, his dad is in Sing Sing. After impregnating the daughter and alienating the

to-Palookaville bumptiousness, both register strongly in
the film. Morrissey tells his story with a fluidity that
never prettifies but does hold out a promise of beauty
amid so much waste. The Italian songs of Pupo and Mas-
simo Ranieri also cut the surrounding sourness. Morrissey has achieved a combination of Kazanian punch
with slapstick energy; it's neorealist farce.

*A*cross the river in New Jersey, John Sayles has emerged
as an independent director of political and social scope,
as a man who tries to make sense of life. His work is
marked by a strong and sober social conscience often,
however, laced with a rich humor of character. Born in
Schenectady, New York, in 1950, Sayles went to Williams College in Massachusetts. After college, he traveled
the states working such jobs as meat packer, day laborer,
and hospital orderly. Sayles's first artistic vocation was
writing; he has always been publishing collections of
short stories; his second novel, *Union Dues,* was nominated for a National Book Award.

Early on, Sayles took an interest in screenwriting and
hooked up with not Andy Warhol but Roger Corman's
New World Pictures, for whom he wrote *Piranha* in 1978,
a cheapo nature-gone-nutty thriller directed by Joe Dante
that verged on being a *Jaws* parody. Striking a theme that
will recur in his later work, Sayles has greedy develop-
ers—here, of a potentially dangerous resort hotel—put
profits before human concerns. The tone may be light, but
the point is made.

The next year saw Sayles writing a film for Corman

called *The Lady in Red;* it was a low-budget feminist gangster movie, telling the story of John Dillinger's moll (Pamela Sue Martin) from her point of view; the film, incidentally, was retitled *Guns, Sin and Bathtub Gin* for video.

In 1980, Sayles wrote, again for Corman, *Battle Beyond the Stars,* in which a peaceful alien (Richard Thomas) seeks help for his planet, threatened by an evil emperor. Once more, Sayles brought to these familiar and cynical genres an optimism and a multicultural awareness that infused new life.

In 1981, he brought his touch to the writing of yet another genre piece—this time the horror flick *The Howling.* Along with an affectionate teasing of Northern California New Age encounter groups, there were genuine werewolf thrills in this Joe Dante move. Sayles has a cameo as a morgue attendant; in 1993, he was to have a cameo in his friend Dante's fine comedy *Matinee.* As a phony fundamentalist protester against scary movies, he snarls, "There's no First Amendment to the Ten Commandments."

By now a master of the slightly-tongue-in-cheek genre quickie script, he had earned from Corman enough money to start his own debut film as a director. With $60,000 of his own money, he made *Return of the Secaucus Seven,* which dealt with a weekend reunion of seven idealistic Sixties types commemorating their unjust arrest (in that comic-sounding Jersey town) on the way to Washington to participate in the very last demonstration ever held against the Vietnam War. In its leisurely exposition of character and its bittersweet contrast of adulthood's responsibilities with youth's unfettered dreams, *Secaucus Seven* anticipated a keynote of the 1980s, as later sounded in *The Big Chill* and the TV series *Thirtysomething* (set in nearby Philadelphia).

The film was a success, winning for Sayles the Best Screenplay Award from the Los Angeles Film Critics. This precise award signaled the centrality of literary composition to Sayles's film career. Throughout the decade, he made (and wrote) films sometimes financed entirely by himself (*Secaucus Seven, The Brother from Another Planet*) and sometimes financed from various outside (but never Hollywood) sources. They were always the films he wanted to make; a prickly independence of character shone through them. And not only did Sayles write and direct; he often acted juicy smallish roles in the films himself.

In 1983, his second film, *Lianna*, dealt with a Jersey housewife of that name (Linda Griffiths) who escapes a confining marriage by finding herself in love with a woman professor of child psychology (Jane Halloren). Sayles appears as a horny professor. What is remarkable in *Lianna* is the empathetic capturing by writer and director Sayles of—not only lesbianism as such—but of the emotional rhythms and inner structures, not male-centered, of a woman.

Also in 1983, Sayles made a cute Romeo-and-Juliet love tale, set in dreary Trenton, New Jersey, around 1966. In *Baby, It's You* we meet a signature device of two generations of filmmakers, emanating from Martin Scorsese's

*Mean Streets* in 1973 and George Lucas's *American Graffiti* in 1973: the use, sometimes ironic, sometimes not, of pop/rock tunes as soundtrack accompaniment. The film tells how a dashing but flaky working-class Italian Catholic boy (Vincent Spano) chases after a middle-class Jewish girl (Rosanna Arquette), who has gone to college after their high-school fling. Coproducer Amy Robinson wrote the story, which was essentially a teen flick given edge by explicitness about class, religion, and money.

In 1984, Sayles made *The Brother from Another Planet*, about a black space fugitive (Joe Morton) who crashlands his saucer in New York Harbor, swims ashore on Ellis Island, and soon winds up in Harlem. (Sayles himself plays a space cop hunting the Brother.) The basic gimmick of the narrative is that folks mistake the hero's mute deadpan for profound wisdom. A busy subplot involving drug dealers is finally only distracting; indeed, as one looks at reaction to early Sayles films, phrases like "the film goes on a bit too long" or "the script loses momentum" or "it falls apart toward the end" tend to pop up frequently. Sayles has been, in fact, a better cinematic short-story writer than he has been a novelist; he can conceive a deft and novel attack on sociopolitical cliché—what if E.T. were black?; what if Nelly Normal, housewife, suddenly turned gay?—but the structural follow-through has sometimes been missing.

In the late 1980s Sayles filmed two historical stories—one from 1919 and one from 1920—about dramatic injustices in American history. *Matewan,* made in 1986 in West Virginia for four million dollars, dealt with a coal miner's strike in Matewan, West Virginia. Sayles's script, supplemented by some made-up labor songs he also wrote for the soundtrack, has a compassionate tone, a socialist idealism, and a slightly generic flavor that recall the John Steinbeck of *In Dubious Battle* and *The Grapes of Wrath*. It was an ensemble piece with a large cast that included Chris Cooper as a gentle union organizer (a typically Saylesian paradox); James Earl Jones as a black labor leader inadvertently, and tragically, decoyed by management into playing the role of scab; David Strathairn as the town constable looking to avoid violence; and Mary McDonnell as a sympathetic boardinghouse owner. Tenderly photographed by Haskell Wexler, *Matewan* was an unabashed homage to the heroic, martyr years of American labor, a subject dear to Sayles's heart. Its big canvas showed a working class kept unnaturally apart and cruelly provoked to violence by an owner class eager to exploit racial and ethnic antagonisms—a topic that recurs in the cinema of John Sayles.

In 1987, Sayles filmed *Eight Men Out*, about the 1919 Chicago White Sox baseball players who took money from gamblers to throw the World Series. Known as the Black Sox, they were expelled from the sport in disgrace. Sayles is, not surprisingly, sympathetic to the working-stiff players, cruelly underpaid by tycoon/owner Charles Comiskey. Taken from a book by Eliot Asinof, the Sayles script highlights the fate of Shoeless Joe Jackson (David Strathairn), an illiterate and possibly innocent victim and a beautiful ballplayer. Sayles himself played sports reporter and short-story ace Ring Lardner, a dream combo, doubtless, for him. The slenderness of the budget is visible, as Sayles himself cheerfully points out, in the tiny Jersey ball park standing in for Comiskey Park. Sayles said he had at most, and for one day only, a thousand extras, who had to be strategically positioned for a third-base-angled shot.

Sayles's dauntless bravery in tackling epic subjects on luncheonette budgets reached a climax in the 1991 *City of Hope*, which sets out to be nothing less than a top-to-bottom panorama of a midsized American city. The city, unnamed in the film, is clearly modeled on New Jersey melting pots like Hoboken, where Sayles lives and which has undergone gentrification in recent years, or Jersey City, which remains more of a decaying machine burg in painful transit from white to black domination.

*City of Hope* is a film about construction in every sense. Its Italians—father Tony Lo Bianco and restless son Vincent Spano—are *in* construction; blacks want *in* the construction unions. Parallels abound in the symphony that is Sayles's city. (*Symphony of Six Million* was the title of a 1932 Depression movie that contrasted Park Avenue with the Lower East Side, then a Jewish quarter.) Decent black councilman Joe Morton has to hold off his hotheads and demagogues while securing justice and well-being for his constituency. The cops on the beat, Irish and Italian, are more or less racist; the top cop brass are political and corrupt; the white mayor is a suave crook; two Catholic women complain, like a Greek chorus, throughout the movie about crime and welfare and ''them'' to stoic (but secretly simpatico) cops; a schizo (David Strathairn) endlessly babbles lyrics and slogans from ads.

Troubled son Spano gets dragooned by two moronic pals into a stupid robbery to get their rock band a speaker; they're caught. In a parallel universe that is in reality contiguous, two black youths, humiliated for no reason whatsoever by cops, turn their rage on a white jogger, whom they mug and then falsely accuse of a homosexual advance (echoes here of both the Tawana Brawley hoax and the Central Park jogger case). The councilman, whose wife is a colleague of the jogger's at the high school where both teach, pretty much knows the kids are lying but dare not say so publicly in the face of local militants.

And so it goes. The city is a mosaic of frustrations and misunderstandings. In its midst, a love flowers between feckless doper Spano and spunky divorcée Barbara Williams, whose ex is a violently jealous cop by whom she has had a severely disabled son. Sayles brings the new pair together in gradually intensifying and isolating two-shots in a club where Spano's band is playing. He walks her home through streets flecked with pools of street-lights intensely lit by photographer Robert Richardson. This time Sayles has cast himself as crippled garage owner Carl, an all-purpose nasty villain he visibly relishes playing.

The plot comes to center on a project inhabited by black and Hispanic squatters; the mayor wants it torched for gentrification and prevails on Lo Bianco (using as black-mail his son's arrest) to arrange the arson. Spano knows what his father has done, for he has seen the son of the family's Hispanic cook die in the fire and met his father's eyes during the blaze; all his illusions topple, as he learns from the vicious Carl that his heroic older brother, dead in Vietnam, actually joined up only to escape jail for killing a woman and crippling Carl while driving drunk. Spano has a moment of sweet camaraderie shooting hoops in the twilight with a black guy who knew his brother and was also in Nam, but the mood evaporates with the light, and he is shortly shot by the jealous cop and, dying, confronts his father about their trashed lives atop a construction site. The father yells for help, but his cry is heard only by the madman, who reiterates the cry uncomprehendingly.

But amid this triumph of unreason, gestures of hope are made. The accusing kid comes by the teacher's home to apologize; they jog in the evening. ("What is it you teach?" "Urban relations." "What's that?") The councilman takes his angry constituents to invade a white-power dinner in order to save their neighborhood from expropriating gentrifiers—a concern voiced very explicitly also by John Singleton in his much rougher *Boyz N the Hood*. *City of Hope* is a brave and humanist canvas, but once again Sayles's melodies are more successful than his architecture. Those resolutions—the angry march, the apologizing kid, even the twilight hoop shoot—seem wishful thinking. But the more important feat is that Sayles, like John Singleton and Spike Lee, is striving to put the urban experience of today, the angry cities we actually live in, into art.

*Passion Fish*, his 1992 film, is Sayles in a private frame

of mind; it's his most intimate movie since *Lianna* and, like *Lianna,* it concentrates on the emotional life of a woman. A woman in a bed in a postop fog turns out to be a soap star slammed by a taxi on her way to have her legs waxed; she is rendered paralyzed from the waist down. May-Alice swims back to consciousness watching her own soap on TV and muttering, "He gave her my fucking close-up." Asked by a patronizingly purring voice if she knows who and where she is, May-Alice snaps back, "She [her soap character] had amnesia, not me." Clearly, a bitter cookie. And when she falls and curses in rehab, it seems likely we are in for a triumph-over-adversity scenario with anger yielding to acceptance. And we are, but not in the way we might think.

The rehab strategy May-Alice chooses is to go home again. Home is the vacant Louisiana house she grew up in, on the edge of a bayou. In *Passion Fish,* Sayles worked for the first time with British cinematographer Roger Deakins, who shot *Barton Fink* for the Coen brothers and *Homicide* for David Mamet. Deakins has a bright, bravura optical style that he employs here beautifully to convey the lonely roads and lazy waters of this rural setting. And it matters, for the local ecology is May-Alice's therapeutic agent; the very places she had fled so eagerly in headlong dash from an oppressive provincialism are now healers. But a human hand is needed, too. Finding the right nurse/dogsbody/friend is a trial for the monumentally cranky May-Alice, she runs through, in a hilarious montage, a martinet (dubbed promptly "Elsa, She Beast of the Gulag"), a motormouth, a weeper, a biker moll, and more. At last, a tentative waif-type called Chantelle (Alfre Woodard) shows up and seems to possess a workable mix of intelligence, guts, and tolerance. Still, though, the stark loneliness and pain of May-Alice, given voice in a bathtub wail and superbly imaged in an overhead shot of her wheelchair, abide.

Local fauna pop in, trying to relieve; they succeed only in annoying. There's an effete, alcoholic uncle out of Beth Henley, who does, however, show May-Alice a shed that used to be a photographic darkroom and thus gives her an idea. She takes to the camera, the still camera, as a return to creativity, a banisher of idleness, a saving instrument of curiosity. Two bitchy girlhood chums (this time out of Tennessee Williams) called Ti-Maria and Precious drip nastiness about Chantelle and "the colored" in general. This scene, with May-Alice writhing in contempt on a hot noon lawn, is very comic. That night, May and Chantelle watch *Whatever Happened to Baby Jane?* and laugh. This is Sayles at his best, desentimentalizing the bonding that is springing up between the two women by a reference to a grotesque version of it.

Both women find local romance, of a sort. Chantelle is courted, and won, by a middle-aged, much-divorced blacksmith, musician, and overall charmer named Sugar (Vondie Curtis-Hall). At first Chantelle is wary; it is only when she sees Sugar's easy rapport with his teenaged daughter—not to mention with his horses ("I'm a blacksmith." "You're a black something.")—that she relaxes with Sugar.

A more difficult encounter still is that between May-

Alice and Rennie (David Strathairn), a formerly sexy high-school heartthrob. Rennie is now a carpenter (he shows up to build her a ramp) with five kids, a religious-nut wife, and a swell flat-bottomed boat. When Chantelle asks if he is "white trash," May-Alice says no, he's swamp Cajun—"It's more complicated than that." Here speaks Sayles's unusually delicate feel for the nuances of class, place, and gender in America. And David Strathairn, a durable Sayles regular, does not turn Rennie into a cutie pie; he is not an Armani model in stubble and denim but a man weathered and a bit beaten by life while still gentle and attractive. May-Alice feels stirrings of the heart in his company, while being brutally and explicitly frank to Chantelle about the range of sexual possibilities open to her.

Alone one night, she watches an inane TV evangelist; religion is not a useful consolation in Sayles's world. When Chantelle returns at dawn from a night with Sugar, it is to have a fight with May-Alice about aspects of Chantelle's hidden past that have been surfacing. A druggie has strolled up to May-Alice on the dock and asked about Chantelle; there had been a detox episode and a sense of past waste. The women make up when May-Alice cooks up a spectacular Cajun dinner; Chantelle cannot cook—a nice Sayles touch, bringing a note of surprise and subversion to the boss-employee formula.

A serious intrusion from the outside world descends: the black woman director and two white actresses from May-Alice's soap in New York. They are full of gossip, some of it unwelcome to May, and actor-babble. It is altogether a much friendlier imposition than that of Ti-Marie and Precious; in a privileged moment nicely compounded of affection and mockery, one actress tells a very funny story of an early show-biz humiliation involving sense memory and an anal probe. But by now the flow of the narrative and the power of the images (some of them made by the character May-Alice herself) have moved things forever away from any possibility of a return (even, as she is later offered, in the role of a blind and comatose paralytic) to New York show biz.

There is, during this visit, a lovely moment in the kitchen between the two black women: they discover they're both Chicagoans, but Chantelle is from a much posher section, being the daughter of a doctor. It is a sociologically rich aperçu, tossed off by Sayles, but in fact more rewarding in later contemplation than the labored ironies of even a well-intentioned Hollywood film like Lawrence Kasdan's *Grand Canyon*.

Two boat trips—one by day, one by night—into the depths of the swamp seal May-Alice and Rennie's friendship. The fauna of the place rise to visibility and importance; Chantelle is afraid of snakes, Rennie catches and opens some passion fish, an owl looks at the gibbous moon. On the haunted isle of Misère, a child's dream recalls to Chantelle her own "lost" child, who is restored temporarily to her—a shy, plain girl—when her solemn and serious father arrives for a trial visit. These almost wordless trips into the alien and watery world serve also for May-Alice, besides being introductions to the guiding skills of Rennie, as Orphic/Eurydicean journeys into the unconscious and the impersonal. One thinks, watching their images of wonder, of Rilke's words about Eurydice: "She was already loosened like long hair, poured out like fallen rain. . . . She was already root."[1]

May-Alice is under the spell of her natal place; a rebirth of soul has come to pass. And in Mary McDonnell's tart performance the character's intelligence holds all easy answers or consolations at bay—while accepting some difficult ones. She finally tells Rennie to visit—and soon. She tells Chantelle, in the film's final words, "You're going to have to learn to cook."

*Passion Fish* is Sayles's most adequately realized film to date. In narrowing his focus, he has achieved depth of character and an unhurried trust in imagery itself. With no loss in human or social meaning, *Passion Fish* breathes artistically.

Fittingly, Sayles has made, in the bars and on the streets of New Jersey, three music videos for the Jersey laureate, Bruce Springsteen. "Born in the U.S.A.," "I'm on Fire," and "Glory Days" are evocations of the economic and psychic misery suffered by working-class victims of the Vietnam War and of home-front, rust-belt unemployment. Sayles has received the John Cassavetes Award for accomplishment in independent filmmaking—a fitting tribute, although Sayles's qualities of balance, irony, and control are in a way the temperamental antithesis of Cassavetes' trademark refusals to put any bounds on rage, anger, madness.

[1]Trans. Stephen Mitchell.

*M*ore in the Cassavetes tradition is Abel Ferrara, an artist of extravagance, of transgression, of outrage. Born in New York City, he started in high school with 8mm shorts. He graduated to features in 1979, around the time Sayles began. *The Driller Killer* starred Ferrara himself (he used the moniker Jimmy Laine) as a rejected suitor turned psycho killer. *Ms. 45,* from 1981, featured Zoe Tamerlaine Lund, billed as Zoe Tamerlis, as a mute raped twice in one day and turned by this unpleasantness into a vigilante manslayer. At first her targets are pornographers, pimps, and street whistlers, but later her rage turns against male desire as such. When she sees an Asian youth kissing his girl, she pursues him. (He escapes.) Even a male dog, belonging to a classically nosy neighbor (Editta Sherman), gets her attention. (He escapes, too.) A masked Halloween dance gives her the opportunity for a climactic rampage. Dressed in a nun's habit, she lets every masked male in her sights have it.

With these over-the-top stylistic and iconic conceits Ferrara hit his stride and bid for the mantle of Samuel Fuller, bold grabber of the filmic Id.

Ferrara's *Fear City* (1984) was a largely conventional thriller about the hunt for a go-go-dancer–slashing psycho in downtown Manhattan. A mild innovation (in the tradition of Fritz Lang's *M*) was to have for hunter-hero a member of the underworld: a tormented goon (Tom Berenger) in love with a junkie dancer (Melanie Griffith) and given to asking, in an expressionistically shot Catholic church, forgiveness for murder *before* he commits the crime. *China Girl* (1987) was a Romeo-and-Juliet tale about a boy from little Italy (Richard Panebianco) and a girl from Chinatown (Sari Chang) who die picturesquely. Neither film was much of an advance on *Ms. 45*. Sayles, too, had done a feminist film and a Romeo-and-Juliet tale.

In the 1980s Ferrara sharpened his eye for vice and crime by directing two episodes of Michael Mann's visually innovative TV series *Miami Vice* and by directing, again for Mann, the pilot for *Crime Story*. Sayles's TV work, by contrast, ran more to serious expose dramas about Agent Orange and to the series *Shannon's Deal*, about a deliberately unglamorous lawyer fighting big business and other big corruption.

In 1989, Ferrara directed Elmore Leonard's *Cat Chaser*, a film that was never released theatrically. *Cat Chaser* is, amid much else, a James M. Cain-esque story about George Moran (Peter Weller), a guy who owns a hotel in Pompano Beach and cleans his own pool, and Mary Delaney (Kelly McGillis), the woman he loves who is married to an evil rich guy who used to be the head torturer in the Dominican Republic. When he asks, "Why did you marry that creep?" and she answers, "I like being rich," we know what line of country we're in and we expect a standard noir tale. But *Cat Chaser* has some surprises up its pretty sleeve: after the best sex scene on the recent screen, Mary and George make a happy ending for themselves, kissing on a balcony with all the bad guys dead and the money in a neat suitcase. *Cat Chaser* has its problems (muddy narrative, inept voice-over), but Peter Weller and a blonde McGillis have never glowed more invitingly. And it is a great Florida movie, in Anthony Richmond's blinding, blue-on-white, Hockney-meets-noir images of pools and sun-blanched walls and far-off sea. To my eye, it looks and feels better than that other Florida noir of the 1980s, Lawrence Kasdan's *Body Heat*.

In 1990 Ferrara reunited with screenwriter Nicholas St. John on *King of New York,* an impudent fable proposing an elegant drug dealer as the fit savior of a rotten town—*cool* as a redemptive force. *King of New York* was Ferrara's bring-it-all-together work, a dense, energized, sexy, funny, deconstructive ode to big-city metabolisms. The subjects are drug lords and ambiguously virtuous cops and tribal explosions—topics as familiar in film today as flowers and beloveds in Elizabethan sonnets. But Ferrara handles it all with twilight verve, like Robert Aldrich creating *Kiss Me Deadly* at the very end of the golden cycle of film noir.

The king of the title is Frank White (Christopher Walken), a smooth drug lord just out of prison. He sets about reestablishing his various empires in the night worlds of uptown and downtown. His base of operations is the Plaza Hotel, a delightful choice for this Trump of crime. He sashays through its Ivana-gilt lobbies guilt-lessly and swans along its vistaed balconies to the music of Vivaldi. Frank White (in what is by far Walken's most amused and appealing screen performance) is a genuine charmer and wit, at home in uptown power circles but really coming to life in the darknesses of downtown. Flanked by two female bodyguards, one black and one white, and relying on streety henchman Jimmy Jump

(Larry Fishburne), he glides sharklike through fathoms of evil. He deals with a traditional Mafia social club with dispatch; the next threat is a Chinese warlord glimpsed watching *Nosferatu*, the silent Dracula classic (a deft allusion to the contemporary function of drugs). The threats are eliminated as easily as breathing.

White takes well to underground, too; he likes subways—he almost fucks and actually kills while riding underground. It is worth noting that, in a Ferrara film, we can be sure the filmmakers know which subway line the characters are on and where they will get off—Frank's final stop is Times Square on the 7 line. And the music downtown and underground switches to aggressive, macho rap.

Running parallel to White's power lines are cops, themselves no moral bargains. A trio of them (older white Victor Argo, young black Wesley Snipes, young white David Caruso—all in powerful form) haunt and manhandle and mess with White after baiting him about getting AIDS in prison. If they are not angels, they have their decencies and their frustrations are understandingly portrayed. Argo, dying, is sadly resigned to things; Caruso is a hothead whom we see presiding boisterously at an Irish wedding reception (a warmly authentic scene). When Caruso sees White being honored on TV by the New York cultural and political establishment for his donations to a children's hospital, he snaps and triggers the final savage, surreal clashes between king and cops.

These last scenes, full of death and silences and love between partners, are almost abstract, geometric, poetic, like the final shoot-out in *Lady from Shanghai* (1948). Ferrara shoots the gunplay chastely. There are no exploding heads. People shot in the chest walk long distances concealing their woundedness, as in old movies. These are true collisions of fate, duels of destiny, exciting no thrill and leaving no hope or lesson except their own beauty. In this, they differ from Quentin Tarantino's violence in *Reservoir Dogs,* for Tarantino really invites a prolonged awareness of blood.

"I've been reformed, I want to be mayor," says Frank, dimly echoing Shakespeare's Prince Hal. A friend is skeptical: "I thought people like you did not believe in the legal system." "I thought people like me *were* the legal system," answers Frank. He is soon seen first-nighting at the ballet, where, prophetically and hilariously, the ballet features cops gyrating near a bridge under blue strobe lights.

*King of New York* is Ferrara and St. John's wittiest and richest film by far. It is also the best acted overall, down to such bits as Steve Buscemi's "chemist" and Giancarlo Esposito's "accountant." With his minions and persecutors all slain, Frank White dies in a taxi, surrounded by cops, in Times Square. A taxi is a pathetically bourgeois place for him to die; he would doubtless have preferred one of his usual modes of transportation: a dark stretch limo or a fluorescent subway car.

There are pleasures, however, in *King of New York.* The film shows a polychrome, multicultural rainbow of New Yorkers getting off on things: liquor, old movies, cards, cocaine, drugs, music, power. And the getting off is enticingly and sympathetically shot and scored. It is a movie of the pleasures and destructivenesses of the nighttime; suave male monsters collide in the dark. It is the real *Bonfire of the Vanities.*

The road of excess leads to the palace of wisdom, William Blake tells us. In *Bad Lieutenant,* Abel Ferrara's 1992 film, the road of excess leads to the Port Authority Bus Terminal off Times Square. The film is a fantasia of decomposition, a devil's parody of the Stations of the Cross as a New York City cop (Harvey Keitel) known as the Lieutenant (he only has this allegorical moniker) executes an itinerary of self-abuse.

He spends a lot of angry time in his car; the first such long shot follows him and his two little sons on the way to school while he ferociously berates them for letting their aunt hog the bathroom. (This is one of the rare notes of home sounded in the story.) The kids get out of the car and Daddy does coke right by the school. This scene rhymes with the Lieutenant's final drive down from Spanish Harlem to the Port Authority with two crackhead kids (same positioning in the car) whom he is, in a unique and hard-won moment of mercy, about to send to freedom and New Jersey instead of to prison—which is where they belong for raping a nun right on the altar and violating her with a crucifix, not to mention stealing a chalice full of hosts. The cop then drives to Madison Square Garden and his destiny, which we see in long shot with loose, random traffic intervening.

Between the two trips intervene, like the Hell panels of Roger van der Weyden's *Last Judgment,* grotesque tableaux of the Lieutenant sampling a lurid menu of sins. His police activity is an uninterrupted and unreined abuse of power: scoring coke, ripping off black kids who have themselves ripped off a Korean grocer. The coke is sex fuel—an orgy with two willing (or least bought) hookers to the soundtrack tune of "I'll Forever Love You" is followed some time later by the Lieutenant's snarling degradation of two unwilling young women (Eddie Daniels and Bianca Bakija) in their daddy's car, beside which the cop stands masturbating in the uncleansing rain.

The guy's days—and the movie—are structured by a baseball play-off between the New York Mets and the L.A. Dodgers; he keeps upping his antihometown bet until he winds up owing the Mob an impossible $120,000. Games four through seven mark his decline, as radio talk shows *about* the games and live TV airings *of* the games thread the movie; the Lieutenant spends a lot of time in, and gives a good deal of abuse (including shooting the radio) to, his car. The Mets, down zero games to three, stage a miracle comeback and take the pennant, but their miracle is the Lieutenant's damnation. These are odds he cannot fix. (Ferrara's play-off is imaginary, of course, but, while he has doctored some real footage cleverly, there are visible mistakes. The play-off is often referred to as the *Series;* games are played at night in Los Angeles while it is still day in New York, for instance.)

But if the Mets doom the Looey, there is Jesus to tug in another direction. The case of the violated nun (played by Frankie Thorn) reverberates throughout the downward spiral of the cop. First, the rape takes place to the beat of heavy-metal rock on the soundtrack; lipstick-red strobe lights blink excitingly on the altar as a blue plaster statue of the Blessed Virgin topples and the ravished sister's leg is stroked. This rape is stylistically of a piece with the cop's coke/come sensibility; it might as well have occurred in his head, as is further emphasized by the obscene rap that roars on the soundtrack while he approaches the nun's hospital room and eyeballs, from behind a curtain and with a gaze perfectly split between lust and sorrowful compassion, her voluptuous nude body on a gurney.

Officially a cynic about Catholicism, the Lieutenant is a sucker for its iconography. He squats on a velvet Jesus while visiting the devout Hispanic mother of his nice dope dealer. Then he pops in on and is popped in the arm by his dreamy junkie girlfriend Magdalena (she, called after the prostitute reformed by Jesus, is the movie's only named character, played by coscreenwriter and erstwhile Ms. 45, Zoe Lund).

Then as he writhes climactically wailing and cursing on the church floor after the nun persists in her refusal to incriminate her rapists, a bleeding Jesus in a soiled loincloth appears and beckons the sinner. The Lieutenant, who had earlier boasted to one of his Mafioso creditors that "no one can kill me, I'm blessed, I'm a fuckin' Catholic," at first takes an angry tack in addressing the Divine Founder of Catholicism, saying, "You ratfuck, you fuck, you got somethin' you want to say to me?"

But he has an epiphany of self-knowledge, which, of course, given Ferrara's lurid style, functions also as a parody of an epiphany, and moans, "I'm sorry, I'm weak." He kisses the feet of Jesus, who suddenly turns into an elderly black woman, who is kindly returning the chalice because it is "a holy thing" and who then inadvertently points the way to the rapists' crack den. There, outrageously (the whole movie is a sustained Ferraran outrage), the veins of his metabolism and the lines of his fate converge as he smokes crack with the rapists and with them watches the Mets win the pennant on TV.

The movie, which was shot for a mere $1.5 million, has an abstract quality to its horrors, as if the Lieutenant were on a trip through Dantesque circles of pain. *King of New York*'s investigations of pleasure and violence had already an unreal feel. Reality is so dark in the tenebrous *Bad Lieutenant* (Ken Kelsch was the cinematographer) it seems trying to negate itself. The scene with the two young women in the car goes on, it seems, forever. In its refusal to stop, in its limited repertoire of shots, in the Lieutenant's stuck-needle obscenities, it achieves a penitential exposure of the emptiness of sin, of death, masquerading as pleasure. And the cop finally does imitate the nun's charity.

And yet Ferrara's art has finally, I think, no religious dimension. There is no redemptive or purgatorial process at work; there is only an infernal toilet. The Lieutenant crying out in church echoes for a second Victor McLaglen, in John Ford's *The Informer* (1935), repenting his treachery, but even that sentimental religiosity is alien to Ferrara, who is rather a negative diagnostician of pleasure—a puritanical Russ Meyer.

Harvey Keitel holds nothing back, stripping body and

spirit bare to give us this soul in hell. For once, the maddening repetitions and egotisms of Method improvisations have justified themselves.

Ferrara's, then, is an antiliterate sensibility, the opposite in texture and in moral flavor to Sayles's.

Ferrara has completed the third version of the alien-paranoia classic, *Invasion of the Body Snatchers.* The first two, both set in California, were by Don Siegel in 1956 and by Philip Kaufman in 1978. Ferrara's is set on an Alabama military base and features a strong young woman heroine (Gabrielle Anwar). His next project is *Snake Eyes,* with Harvey Keitel, Madonna, and James Russo. The script, by Ferrara and Nicholas St. John, deals with a movie director, an actor, and a TV actress the director is persuaded by the actor to hire. It will involve extensive use of videotape, film-within-film, and art-mirroring-life. Ferrara has likened *Snake Eyes* to *Who's Afraid of Virginia Woolf?*—and the names of Pirandello and Cassavetes come to mind as well.

*F*rom the Bronx has come a softer—softer but not less tough—analysis of New York lives in the work of Nancy Savoca. Her debut film was *True Love,* made in 1989. Savoca is a Bronx native, daughter of a Sicilian father and an Argentine mother. Graduating from NYU's film school, she married Richard Guay, an accounting student she knew from the deli around the corner. Wed for more than ten years, they are partners in film as well and co-wrote *True Love,* which Guay produced. They still live in the Bronx.

*True Love* looks with fresh eyes and warm humor at one of the oldest of human dramas. The story covers a few days preceding and the day of the wedding of Donna and Michael, two attractive kids with lots of smothering familial and social ties that bind. The setting is deep in the East Bronx, an almost exclusively Italian neighborhood of two-story houses and tree-lined streets that might be where Marty the butcher and his wife moved to from the cramped apartments of the West Bronx, where they met in the 1950s. It is also a mythic movie neighborhood in the image of Vincente Minnelli's *Father of the Bride*. Savoca knows this turf intimately, as well as Spike Lee knows Brooklyn or Singleton knows South Central L.A.; she knows just how to move about its streets and bars and kitchens and bathrooms. She shows a traditional culture enacting its rituals—rituals that fit some like a gown or a glove but that might prove too confining for others, like a rented tux.

The film drags the young pair through the mercilessly enforced mating rites: Donna insists on color-coordinated food for the reception (she wins), she wants Michael to wear a blue tux (she loses), a smoothie jeweler pushes multiple rings (he loses), the guys watch porn at the bachelor party, Donna has last soulful talks with her father and her mother.

Savoca beautifully notices the separate gender cultures at work. Guys have their things to do: they get drunk and look at porn and cruise for girls (not Michael, though) and go to Atlantic City. Girls sit around laughing about guys and worrying about apartments. Donna's friend J.C.

is the freest character. She drives a taxi; she is shouldering the responsibility of taking her twelve-year-old sister away from her alcoholic parents; she is just at the start of a relationship with fat, smitten Irish Brian. J.C. is the old Eve Arden character of the cynical best friend, given a contemporary reality check.

But beneath the comedy there is terror. Michael is gripped by panic at the structures about to enclose him. He'll become a partner in the deli he works in; above all, he'll be married. And he rebels—he goes to a stag all-nighter in Atlantic City and has a fight with Donna; he drunkenly dances the hucklebuck with one of those girls who hang out in the local bar (actually, it's his happiest, because least committing, moment); even on the wedding night itself he wants to go out again one last time with the guys, which leads to a hilarious and poignant sisterly consolation scene and spousal-reconciliation scene in the ladies' room at the reception. Michael had voiced his deepest terrors to a bartender earlier: "She tells me things and she says they're important and I don't know what the fuck she's talking about—it's very complicated—I just don't want to end up hating my life."

The film solves nothing; this is not Vincente Minnelli Land. The pair are sexually attracted to each other, as we see when they make love, against all taboos, on the wedding morning, which leads to the film's neatest cut: Michael pulls Donna's nightgown up/her bridesmaid pulls down her wedding dress a few hours later. But Savoca has let us feel too many insecurities: the ceremony will not magically solve real anxieties; it rather signals the real beginning of a real marriage. It is a maturer finale than the fantasy conclusion of Steven Soderbergh's *Sex, Lies and Videotape,* where a purring guru is empowered by Love to overcome impotence and bestow orgasms. Videotaping, incidentally, while an act of alienation in *Sex, Lies and Videotape,* is an act of community, continuity, and humbling humor in *True Love,* an amazingly wise movie that actually seems at moments fairer to the guy than to the girl. The playing is as honest as everything else. Annabella Sciorra in her film debut acts Donna gutsily; she is not afraid to hit the character's obnoxious insecurities hard. As Michael, Ron Eldard masterfully shades desperation and fear into everybody's favorite local kid. And the stunning Star Jasper almost steals the movie as J.C.

Savoca's second film was *Dogfight* (1991), from a script by Bob Comfort. In San Francisco in 1963, a Vietnam-bound marine initially picks up a folksinging waitress in order to enter her in a Most Ugly Date contest with some jarhead buddies. Cruelty yields to remorse and then to attraction in the course of a long night. The nastiness of the premise—not to mention the unsuitability of Lili Taylor to play a "dog"—is never overcome, even by the shrewd and sensitive playing of Taylor and of River Phoenix as the marine. But there are Savoca-like moments about the alternating terrors and joys of commitment, as well as a signature sisterly moment in the ladies' room. A powerful epilogue in which the traumatized marine, his buddies all wiped out in combat, returns in 1966 to an unimaginably altered, hippified, radicalized San Francisco, and to the café where he met the singer is the film's best moment.

Savoca's next film was *Household Saints,* which she wrote with Richard Guay from a novel by Francine Prose about three generations of women in an Italian-American family. Mother Tracey Ullman has to cope with the various religious manias of her mother-in-law, Judith Malina, and her daughter, Lili Taylor. Very much Savoca territory.

# CHAPTER TWO

# *A*round Long Island

*L*indenhurst is a working-class town, a commuter suburb on the south shore of Long Island. It has the flatness,
the bleakness, the proximity to industrial ugliness, the
curious love-hate relationship to the big city and its values (symbolized by the Long Island Railroad that goes
into Manhattan) that characterize that uniquely American phenomenon, the prole exurb. Lindenhurst has also
produced an artist, an artistic chronicler of its ways, in
Hal Hartley, product of a large Irish-Catholic family there.
Born in 1960, he took early to painting and went to college at the Massachusetts College of Art in Boston to
pursue that interest. But while there, he took some
courses in filmmaking and got bit. He told Ellen Paul in
the *New York Times* that, when he saw the first images he
had filmed, "some of them very mundane, like water
glasses in the window with light coming through them,
I was just crushed with sadness—a good sadness, totally
life-affirming." He went on to study film full-time at the

State University of New York at Purchase, north of New York City, a school that is in some ways a working-class NYU.

At Purchase, Hartley began collaborating, in student films, with a group of actors and technicians who have continued to work with him over the years. He graduated in 1984 and came to New York City, where he worked in and around film until 1988, when, for well under $100,000, he shot his first feature, *The Unbelievable Truth,* in eleven days. Using a bank loan (supposedly to buy a computer) he shot at the homes of relatives.

The peculiar flavor, the aromatic blend of deadpan and despair, of Hartley cinema is evident from the first shots as Josh (Robert Burke) is seen hitching rides back to town. One of his hitching posts is the Wall Street statue of George Washington. Cut to beautiful young blond Audrey (Adrienne Shelly) waking up in a suburban bed that is dominated by a huge blowup of a dollar bill featuring Washington's kisser. An unlikely obsession with the first President is to unite the two central misfits.

At breakfast, Audrey is nagged by her gruff father about earning money for a good college. "Dad," she apocalyptically replies, "the world is coming to an end . . . Mom, got any Valium? . . . I quit Burger World." She is reading a book called *The End of the World.* This is a young woman too wild and large in spirit for the anemic proprieties of a suburban bourgeoisie.

Her old boyfriend, dumb, plump Emmet, shows up in an aqua suit and whines. Rejected, he accuses Audrey of promiscuity in front of her father. A local photographer has convinced Audrey to let him take some model shots. Josh's reentry into town is marked by weird events and coincidences: a woman, Pearl, faints and is laid out on a soda counter.

In a bookstore, Josh meets Audrey while looking for a book about Washington. At once she articulates her credo—''I don't trust anyone''—but sends Josh nevertheless to her dad's garage for a job. He proves a whiz at engine-fixing, explaining, ''I fixed cars in prison.'' What exactly Josh *did* to go to prison is a subject of confusion and controversy all over town. It seems he killed Pearl's sister and then threw her father fatally down a flight of stairs. But Audrey's attraction to and moral surety about Josh holds: she brings him his George Washington book at the garage, and they discuss Molière's *The Misanthrope,* a label that seems to fit Josh better than his baggy blue garage suit.

Back in the blue garage amid the tires and jacks, the likable and funny Mike (Mark Chandler Bailey, who will also work a garage in *Simple Men*) plays guitar and teases the laconic, possibly menacing Josh about his seeming celibacy, querying, ''You're not a homo? . . . I thought *I* was, but I joined the marines.''

But romance is about to bloom. A huge glass of orange juice in Audrey's kitchen dissolves to a hilarious, formalized quarrel out in the street between her and Emmet, who is still outraged by his rejection and takes out his frustrations on an innocent passerby. Then, in extreme close-up, Audrey and Josh kiss down by the LIRR. Her alarmed dad demands she give up the homicidal Josh or he'll lose his job at the garage. Audrey agrees.

Josh and Pearl try to communicate at a bench by the sea, a sea felt as a warm and liberating, if rarely visible, presence in *The Unbelievable Truth*. Audrey's first big underwear ad in the *New York Times* freaks out Dad, half proud, half scandalized.

Audrey goes to sit on Josh's stoop; she asks, "Will you make love to me?" "Wait here," answers Josh, who returns with a bandage for her scraped knee and says, "Get out of here!" The stoop as middle ground between interior and exterior seems quintessentially American and is featured again in the final scene of *Sex, Lies and Videotape*.

Love has met a bump. On a rubber raft in her dad's pool, Audrey decides to move to Manhattan and become a model. At a last confrontation in a coffeeshop, Audrey and Josh fight, she declaring more misanthropically than ever that "you can't have faith in people, only in the deals you make with them." At his Sunday backyard barbecue, dad does a volte-face and tells Josh to go to New York after his daughter. Mike, who has vouched for Josh to Dad, sneaks a lewd look at an even more revealing *New York Times Magazine* spread on Audrey that is out that Sunday, to Dad's righteous consternation.

Josh takes his quest ritual seriously: we see him shave and primp. In town, he heads to her SoHo pad, pausing to explain to a bum slumped in the street that Pearl's sister died in a DWI accident for which he was indeed responsible but that he only killed Pearl's father in strict self-defense. This Hartleyan parody of clear-up exposition renders Josh not blameless, but not dangerous, either. Then he espies Audrey cavorting amorously (he thinks) in the street with her photographer; he angrily throws the George Washington book through her window, shattering the yuppie photographer's exquisite vase into the bargain. Audrey sees all at once.

At this point of romantic misunderstanding, Josh takes the LIRR back to the garage, locus of male self-pity, and starts drinking—something his past has kept him away from thus far. He drives a van to that strip of beach, where Emmet and Pearl and Mike (who is after Pearl) all happen to turn up. The action shifts back to Josh's place, and the tone and pace get farcical: Dad and Audrey and Pearl and Josh all skulk about just avoiding bumping into one another. We end back at the sea with reconciliation, trust, and faith all around—almost. Josh piggybacks Audrey; their two faces near each other; we hear the susurrus of the surf and birds calling.

Hartley has cited as among his admirations the filmmakers Wim Wenders, Jean-Luc Godard, Robert Bresson and Chantal Akerman, and one can see what he responds to in their droll, ironic stylizations of life. Hartley uses distancing signs such as cards that say MEANWHILE and BUT and THEN. Hartley and his director of photography, Michael Spiller, do have an eye for the pale washes of pastel color that suburbia so generously displays. But there is in Hartley, too, a peculiarly American affection for the lurid, both chromatically and behaviorally. He has a quick nose for the believe-it-or-not tragicomic horrors and hilarities of Long Island (for which read *generic suburban*) split-level living. He refrains, though, from pushing his take over the edge into surrealistic absurdity, as the dazzling satirist John Waters does in his *Pink Flamingos* and *Female Trouble*. Hartley is, in fact, a tenderhearted combination of Michelangelo Antonioni and *Hard Copy*.

In 1991, Hartley made his second movie, *Trust*, for $650,000. It deals with a similar pair of family-values misfits, but this time the hues are darker, the problems tougher, and the tone angrier. The patriarchal figures in *Trust* are real monsters, not sitcom bluffers. Pregnant, unwed, and yelled at by her dad, Maria, the heroine (Adrienne Shelly again), slaps him right back only to have him promptly drop dead. She is also ditched by her jock lover and has to fight her way through protesters to enter an abortion clinic, where no-nonsense nurse Paine (Karen Sillas) unsentimentally and in extreme close-up gives her a shot.

Meanwhile, Matthew (Martin Donovan), an electronics repairman, refuses to take money for pretending to fix a hopeless set, puts his boss's head in a vise, and gets fired. At home, his sadistic, pathologically neat and anal father makes Matt clean the toilet endlessly and whips him at the sight of a cigarette butt.

Ejected from her home by her widowed mother, Maria listens sympathetically at a bus stop as a housewife mourns her childlessness and imprisonment in routine. Maria later jabs a cigarette into the face of a liquor store owner assaulting her in the back room.

It is a mean, brutalizing world, the world of *Trust*.

When the two emotional desperadoes meet, they exchange verbal tokens of nihilism: "I want nothing"; "Nothing's going to help." He tells her he carries with him at all times his father's grenade from Korea; she purrs, "Are you emotionally disturbed?" It is also, in *Trust*, a violently dysfunctional universe on the material level: thousands of TVs break down at once, milk falls off tables, milk does jigs atop washing machines, toasters break into flames, cigarettes wind up in coffee.

The central pair go on speaking in minimalist haikus: "I like librarians," says he when she deprecates her homeliness; "Give me your hand grenade," she asks. At Maria's urging, Matt attempts respectability; he studies the lathe and moves in with her mother, a nasty and manipulative woman. After a bit of her, Matt says, "A family is like a gun; your mother is a psychopath." The three—boy, girl, grenade—cuddle in bed. He wants a bourgeois setup: "Marry me, have a baby, and we'll be a family." Her response: "You're delirious."

But the next day, down at the LIRR station, the hope in Hartley surfaces. He finds something to cherish in the marginalized and the mad. Maria wants love from Matt. He: "I respect and admire you." She: "Is that love?" Extreme close-up. She: "I'll marry you if you admit that respect plus admiration plus trust equal love." And she proceeds to act out her trust by jumping off a mild height and assuming he'll catch her. Although she carries a thesaurus, she does not know the meaning of the word *naïve*; but, in the passionately alienated and alienatedly passionate performance of Adrienne Shelly, she incarnates naïveté.

Robotic, raincoated consumers pile off the train, embodying the deadness of bourgeois routine (this is not the freshest insight or image in Hartley); this sparks a detective hunt by our pair for the childless woman who has, Maria realizes, kidnapped a baby—a powerful thematic counterpoint to her own urge to abort. They find the woman, who has already returned the purloined baby. The lovers have a fight. She: "Your job is making you boring and mean." He: "My job is making me a respectable member of society." It is the eternal Hartley dilemma. She goes off to get the abortion, which proves an ugly and degrading experience, leaving Matt at home in the hands of her mean mother, who mischievously gets him drunk and puts him in the bed of Maria's divorced sister. Once again conscience-stricken at being ordered to do shoddy work, Matt quits his job, gets into a violent confrontation with his father, who has tracked him down, and finds out about the abortion. He snaps.

We realize this when we see a red fire engine streaking toward Matt's plant, where he has terrified coworkers by curling up threateningly with the hand grenade. Matt's collapse is especially terrifying after Martin Donovan's earnest charm is brought to this pass. The grenade is, apparently, a dud. Maria sneaks in; the two lie head to toe—an oddly touching frozen pose—on the floor until he is removed. He pokes his head out of a receding cop car. Standing in the road, she puts her glasses on to keep in contact with his vanishing gaze.

The heroes of *Trust* crouch warily in the corners of the screen; they speak reluctantly and in slender, chiseled words. We can feel the inner pain and the surrounding

emptiness that have driven them into their corners and
their silences. But for all the stylized grimness, Hartley
offers glimpses of qualities that might liberate these prisoners of family and prisoners of the job: trust, trueness,
love.

The romantic pair in *Trust* have been wounded more
deeply than the couple in *The Unbelievable Truth*, and the
mantras of trust may not be enough this time to save the
lovers—but maybe they will. It is a heartbreakingly ambiguous ending. Hartley likes to make coolly formalist
claims that "what we're creating is a flat surface with an
image on it," but beneath the rigid formalism is a romantic humanism. It is hard to imagine lovers in Antonioni
opening up as vulnerably as the lovers of *Trust* do at the
train station.

Hartley's 1992 film, *Simple Men*, cost two million and,
though set on Long Island, was actually shot in Texas,
whose sad, flat, desolate spaces fooled me in their aping
of Long Island. Old colleague Robert Burke, who is by
way of being Robert De Niro to Hartley's Scorsese, returns
as Bill McCabe, a professional robber who has just bun-
gled a job and been dumped by his girlfriend. Angularly
handsome William Sage is his younger brother Dennis, a
respectable college student.

They meet at an LIRR station ticket counter on their
way to Lindenhurst, that by now almost mythical locus of
home and family for Hartley. They discuss (a bit improbably for seasoned locals) whether Queens, the borough of
New York City, is a part of Long Island or not. (It is.) They
buy, for $15, two tickets to Lindenhurst. It is almost a

parody of the quest for home—not dissimilar in its mix of poetry and fun to the wacky quest for his mother engaged in by the hero of Gus Van Sant's *My Own Private Idaho.*

Arrived in Lindenhurst, the brothers are posed, pathetically solitary, in a long shot of a road. "Don't do anything suspicious," warns Bill, as if they were in Dodge City. A guy inexplicably trashing his motorcycle asks where they're from. "New York." "Big deal." An acoustic guitar plucks again and again the same plangent chord; the music is written and played by Ned Rifle, a Hartley pseudonym.

Our guys find a café—blue walls, red banquettes, red phone booth. (In this film, cinematographer Michael Spiller seems to be paying overt homage to Antonioni's *Red Desert* and to Raoul Coutard's chromatic reifications in such Godard pictures as *Pierrot le fou.*) Bill and Dennis discuss the law and their father's internal exile in the USA. Dad, it seems, was a Brooklyn Dodger shortstop who turned radical activist and fled suspicion of having bombed the Pentagon in 1968; it's a typical piece of Hartley impudence to link in one man—and in one *father*—the most cherished and the most feared of American institutions: baseball and terrorism. Dennis wants to find Dad; Bill despises Dad and discourages the quest, saying, "There is no such thing as adventure, no such thing as romance. There's only trouble and desire." The movie will vouch, finally, for the coexistence of all four elements in life.

They then discuss love. Dennis, his heart broken, has determined to break hearts in his turn and to "fuck a piece of ass'' without the complications of love. During this heart-to-heart talk, wry mayhem erupts in the street outside: a girl is in a faint (that Hartley signature image), a smoking nun roughly corrals leather-jacketed school-girls onto a bus and winds up wrestling with a cop over who owns a miraculous medal of Mary. The nun had earlier swiped the medal from a pious student, who had remarked of Mary: ''Not only is she pretty; she has a nice personality *and* she is the Mother of God.'' Hartley's comic evocations of cosmic chaos often come, it is not surprising, from the Catholicism of his background.

The brothers leave Lindenhurst and hit the road for Sagaponack, a beautiful Indian name for a plain fishing town on the ocean out in the Hamptons. En route, they stop at Homer's Oyster Bar, run by cool Kate (Karen Sillas), a formidable woman who wears a cardigan, a lilac dress, and boots—and has a possibly violent ex-husband somewhere in the background. Homer alludes to the *Odyssey*, another tale of a man anxious to find his family. The brothers linger about the bar, speaking laconically: ''I want to play pool''; ''You don't play pool, you shoot pool.'' Martin Donovan, of *Trust*, turns up at Homer's as Matthew, a platonic pal of Kate's. Kate is also a gardener and tree planter, with dreams of opening a greenhouse. Bill drives out with her to look at her shoots, which are in terrible shape after a fire.

A local gas station plays a sort of choric role in *Simple Men*. A long, long establishing shot burns its palette—pump, yellow pillar, red newspaper dispenser, pump—into our eyes, while a goofy gas jockey (Mark Chandler

Bailey, reprising his job in *The Unbelievable Truth*) plays
"Greensleeves" on an electric guitar and practices French
grammar. The local sheriff shows up to voice his gloomy
thoughts on love and on grammatical abstraction. Although the *New York Times*'s critic complained of Hartley's
"long shaggy-dog story, comprised of purposely flat dialogue" and "chic decor" and contrasted *Simple Men* unfa-
vorably with Godard's "wit, humor, and spontaneity,"
the unbelievable truth is almost the opposite. It is Godard
who firmly keeps a distance from his cerebral characters;
it is Hartley whose affection for them—for all of them,
practically—peeps through their deadpan, fortune-cookie
patter. And the stories are actually well-groomed dogs.
Trust me.

Loitering about Homer's is a young woman called Elina
(Elina Löwensohn), a mannered and epileptic Romanian
performance artist who is drawn to young Dennis but,
alas, turns out to have a mysterious liaison to his father,
believed to be in Sagaponack. First seen fainting in a
field, she later sits on steps and refuses a cigarette—all
familiar Hartley images. Dennis's act of carrying her in
from the field and her epilepsy are images and signs that
have echoes in *My Own Private Idaho,* where, too, unconsciousness is seen as a sign of grace. Elina sits at a table
with Dennis (hand static on glass, red shirt) and suddenly
slaps him, overturning table and chair. Elina is not Hartley's most successful character; her mode of stylization,
shrill and confrontational, is discordant with his tones.
And, too, she is pretentious and obnoxious.

Meanwhile, amid the tree shoots, Bill kisses Kate; the

camera lyrically circles them in seeming acceptance and abandon, but Kate, once unclenched, smacks Bill. Love is tricky on Long Island. Later, guy-talk: Bill tells his brother that both hostile women are undoubtedly lesbians. Dennis tracks down Elina through the upstairs rooms; it gets a bit like the end of *The Unbelievable Truth*. Elina melts a bit and confesses that Dad, her lover, is "a womanizer" and that she was perhaps taking that out on Dennis.

Next a sequence of dance and music serves to relax romantic knots. Elina and the brothers execute a sort of modern, free-form dance; Bill and Kate then slow-dance in blue light. At dinner later, discussion turns to the significance of Madonna, whose meaning is also discussed, much more sexually, at the beginning of *Reservoir Dogs*. It is possible that this topic will carbon-date these films to the early 1990s as easily as, say, Hula Hoops in earlier years. Dennis lists his favorite bands, Kate her favorite trees.

Later, outside, Dennis tries to be nice to the ever-touchy Elina, saying, "I respect his [my father's] taste in women." She shoots back: "So then go make love to your mother." But Dennis is not into the oedipal scenario. Inside, things are going better for the older, more life-hardened pair. He: "I'm gonna stay here." She: "You mean for good? You'd give up crime?" He: "Crime isn't a way of life for me—it's a knowledge—but, yeah, I'd give it up."

Blue light (color of the Virgin Mary, by the way) signals potential happiness for this pair of lovers, but trouble is on the way both in the form of Jack, Kate's sprung ex, and in the form of the law, which is after Bill. Jack is driving to Homer's; "I can't stand the quiet," he comments about Long Island. Elina, trailed by Dennis, heads for the boat in Sag Harbor that Dad is living on.

The father-son confrontation that ensues lurches from tragic to farcical: "Who do you think you are?" "Your son." He hits Dennis: "Keep your hands off my woman . . . you want some coffee?" Dad stages a solemn reading from Mao's *Little Red Book* on his boat, just to manifest his continuing radicalism, and then, in another Hartleyan parody of exposition, explains he did not really bomb the Pentagon. Dennis is relieved.

Back at Homer's, events are reaching a film-noir climax. Jack turns out not to want vengeance but a drink and a leather jacket and splitsville. Bill and Kate sit on the porch in long close-up. "Why," she wonders, "are all the men in my life criminal?" The soap-opera sheriff has traced Bill to Kate's place through a gun stupidly forgotten in the bike he left for repair at the garage. "Lie for me," he begs. She says she won't, but in effect does when Bill drives off and the sheriff squats on her stairway (photographed through the railings) moaning about his marital woes.

Bill, after a brief visit to the boat and a sort of reconciliation-at-a-distance with his father, drives back to Homer's and into the arms of the cops—and of Kate. He lays his head on Kate's shoulder as a cop needlessly and ridiculously, in voice-over, warns the unmoving man, "Don't move." Bill has found home (if maybe not immediately) and has no intention in the world of moving. Dennis, recognized by his father, can begin his life journey.

A lingering image from *Simple Men* is the plain cardigan strength, solidity, and beauty of Karen Sillas as Kate—a Willa Cather pioneer in a Samuel Beckett landscape. *Simple Men* is testimony both to the ease and inventiveness and humor with which Hartley creates his world and also to certain dangers present therein: preciosity, monotony. But far oftener than not, Hal Hartley trumps his limitations with visual and verbal wit and with a real affection toward his creatures, who so often seem to be irredeemably doomed in a noir, or Bressonian, way but then spring sudden shoots of hope, also in a Bressonian way. *Trust* and *Simple Men* both end with lovers being or about to be separated by the police, but both endings are wonderfully life-affirming for all that.

Hartley has directed a one-hour TV drama, *Surviving Desire,* for PBS's *American Playhouse.* Dealing with a literature professor's (Martin Donovan) briefly successful crush on a student (Mary Ward), it took place in a recognizably Hartleyan universe of bookstores, madness, and frustration. It was a joyless work, as epitomized in a stiff and musicless dance of love executed by the hero and two anonymous guys at night behind a building (a tip of the hat to the little dance in Godard's *Bande à part* here). It ends with the professor's head upside down on a sewer grating (''I'll be okay, but let me rest my head here in the gutter for five or ten minutes'') and the student wandering around the bookstore she works in, repeatedly enquiring, "Can I help someone?" *Surviving Desire,* while not without visual interest, is on the whole charmlessly pretentious. Hartley is next to film *Amateur,* a story of love and amnesia with Martin Donovan and Isabelle Huppert. Hartley is a brilliantly, sometimes even a rigidly, idiosyncratic artist; he has become, in the words of a coworker, "a genre unto himself."

*B*oston-born Alexandre Rockwell, now in his late thirties, broke into the front rank of independents in 1992 with *In the Soup,* which he directed and cowrote with Tim Kissell. Rockwell is not a product of film school; his film school was the films of Truffaut and Godard (he lived in Paris for a time) and, more recently, of John Cassavetes. In 1983, Rockwell released *Hero,* which was described as a "surrealist journey to nowhere"; it was a road movie that took a handicapped American boy, a Mexican cab driver, and a silent Japanese girl in a yellow checker cab to Truth or Consequences, New Mexico. On the way, they run into various symbolic figures such as a Cowboy and a Native American.

In 1989, he made *Sons,* about three New Jersey brothers (William Forsythe, D. B. Sweeney, Robert Miranda) who contrive to bring their old father (Samuel Fuller), sullenly vegetating in a veterans' hospital, back to Normandy to see the woman he loved there in World War II (Stéphane Audran). *Sons* was notable for giving a rich part to director Fuller, that great, grizzled, curmudgeonly, cigar-sucking icon of personal cinema and for reuniting Fuller with Stéphane Audran, that superb actress who had played in

Fuller's magnificent World War II memoir-movie, *The Big Red One* (1980). Jennifer Beals played a Parisian transvestite in *Sons*. All three early films of Rockwell's were made for roughly twenty to thirty thousand each.

Set in a wintry, black-and-white New York, *In the Soup* is pretty clearly autobiographical, a filmmaker's film about a young man desperately eager to cobble together enough dough to make his debut dream movie. The story behind *In the Soup* replicated the story *in* the film. "We were up against a wall from the first day of shooting," remembers Rockwell. "We ran out of production money and I had to borrow from my mother-in-law's pension fund; then the New York unions tried to close us down with baseball bats. . . . It constantly reminded me that it's people who make films, not money." With some help from Japanese financing, Rockwell finished *In the Soup* for about $800,000.

It is very much a New York movie, acknowledging Jim Jarmusch (who is, indeed, in it) and John Cassavetes, who, says Rockwell, "taught me to come toward people." He chose black-and-white not, he insists, for economic reasons but to pay homage to Truffaut and Godard and Cassavetes.

The film's look is indeed raw; we see a grainy, chilly, bleak New York City. Our hero, Adolpho Rollo, lives in a grungy Lower East Side walk-up and supports himself as a house painter. He placates his intimidating, petty-racketeer landlord by means of regular rent assists from his mother; he has a crush on his beautiful Hispanic neighbor Angelica (warmly played by the beautiful Jennifer Beals, Rockwell's wife), who is a waitress in a nearby café and high-hats Rollo's lame attempts to chat her up there. But at heart Rollo is a film nut: his walls are adorned with posters of Tarkovsky, Godard, and Renoir; he has written a huge, five-hundred-page script called *Unconditional Surrender* that somehow blends Dostoevsky with Nietzsche and that he is desperate to bring to the screen.

A sadsack, Rollo is played with perfect mournful pathos by big-eyed, Brooklyn-born Steve Buscemi, an emerging light of independent cinema who was memorable as Charlie, the uptight barber lured into mischief in Jim Jarmusch's *Mystery Train;* as Chet, the friendly hotel clerk in Joel Coen's *Barton Fink;* and as the whiny, petulant Mr. Pink in Tarantino's *Reservoir Dogs.* He is to be in Joel Coen's *Hudsucker Proxy* in 1994.

Rollo tries peddling his script to Monty and Barbara (played with sleazy relish by Jim Jarmusch and Carol Kane), a couple who bill themselves as independent producers but who in fact run a soft-porn cable show called *The Naked Truth,* for which they promise Rollo $100 to strip and talk. He is broke; he does it; he then gets $40, take it or leave it.

Back home and bummed, he slumps, smoking, on a filthy couch where mice are nibbling at an old, derelict pizza. He gets a bright idea: why not take an ad and offer to sell the script? Sure enough, he gets a phone call summoning him to a Gramercy Park hotel, where he meets Joe and a nude party girl in a Santa hat (it is Christmastime throughout *In the Soup*). Joe offers him $100,000 for his script; Joe is a crook, using Rollo as cover and gofer—a state of affairs Rollo is very, very slow to appreciate. And by the time he *does* get it, it doesn't matter, for Joe is irresistible, as incarnated by the wonderful Seymour Cassel—Panama-bred, white-maned, gravel-voiced veteran of eight Cassavetes films including *Shadows, Faces* (Cassel's greatest and most brutally revealing performance), *The Killing of a Chinese Bookie, A Child Is Waiting, Too Late Blues, Minnie and Moskowitz, Love Streams,* and *Opening Night.*

Joe looks at a bit of Rollo's home movies and promises him the world. What Rollo gets is unceremoniously dumped in remote Jersey at night by Joe's crazy goombah brother. To be fair, Joe does get his landlord off Rollo's back by suave threats. There are fantasy sequences in which Rollo's lovemaking with Angelica is interrupted by a homicidal Joe. Joe, though unquestionably heterosexual, is forever pinching and caressing and slapping Rollo in a crazily avuncular way; Rollo squirms. Joe dresses up as Santa and goes out to Staten Island with Rollo to steal cars; Joe squirms. Breaking into a house at night, Joe collects the valuables upstairs while Rollo is left downstairs to squirm and listen to the confessional babbling of an old man with Alzheimer's.

Rollo meanwhile gets a bit closer to the elusive Angelica, whose green-card husband, Gregoire, goes through Rollo's apartment one night to get to the connecting fire escape and confides: "My wife, she *eeets* me." "Huh?" says Rollo. Punching motions. "My wife, she hits me." "Oh." But it is Joe whose joie de vivre unthaws

Angelica. Next thing, Rollo is filming Angelica and her retarded brother and himself dancing in the dirty snow on the rooftop. Rockwell intercuts these sweet home movies of Rollo's with lewd and violent fantasy movies.

Ever the touchy-feely life force, Joe gives Rollo a cha-cha lesson on New Year's Eve while a deadpan instructional record plays. Rollo whines, "I can't dance." Joe moves with sexy grace. But Joe's party later goes awry when Joe comes on to Angelica during a merengue lesson; to make it up to Rollo, he brings two hookers to the grimy walk-up. Rollo is merely friendly, and he and his hooker just watch TV.

Rollo has at last gotten the picture: "Instead of making my movie, I was living in his." Joe's scams get wackier and riskier. Rollo at one point has to pick up drugs from a guy in Brooklyn wearing a gorilla head. "Oooooh, drugs are *so* bad," mocks Joe about Rollo's squirmy scruples—the William Burroughs character in Van Sant's *Drugstore Cowboy* makes more savage and thorough mock of drug paranoia, but the note struck is the same. A little boy Joe claims is his son is kidnapped and released; Rollo squirms. Joe's brother is killed in the hotel.

The colorful whirligig winds down with Joe, Rollo, and Angelica on the sands of Brighton Beach on a pale, sunny afternoon. There is a teddy bear stuffed with cash. There is a gun. A scuffle and a shot. "Don't call me baby," insists an angry Angelica to a patronizing Joe. "Women are hysterical" is Joe's take. Joe and Rollo sit on a swing. Joe: "Basically, I'm fucked." Rollo: "I forgive you for using me." Joe: "I love to watch the sunrise by the beach." Rollo: "It's the afternoon, Joe." (This line, in its mixture of deflating absurdity and dry lyricism, seems to me typical of the tone of so much recent independent American cinema.) Joe says, "Well, you can't have everything. . . . Make that movie. Make that movie. Make it a love story. Do that for me." Rollo: "What if we made it a film about us?" And that, of course, is what "Adolpho Rollo"/Alexandre Rockwell has done.

Tight close-ups as Joe tries to light one of his omnipresent cigars, but, since, he has been accidentally shot by Angelica, he cannot succeed and slumps down. Angelica runs toward him as Rollo holds him.

*In the Soup* has the urban poetic look of a bleak winter metropolis. Its weakest side is its attempt to reproduce authentic street crime life. Rockwell does not have it in his bones like Scorsese, nor does he grab it with the take-no-prisoners formalist wit of Quentin Tarantino. But his central story works well. It is, at heart, the story of Falstaff and Prince Hal—the bad teacher who turns out to be the good teacher, the opener-up of life, and the uptight pupil. It is the story whose readiness for a revisionist take also struck Gus Van Sant in *My Own Private Idaho*, where Shakespeare's political message was turned upside down. Here Rockwell paints a Hal who learns to follow Falstaff. Both films might be, from one angle, called *Falstaff's Revenge*. As Rockwell said about his film, "It's not about filmmaking; it's about love and friendship and dreams."

# CHAPTER THREE

# *A*round Brooklyn

*I*f some characters in Hal Hartley are shaky about where Queens is, no one will ever be uncertain, after the work of Spike Lee, where Brooklyn is. Spike Lee seems by now as much a mythic presence in modern American cinemas as figures of an earlier generation like Francis Ford Coppola, born in 1939, Martin Scorsese, born in 1942, or Jonathan Demme, born in 1944.

Lee was born in Atlanta, Georgia, in 1956, the son of musician Bill Lee, and attended Morehouse College there. He went on to take an MFA in film production at NYU's Tisch School of the Arts. Taking up residence in Brooklyn's Fort Greene neighborhood and founding his Forty Acres and a Mule production company (the title refers to what the U.S. Federal Government promised each liberated black after the Civil War), Lee had by 1986 raised a relatively small sum, some $175,000, and undertook his first feature.

*She's Gotta Have It* was photographed in black-and-white by a genius named Ernest Dickerson, who has shot all of Lee's films. A native of Newark, New Jersey, Dickerson went to Howard University, where his first film job was photographing surgical procedures for the medical school. (He met Lee at NYU, where they began their long collaboration by working on Lee's student film, *Joe's Bed-Stuy Barbershop: We Cut Heads.*)

*She's Gotta Have It* is a dazzlingly accomplished and sophisticated erotic comedy that has not even today received its due. An investigation of the sexual sensibility of a bright and beautiful young woman called Nola Darling (Tracy Camilla Johns), a magazine art director who is having *it* with three men simultaneously, the film opens with an observation by Zora Neale Hurston on the different ways men and women dream. Before Nola rises from her bed to address the camera, the Brooklyn-ness of the movie is established by images of the patterned cables of the Brooklyn Bridge.

After Nola has introduced herself to us, key figures in her life do the same: suitor Jamie Overstreet (Tommy Redmond Hicks) sits on a park bench and recalls in flashback sex with Nola on top; ex-roommate Clorinda Bradford (Joie Lee, Spike's sister and a performer in many of his films) recalls Nola's annoying promiscuity; Mars Blackmon (Spike Lee, who acts in all of his own films), a sneakered bicyclist, remembers his first meeting with Nola, when she told him her birthday was the same as Malcolm X's; Opal Gilstrap (Raye Dowell) perches on a stoop on a block full of pretty brownstones and whiningly tells of her unsuccessful lesbian courtship of Nola and clashes with Jamie; Greer Childs (John Canada Terrell), a vain and fastidious male model in a sports car, patronizes Nola and Brooklyn; Sonny Darling (Bill Lee, Spike's father) plays on the cello a song he wrote for his daughter.

Narrative economy, formal inventiveness, confrontational and bracing wit, sexual and sexy candor—many hallmarks of the Lee style are evident in this first bravura passage. Not to mention an awareness of Malcolm X and a fetish for sneakers. Lee's is the most profoundly Godardian sensibility of American filmmakers, and this is the most Godardian of his films both in its impish eagerness to interrupt, indeed to shape, the narrative by direct address, meditation, revelation, and in its humble confession of inadequacy before the mystery of woman.

Jamie is Nola's most serious and passionate suitor, for Mars is too much the comedian and Greer too much the fop. For her birthday, Jamie treats Nola to a picnic in Prospect Park, complete with balloons and a pair of ballet dancers. Dickerson's camera treats us to the movie's only color sequence, with a burst of sudden Minnelliesque gorgeousness. And Jamie writes poems to her. What Jamie feels is love. Talking to us, Mars mocks Jamie's poetry and concocts an inept Freudian explanation of Nola's promiscuity. (In fact, as we see, she maintains a good relationship with her father.) Mars makes Nola laugh, even (or rather especially) in bed—asking if he is as good as the others, putting her panties on her head. There is a wonderful shot of her belly laughing as Mars licks her navel: Dickerson is one of the great erotic image-makers.

When Greer calls Nola a "sex addict," she goes to a sex

therapist. But Nola eludes all labels, both damning and therapeutic.

November brings snow on the trees and a Thanksgiving dinner Nola optimistically makes for her three lovers. At the table Mars scorns Greer and proposes to divide Nola with Jamie, saying, "You get four days. I get three." Jamie answers, "That's mighty black of you," but Mars has a hidden ace: "I get the weekends, though." After a contentious game of Scrabble, they all fall asleep clothed.

The amorous quartet goes on until summer, whose arrival is signaled by an image of Nola and Greer solemnly sunbathing. But by this time Jamie has started seeing someone else (the ballet dancer, in fact) and poses an ultimatum to Nola: me and only me or else. Nola dithers, saying, "I'll decide soon." When Opal shows up, Jamie stalks out, snarling, "You can have her."

Then Lee shifts gear for an angry, ugly episode: in the middle of the night Nola, playing with herself in bed, calls Jamie and begs him to come over. Blurred, jerky shots of his sullen, sleepy face on the subway over. When he gets there, he sexually brutalizes Nola. "Make love to me," she pleads. "You don't want me to make love to you," he rages. "You want me to fuck you." And he does, with force and macho possessiveness.

After this traumatic, almost pornographic experience Nola arranges her life. Down by the bridge, she bids farewell to Greer, who puts her down as a Brooklyn provincial unworthy of Manhattan anyway. Also by the water, she says a laughing goodbye to a wheedling Mars. On Jamie's bench, she accepts his apology for the "near-rape" and accepts his "love"—sort of, for she adds the proviso that she has decided to be celibate for a spell. In slow motion she walks away from, but then back to, him.

A lesser, sweeter movie might have ended there, but a final scene shows Nola alone in bed. Celibacy and Jamie only lasted a while, she informs us. For her, it was finally a matter of "control," or who was going to own her. The answer was easy for Nola: herself. She pulls the blanket up over her head and snuggles, alone, into her candle-surrounded bed, like an African priestess.

Tracy Camilla Johns manages to be at once a sexy young woman of independent outlook and a smilingly enigmatic archaic goddess. And the three guys are excellent as almost allegorical slices of a trisected male sensibility, a "three-penised monster" (as Greer says at one point): John Canada Terrell as Body, Tommy Redmond Hicks as Heart, Spike Lee as Wit.

*She's Gotta Have It* has a Mozartean mastery of structure and tone, above all in its faces and images. A seemingly superficiality hides much wisdom about the ways of female Eros and of male ego. The movie disdains mere sociology: we barely know what the characters do for a living, and the only interior we see anything of is Nola's. It is not sociology, but a hymn to . . . I was going to say to love and to lovers' Brooklyn . . . but the truth is that it is a hymn to independence and to an independent person's Brooklyn.

After *She's Gotta Have It*, Lee's second feature was *School Daze* (1988), a serious musical about the soul of African-American higher education. Set at imaginary black Mission College in Alabama, it pitted activist Dep (Larry Fishburne), who was agitating for South African divestment, against Julian (Giancarlo Esposito), head of the Gamma Phi Gamma fraternity and obsessed with its grotesque and fascistic hazing rituals. The only human link between these two antithetical figures was Dep's nerdy cousin Half Pint (Spike Lee), a Gamma pledge. A parallel gender war saw the light-skinned, boy-toy Gamma Ray auxiliaries clashing with the darker-skinned independent black women students. The intention was to toss a hand grenade into the *Grease* genre, and there are moments when it works, such as the musical production number between choruses of insult-spitting young women ("tar-baby" vs. "wannabe"). But on the whole the good guys come off as killjoys, with the bad guys having the fun. A long episode of a big college dance with everybody in bathing suits seemed, if pleasant, not far removed from Frankie and Annette. Finally, Lee seemed a prisoner of the insipid college-musical genre.

But the soft energies of *School Daze* were to find hard and blinding force when Spike Lee turned his attention back to Brooklyn in 1989 to make *Do the Right Thing*, which, like all of his movies until *Malcolm X*, he wrote entirely by himself. *Do the Right Thing* is, like *School Daze*, a choral movie: it's about twenty-four hours, a summer day, in the life of a Brooklyn block in the black neighborhood of Bedford-Stuyvesant. Looking back in one respect to the realist, 1930s canvases of such neighborhood films as King Vidor's *Street Scene* or William Wyler's *Dead End*, it jump-starts the old social prose with Spike Lee's brand of poetry: staccato narrative rhythms, music, specifically African-American anger. That note is struck immediately as Rosie Perez, a dancer making her debut as an actress in this film, dances over the opening credits, sometimes in boxing togs and gloves, to "Fight the Power," an in-your-face-whitey rap song by the group Public Enemy.

The movie opens with a mosaic of choral voices: a DJ called Love Daddy, headquartered on the block, wakes the locals up with a forecast of "hot" ("color—black"). Residents seen arising include an old drunk called the Mayor (Ossie Davis); simple Smiley with his old collection of photos of Malcolm X and Martin Luther King, Jr.; delivery boy Mookie (Spike Lee) counting his cash in bed and being hassled by his sister; Mother Sister (Ruby Dee), a watchful matriarchal presence brooding over the block; Radio Raheem (Bill Nunn), a hulking carrier of a huge boom box; three dudes who are to sit all day under an umbrella complaining about the lack of black business enterprise; hothead Buggin Out (Giancarlo Esposito); five stoop-squatting Hispanics; a bicycle-riding, orange-juice-quaffing white yuppie (John Savage) who has bought a brownstone on the block. And more, until a vibrant, crowded, tightly packed human grouping is suggested. Ernest Dickerson's camera moves restlessly, nosily, urgently up and down the block, poking with a fish-eye lens into everybody's business as the sweltering day wears on and tempers get rawer.

At one end of the block is the node of the action—Sal's Famous Pizza, a twenty-five-year-old enclave of Italian enterprise run by tough-but-benign Sal (Danny Aiello) and his two sons: angry, racist Pino (John Turturro) and simple, intimidated Vito (Richard Edson). These Italians live in the nearby enclave of Bensonhurst—nearby but a million miles away culturally, as can be seen in Morrissey's *Spike of Bensonhurst*. This pizzeria immediately becomes the focus of an iconic controversy: its walls sport glossies exclusively of Italian-American celebrities like Sinatra, DiMaggio, Pacino, De Niro. "No brothers," protests Buggin Out. "Get your own place," ripostes Sal. "Boycott!" screams Buggin Out, as peacemaker Mookie, the delivery boy, hustles him away. Across the street from Sal's is another potential focus of community resentment, a Korean grocery.

Cops (white) make their first appearance, turning off a hydrant kids have opened to beat the heat. This wrenching off of a source of relief and play by the powers that be is symbolic.

Mookie has a Hispanic girlfriend, Tina (Perez), and a son, Hector. Tina, whom we see only in her apartment, is largely present to harass Mookie for his familial irresponsibility: "Make this relationship work or I don't want to be bothered with your ass." Mookie promises to improve. He also tries to put some spine into Vito, to get him to stand up to big brother Pino's abuse; they have a friendly rapport, fighting over the merits of Dwight Gooden and Roger Clemens. (Guess who likes whom.) Mookie and Pino, on the other hand, are natural enemies. Pino: "How come niggers are so stupid?" Mookie: "How come all your favorite athletes and singers are black?"

The Italians are allowed a humanizing moment in Lee's panoramic vision: in a long single take Sal and Pino sit in the window of the pizzeria in the late afternoon. "Maybe we should sell this place, open one in Benson-hurst," suggests Pino, adding, characteristically, "I'm sick of niggers." "Why you got so much anger in you?" wonders Sal, who reminisces fondly about the local chil-dren who "grew up on my food." (Aiello has said he improvised this memorable line, with Lee's enthusiastic encouragement. This collaborativeness seems typical, even with the strongest directors, of the best of indepen-dent cinema.) In the same shot, Pino and then Sal go out into the street to shoo away Smiley, who is sticking his Malcolm photos in the windows.

But Spike Lee is no sentimentalist, especially about males. The knife of skepticism is always sharp. A suspi-cious Mookie tells his sister to stay away from "old letch" Sal. Aiello has been playing his fondness as merely avuncular, but Lee clearly means to endorse Mookie, whom he poses by a graffito reading TAWANA [Brawley, a black woman who claimed to have been raped by whites] TOLD THE TRUTH.

In a foreshadowing incident, Radio Raheem stomps into Sal's with boom box blaring and angrily orders two slices in fisheye close-up. A sweating, hard-worked, ex-asperated Sal insists he turn the machine off. He does. Raheem later has a nasty, profane set-to with the Korean family across the street in the course of buying new batte-ries for his fatal radio. As the day grinds on, kids eat flavored ice; the old Mayor saves a kid from a speeding car—a somewhat Thirties piece of sentimentality ex-tended to this character.

Although the film superbly registers tempers fraying

and frying under the backing sun, *Do the Right Thing* is also surprisingly funny throughout. The three street philosophers, including one called Sweet Dick Willie ("You Negroes kill me, always talkin' about your dicks," says one), are especially valuable at undercutting any idealizing partisanship. Looking at the pictures of Mike Tyson that adorn the block, one says, "I remember when he mugged that woman; if he's dreaming about muggin' my ass, he better wake up and apologize." About the Koreans' business hustle: "Either those Korean motherfuckers are geniuses or you blacks are dumb." To Buggin Out, who demands they join in his boycott of the pizzeria: "Boycott the goddamn barber that fucked up your hair." To Radio Raheem: "Turn that shit down." But as the cop car drives menacingly by, the three gaze stonily back. These three—and, more humorlessly, Mother Sister—are the block's self-critical conscience and common sense.

In one electrifying heightened sequence, Lee choreographs a symphony of racial malevolence and demonic insult. Face into camera, five representatives of their tribes let loose: Mookie in the middle of the street ranting against Italians, Pino in the pizzeria against blacks, a Hispanic on a stoop against Koreans, a white cop against Hispanics, the Korean grocer against Jews. DJ Love Daddy, somehow hearing it all, counsels, "Cut that shit out." There is a sense for a moment that these orgasms of hatred might have been cathartic, might have lanced the boils. No such luck, though. It is a sensational moment. Lee is at home with anger, insult, contempt. But his ability to orchestrate them so beautifully into art, into Brechtian displays of exaggeration, shows a profoundly moral, self-transcending impulse at work in the filmmaker.

Mookie takes a break to deliver a pizza and some loving to Tina. She protests, "It's too fuckin' hot to make love." "Don't curse." "I don't fuckin' curse." Mookie runs an ice cube slowly over her and thanks God explicitly in a litany for her: lips, neck, knees, elbows, thighs, nipples, which we see in Dickerson's rapturously light-silhouetted images. A hot sex scene in every sense, it flaunts the delightful Lee mix of horniness and humor.

As evening falls, Sal tempts fate by saying, "We had a great, great day—there's nothing like a family working together. I'm gonna rename this place Sal and Sons." Three confrontational customers enter the store just at closing time: boycotter Buggin Out, Smiley with his black glossies, and Radio Raheem with box at full blare. Sal snaps and brings out a bat, screaming, "Turn that shit off. I'll tear your nigger ass." General melee, which results in Sal smashing the radio and being choked by Raheem, who is in turn choked—to death—by a cop with a stick. Buggin Out is arrested. Smiley weeps.

This use of inordinate police force brings the block to a boil. Mookie turns against Sal and heaves a garbage can through the pizzeria's plate-glass window. As the Mayor escorts the three Italians to safety, the gathered residents torch the place. Mother Sister gives her blessing—"Burn it down"—while the three philosophers turn on the Korean, who pleads, "I black. You me same." The Korean is spared, which seems rather disingenuous of Lee in light of the later black boycott of a Korean grocer in

Brooklyn and in light of the fate of some Korean businesses during the L.A. riots. As "Fight the Power" insistently rises on the soundtrack, Smiley enters the burning pizzeria and affixes a photo of Malcolm, on the wall. He smiles.

In a coda the next morning, Tina is in bed nagging Mookie, who insists on going down to the ruins of Sal's to collect his wages. Sal, improbably, gives him double pay. They talk a bit about the insurance money and the hot weather, and Mookie leaves to "go see my son"— perhaps a new birth of parental responsibility to go with his newfound activism.

As the camera cranes panoramically above the block, the radio announces a visit by the (white) Mayor, shocked by the destruction of property, to the block and urges listeners to vote (in order, presumably, to turn that mayor out). A basketball game starts.

Two texts appear in sequence: Martin Luther King calling violence "both impractical and immoral" and Malcolm saying, "I am not against using violence in self-defense. I don't even call it violence, I call it intelligence." There seems little doubt, both from what happens in the movie and from the greater vigor and bite of Malcolm's prose here, which of the two attitudes *Do the Right Thing* finds more congenial—although the presence of King's words do not rule out that utopian possibility, either. If the violence that climaxes *Do the Right Thing* seems not intelligence but another injustice to add to the ones the residents of the block have suffered, such illogic is perhaps in the very nature of violence.

The performers each sound one strong, separate clear note in the block's symphony. Lee gives himself his own best role here; in his baggy baseball shirt (saying Dodgers on the front and Robinson on the back) and striding knobbily along the street, Mookie is every hardworking gofer who finally decides to turn on the boss. Rosie Perez vividly establishes her irresistible blend of sassiness, sexiness, and spunk. Although Tina is another of Lee's strong, take-no-nonsense women, it is noticeable that she is here confined to an interior, away from the action. Esposito as Buggin Out and Nunn as Radio Raheem are powerful presences. Two equally strong characters are the Aiello's Sal and Turturro's Pino. Neither actor has ever been better, and the credit for giving both performers space to go beyond the stereotype is Lee's.

In 1993, Turturro made his directorial debut with *Mac*, which he cowrote with Brandon Cole. It is the story of three second-generation Italian brothers in the 1950s jointly venturing into the construction business. Its feel for the claustrophobic tightnesses of family life was typified by a scene of all three brothers together in the bathroom making plans; its sense of fantasy was visible in a scene where the youngest brother has a silent sex scene with a strange woman on a bus. Turturro, Carl Capotorto, and Michael Badalucco were the brothers.

Let me mention here another director-screenwriter debut by a strong actor: Sean Penn's *The Indian Runner*, a 1991 film about a morosely suicidal father (Charles Bronson in a perfect performance) and his two sons, a sane cop (David Morse) and a psychically wounded Nam vet construction worker (Viggo Mortensen). An original story inspired by a Bruce Springsteen lyric, *The Indian Runner* suffered from symbolism and general overcooking, but it had at best the power of an artist—Penn— learning how to work his obsessions into art.

At any rate, *Do the Right Thing* is Spike Lee's masterpiece to date. He shows himself a master manipulator of societal energies on a broad canvas. If he recalls Brecht's corrosively analytic but bracing cynicism, he has a sharp tang and a restless metabolism all his own. Lee's range— from street naturalism to erotic reverie to surrealistic musical numbers—his aggressive use of music, his fearless originality and daring in formal experimentation are all unique. He achieves here a breathtaking synthesis of old-fashioned social realism, Brechtian formalism, African-American anger, rap energy, and Spikean wit.

Lee's next two films were more conventional formally. *Mo' Better Blues* (1990) told of a jazz trumpeter (Denzel Washington) trying to balance art, success, and love. Cynda Williams as a songbird and Wesley Snipes as a rival instrumentalist stole the film, which kept turning into a solemn, if fictional, biopic. *Jungle Fever* (1991), a tale of an interracial, interclass (he middle, she working) affair between Wesley Snipes and Annabella Sciorra, was better, as it gave Lee a chance to range over and to have serious fun with the spectrum of race and class nuances.

His sixth film was the expensive Warner Brothers biopic, *Malcolm X* (1992). It was an impressive accomplishment, certainly the equal of *Gandhi,* with a superb title performance by Denzel Washington. But reverence comes less naturally to Lee than irreverence. The earlier scenes of Malcolm the sinner have a life not always present in those of Malcolm the saint. Spike Lee has remarked in interviews that he was skeptical of the claims by Betty Shabazz, Malcolm's widow, that she and her husband *never* fought. Here spoke Spike Lee, the probing realist about human nature. But Spike Lee, the brilliant director of actors, was evident in the intelligent performance by Angela Bassett as Betty Shabazz, as well as in the rich, subtle performances by Al Freeman, Jr., as Elijah Muhammed and by Delroy Lindo as West Indian Archie.

*Malcolm X* is certainly an instance of a strong-minded independent filmmaker deliberately opting to work in a Hollywood genre with a Hollywood-scale budget but with no danger whatsoever that his integrity would be in peril from *those* circumstances. Lee's next film, *Crooklyn*, is a return to . . . Brooklyn.

In 1992, Ernest Dickerson made his own directorial debut with *Juice,* which he cowrote with Gerard Brown from his own story. A tale of four black Harlem high-school buddies, it opens with a quick montage of their four homes, which seem to range from middle- to working-class: Quincy (Omar Epps), the hero, has a mother who is pushing him toward education (that omnipresent, insistent theme in African-American cinema); fat Steel (Jermaine Hopkins) has a disciplinarian father; smooth Raheem (Khalil Kain), a father himself already, fights for the bathroom with his sister; enigmatic Bishop (Tupac Shakur) broodingly watches his father staring zombielike at a television.

These four constitute a "crew"—not a gang exactly but

a social and operational unit going back to the second grade. Skipping school, they spend the day fighting a Puerto Rican gang, playing pool, dodging cops, and stealing records. Except for Quincy, who has an older, sensible nurse girlfriend (Cindy Herron) and an obsession with winning a local Saturday night contest to become a "mixmaster" DJ, the four see their lives as one humiliation after another. They watch Raoul Walsh's *White Heat* on television, with Bishop especially getting off on the scene where demented gangster Cody Jarrett (James Cagney) goes berserk in a prison mess hall and later laughingly blows himself up.

Around this point, it becomes clear that Bishop, he of the disturbed father, is a high-school Cody Jarrett himself. He envies an ex-con pal who has just gotten himself killed holding up a bar. He bullies the other three, who are reluctant, into joining him in robbing a grocery. In the course of the heist, as his crew look on horrified, he wantonly kills the grocer. When, in their bunker afterward, Raheem objects, Bishop coldly kills him, too.

Quincy and Steel are from now on in the grip of a lunatic and in fear of three suspicious cops (tight closeups of cop faces grilling the three). After Quincy warns Bishop at school, Bishop just calmly threatens to kill him: "I *am* crazy." Quincy gets a gun—he naturally knows where to go for one—from a mysterious woman called Sweets.

Bishop shoots the quivering Steel, who survives and tells the hospital nurse (Quincy's girlfriend) the whole story. But by now the narrative is heading inexorably for the lengthy riverside-then-rooftop confrontation between mad Bishop and sane Quincy. It is a confrontation and not a shootout, since Quincy has tossed his gun into the Hudson River. "What am I turning into?" he asks himself when he inadvertently terrifies a homeless man. "I'm not you," he courageously tells Bishop, who has no notions of a fair fight and shoots Quincy as he runs up a monumental granite staircase on which a graffito says CRIME STOPPERS. The chase continues through an elevator and a crowded party onto a rooftop, from which Bishop falls despite Quincy's efforts to hold on to him. An awed spectator tells Quincy that he has the "juice" now—street respect, gun power—but Quincy sadly shakes his head no. He has won the DJ contest, but his life is inevitably going to be derailed.

Dickerson's fluid, fast-moving direction and Larry Bank's unshowy but telling camerawork capture the sunny sloping streets, the underground caverns, the bridge-y night spaces of uptown riverside Manhattan. This neighborhood has a verticality and a sense of secret places that Brooklyn does not. Manhattan is somehow an older and trickier place than the other, more horizontal boroughs. The black-and-blue night-action scenes at the end recall those at the end of the similarly Manhattan-bound *King of New York*. Manhattan is a place where destiny can grab you by the throat very suddenly, and there is a Hitchcockian sense of destiny, recalling *Strangers on a Train* (1951), in the way *Juice*'s good man is possessed by its demonic man. Potent in conveying this power of destiny are the strong, very cinematic perform-

ances of Epps as Quincy and Shakur as Bishop. Ernest
Dickerson definitely displays a distinctive directorial sensibility in *Juice*.

Brooklyn's Greenpoint, a white ethnic enclave, was the
setting for *Laws of Gravity*, a debut film written and directed by Nick Gomez, a Boston native of thirty who
studied film at SUNY Purchase, which Hal Hartley was
just leaving as Gomez arrived. (Gomez later worked on
Hartley films; he cut *Trust*, for instance.)

*Laws of Gravity* details the self-destructive activities of
that familiar binary pair of (here, white) marginal crooks:
the smartish one trying to get on top of things (Peter
Greene) and the anarchic whacko (Adam Trese). The
smart guy has, as usual, a sensible, reality-oriented girlfriend (the remarkable Edie Falco). What gives *Laws of
Gravity* original power is, above all, the amazingly supple
camerawork, totally hand-held, of documentarist Jean de
Segonzac; he pokes in faces; he circles; he bobs and
weaves. The camera itself seems almost an equal inciter
with the characters of the raw fights that *every* scene de-
generates into.

Gomez, an angry, naturalistic talent, did the movie in
twelve days for $38,000. Although Martin Scorsese's
*Mean Streets* was cited as a model by many critics, Gomez
told me his style came out of a need to work quickly,
practically, economically. "My aesthetics were econom-
ics," he says, and he professes admiration for "guerrilla"
pioneers like Samuel Fuller, Joseph H. Lewis, and Roger
Corman. His next film is being produced by Spike Lee for
Universal. Called *New Jersey Drive*, it is based on true sto-

ries of young Newark, New Jersey, car thieves and their lethal clashes with the cops. Clearly, Gomez is keeping his eye on the streets.

*Straight Out of Brooklyn* is a cry straight from the heart of Brooklyn's projects. If *She's Gotta Have It* was set in upwardly mobile Fort Greene and *Do the Right Thing* amid the tenements of Bed-Stuy, *Straight Out of Brooklyn* is a Red Hook movie taking place in its rundown apartment blocks, its projects. It wrenchingly depicts the wreckage of older African-American lives there and the desperate urges of younger blacks to escape. The film was written, produced, and directed for *American Playhouse* in 1991 by nineteen-year-old Matty Rich, an NYU film student who gathered the slender financing from grants and friends.

The movie opens, appropriately, with an aerial view of the Red Hook projects in winter, for it is these bleak structures that structure the lives within. Next we are inside the apartment of a tragically dysfunctional family: as son Dennis (Lawrence Gilliard, Jr.) lies awake listening, father Ray (George T. Odom) is drunk again, smashing crockery and beating his wife, Frankie (Ann D. Sanders). Next morning, Dennis and his sister (Barbara Sanon) survey the wreckage—human and material—in the apartment. Her face covered in bruises and scars evidently dating from long before last night, Frankie defends Ray in a long, tender scene shucking beans with her daughter: he is a lifelong victim of racism and so "we got to stand by him, you gots to understand." And indeed we watch a cloth-capped Ray being contemptuously patron-

ized by his white boss and by a white customer at the
garage where he works. There is, too, a brief and affecting
moment of father-son bonding at a project door as Ray
reminisces about *his* hardworking parents and his long-
abandoned dream of becoming a doctor.

In a moment of gentleness, Ray, still in his cloth cap,
puts on an old blues record and dances alone until
Frankie comes in, very timidly, as always, in his presence. He coaxes her, wearing his cloth cap and coat still,
into dancing with him. For a tiny minute, she is young
again. He strokes her bruises and promises to quit drinking. But it is too late for this tragic couple. On his next
self-pitying bender, he sends her to the hospital, where
she dies from his battery.

This hopelessly violent family situation makes Dennis
crave an immediate escape, *any* escape, from Red Hook.
He rejects the respectable, plodding routes out: college, a
job. He wants a quick fix for his imprisonment. Dennis's
fantasies of elsewhere are visualized both on the airy,
sky-blue roof of his own building, where he plots with
pals to rob a drug dealer, and on Brooklyn Heights, a
waterfront promenade with a postcard view of the Manhattan skyline. Dennis has taken his realistic, intelligent
girlfriend, Shirley (Reana E. Drummond), there; he
points to the view and bitterly calls it "the American
dream my parents have worked like dogs all their lives
for." (Some Brooklyners, as we know from *She's Gotta
Have It*, have a love-hate relationship with Manhattan.)

Dennis's impatient rage is comprehensible, but his
scheme is stupid and costly. It results in his getting his

walking papers from Shirley ("Have a good life . . . in Red
Hook" is his sneering exit line), his father shot dead by
the robbed dealers, and his mother dead at the hands of
his father (and, a little bit, out of worry for her foolish
son).

*Straight Out of Brooklyn* is, at heart, a film about family,
about wrecked dreams wrecking a family. It ends with an
image of the dead mother and an exhortation for
"change." The film's young people are sketchily realized, with little of the moving individuality and par-
ticularity of the similarly situated youths in *Juice* or *Boyz
N the Hood* or *Just Another Girl on the I.R.T.* But the parents
are unforgettable: Odom is terrifying and pathetic at the
same time; in Sanders's fearful gestures, loving eyes, and
forced optimism is every wife and mother who has ever
striven to understand and forgive domestic violence. It is
a beautiful performance, not least in making us feel that
Frankie's passive saintliness is not enough.

Rich's next project is *The Inkwell*, from a script by
Trey Ellis. A coming-of-age romance about an eccentric
African-American teen finding love, it is budgeted by
distributor Buena Vista at the (for them) low figure of
"under eight million." Still, that's nicer than under eight
dollars.

*L*eslie Harris's 1993 film *Just Another Girl on the I.R.T.* is,
at first glance, remarkable as the first inner-city feature
film by an African-American woman writer-director.
Harris, born in Cleveland, studied film at Denison University in Ohio and had a successful career in advertising in

New York City. But film was her dream and, with the aid of grants, friends, and family, she achieved her amazing first movie, which is as truly a revelation of a culture as was Spike Lee's *Do the Right Thing*, similarly set in Brooklyn, or John Singleton's Los Angeles–themed *Boyz N the Hood*.

Filmed in seventeen days and very largely within a five-block radius in a project area of Brooklyn, *Just Another Girl on the I.R.T.* recounts a few months in the life of seventeen-year-old Chantel Mitchell (Ariyan Johnson), a high-school student and child of the projects; she has two hardworking, exasperated, exhausted parents and two pesky little brothers. Her dream is to go to college, to become a doctor, to get out of the projects, to not become her parents. We first see her on the el (the I.R.T. is a New York City subway line), going to her weekend job in an Upper West Side Manhattan gourmet deli; she talks to the camera; she is sassy and bright and laughing and bold and in our faces. Female rap and hip-hop energize the soundtrack throughout, beginning with "Chantel's Theme," sung by Nikki D and Cee Asia. Harris says, "I thought it was very important to put it all out there in the music, the visuals, and the attitude."

When Chantel gets home from work, the elevator is broken. She walks up. Her parents are quarreling. In school the next day, Chantel, who has a Malcolm X book on her desk, challenges her history teacher, Mr. Weinberg, by insisting that African-American suffering today is more worth discussing than the Holocaust, which is what he wants to talk about. The fuddy-duddy black principal backs up the teacher.

Chantel and her girlfriend Natete (Ebony Jerido) get together after school and talk about ways to not get pregnant—some sensible, some silly. It's hilarious girl-talk, but it will come to have a serious edge. These girls are loud and brassy, just the kind of girls, as Harris says, that New Yorkers see but do not see on the subway every day. The film arose from Harris's wish to follow, in imagination, one of these young women home and find out what her life was all about. And the roughly textured, cinéma-vérité style of *Just Another Girl*, with its addresses to the camera, hand-held jerkiness, occasionally muddy sound, and urgent excitement, feels—and this is brilliant—like a film both *about* and *by* Chantel.

A big weekend party brings love and trouble to Chantel, who disses and ditches her plain, plump, poor boyfriend for lean, flashy, jeep-driving Tyrone (Kevin Thigpen), who courts her in fancy style, with restaurant dinners. Impressed more than she wants to be, she is soon in bed with him. Next thing, there is an overhead shot of her vomiting into a toilet—she is pregnant. Actions have pitiless consequences, Harris shows.

At once, Chantel enters the bureaucracy of pregnancy: a wise black woman doctor explains the law at an abortion clinic; a welfare worker explains her ineligibility. She talks to the camera about her situation—and here what might have seemed a lighthearted filmic device becomes wholly serious and very much a woman's artistic tool. Chantel's debating with herself represents a powerfully moving female registration of life and suffering.

Harris is not just a woman directing, but a woman inflecting an art form to express women's sensibilities.

An art grows in front of our eyes, and it is exciting to see.

Tyrone, at first sullen ("It ain't my problem, bitch"), grows into some responsibility and gives Chantel five hundred dollars for an abortion. Ty is a complex figure in the movie, a bit remote, vain, spoiled, but not without compassion and humanity. He is not a feminist's villain, although the movie's only two whites—Mr. Weinberg and a nasty customer in the gourmet deli—*are* racial stereotypes. In a superb long-held shot of a flight of concrete steps, Ty descends to Chantel, who sits unmoving at the bottom right—an eloquent image of the solitariness of the woman in this dilemna. But irresponsibility possesses Chantel, and she and Natete (who does not know Chantel is pregnant) blow Ty's money on a giggly shopping spree at a mall.

Ty later confronts Chantel in the women's room at school. They reconcile. She goes to his apartment to make love and has the baby there prematurely. A terrified Ty delivers the child, with phoned help from the clinic doctor.

This gripping scene, full of raw pain and screaming and fear, conquers new territory for naturalism in film. Once the little girl is born, Chantel insists that Ty dump her in a garbage can, saying, "I don't want to end up like my parents"—and foreseeing, perhaps accurately, that motherhood will lock her in the projects forever. After some suspenseful scenes, it emerges that Ty could not bring himself to commit the deed.

Cut to next winter: Chantel is walking across the windy campus of a community college (not her cherished premed school) and tells us that she is bringing up the child, with financial help from Ty. She is living not with Ty but with her family. It is an ambiguous, unsettling, but not hopeless ending. Harris clearly wants viewers to see how the prison of thoughtlessly incurred commitment can lock up a bright spirit for life. But Chantel's energy and dynamism are so strong that she may yet be able to shape her own freedom.

The astonishing debut performance of twenty-one-year-old Ariyan Johnson, a Brooklyn dancer, truly galvanizes the film. Both Harris and Johnson are unafraid to explore the flawed, irresponsible, thoughtless, obnoxious sides of Chantel along with her quick wit, impudent charm, and academic brilliance. (This last, in fact, is laid on a bit too thick and too implausibly.) There are aspects of *Just Another Girl* that savor of the preachy and the didactic, but the film's energies transcend this aspect. It is not just a cautionary tale about teenage pregnancy, it is a living, breathing movie and a good augury for future Harris work.

*T*he Sundance Institute was founded in Park City, Utah, in 1981 by Robert Redford and other film professionals as a working community for emerging and established writers and directors. It provides a variety of programs in support of emerging filmmakers. The Screenwriters Lab is a five-day writers' workshop that takes place in January. Then in June occurs the Filmmakers Lab, a three-week-long workshop for writers and directors where opportunities to rehearse, shoot, and edit scenes on videotape with the advice of seasoned writers, directors, editors, cinematographers, and producers are offered. The Producers Conference is a weekend-long conference in July that focuses on the state of the marketplace for independent production.

Filmmakers and producers who have participated in yearlong programs are invited back to focus on the strategies for moving their projects forward into production. Sundance also provides follow-up in this area through networking and advisory support that assists projects in assembling financing, in putting together the creative and the business team, and in other areas of need as the project moves forward.

The Sundance Film Festival, usually in January, is the premiere showcase for American independent cinema. It showcases the talents of emerging filmmakers and offers a diverse program celebrating innovation and vision in national and international cinema.

One of many artists Sundance has helped is Tony Chan, who was born in Hong Kong, came to New York at thirteen, and studied film at New York's School of Visual Arts. With financing from friends and family, he made, in 1992, his first feature, *Combination Platter*, which he and Edwin Baker scripted. He spent a year cutting it in his Queens, New York, kitchen and got a postproduction grant from Sundance. The movie is a sweet-and-sour comedy about Robert (Jeff Lau), a Chinese immigrant who works as a waiter in a restaurant in the newly burgeoning Chinatown of Flushing, Queens. (It is delightful that one of the best recent cinematic chroniclers of that forgotten borough of New York City should be a member of one of its newest communities.)

Robert writes soothing letters home to his parents, but in fact his life is dominated by his lack of a green card and his consequent fear of the Immigration Department. To remedy this, he allows himself to be fixed up with a naive American woman by a cynical friend. Robert's honesty eventually torpedoes this relationship. But the heart of *Combination Platter* is its detailed picture of the internal life of a small restaurant, as seen from backstage: the gradations of obnoxiousness/pleasantness in customers (a quarrelsome interracial couple, two garrulous Mets) and the currents of hostility/friendship among the employees (a cheating waiter, a white busboy).

Chan shows an impressive command of place and mood in this setting, and in Jeff Lau, a real-life stockbroker, he has an actor whose sad, wise, decent face is one the camera loves. Chan's film admirations include Kurosawa, Ozu, Godard, and, above all, Welles—especially Welles's *Touch of Evil*. Chan's touch for what he handles is sure, and his gentle but tough presence is a welcome one in American cinema.

CHAPTER FOUR

# Around Los Angeles

The city of Los Angeles has been the natural, almost the automatic, backdrop for so much of American cinema that viewers may think they know it. Los Angeles was where Norma Desmond dwelled in eerie splendor, where James Dean rebelled without a cause, where Chinatown kept its secrets. Film noir especially loved Los Angeles— all the way from Billy Wilder's *Double Indemnity* (1944) and Robert Siodmak's *Criss Cross* (1949) through Robert Aldrich's *Kiss Me Deadly* (1955) up to the rich twilight of noir in the 1970s in Robert Altman's *The Long Goodbye* and Roman Polanski's *Chinatown*. The town's visual sprawl and variety, its dependence on cars, its fondness for eccentric use of space, its light that could go from horizontal and bakingly tropical to slanting and dangerous, its sense of odd little houses hiding nasty things—at times it seemed noir was *about* Los Angeles. The city became a poetic landscape of darkness and betrayal.

It is typical of the fresh eye and innovative sensibility

of new American cinema that it has revealed totally new, shamefully unknown, compellingly fascinating sides of Los Angeles. Singleton's *Boyz N the Hood* and Tarantino's *Reservoir Dogs* both offer sunny sections of the city in prey to evil; Carl Franklin's *One False Move* opens in a sadistically depraved Los Angeles and then takes us away into the heart of a country that has brought its problems to California; Gregg Araki's *The Living End* is a road movie for the AIDS age that commences in a confrontational L.A. And Joel Coen's *Barton Fink* gives a retro-surrealist vision of Golden Age Hollywood as hell; Charles Burnett's *To Sleep With Anger* is deeply rooted in the Watts community of Los Angeles.

**J**ohn Singleton was twenty-three and a recent graduate of the USC film program when he wrote and directed *Boyz N the Hood,* his first film, an anguished, unflinching look at the life possibilities for African-American youth in South Central Los Angeles. The hood of the film looks pleasant—small, well-kept houses, lawns, cars. But, as the intrusive, all-pervading, nocturnal noise of circling police helicopters and the inquisitive probe of their searchlights bring home to us, this is an occupied zone, occupied by police from without and by gangs from within. Singleton focuses on two single-parent families and begins his story with a prologue when all the kids were young. A harassed single mother (Tyra Ferrell) has two sons, one a pampered athlete, Rick (Morris Chestnut), and the other an overweight and feckless boy, Farris (Ice Cube). When we hear her say to Farris, "You'll never amount to anything," we feel in our bones that this will be a self-fulfilling prophecy.

In stark contrast, Furious Styles (Larry Fishburne), divorced from his upwardly mobile wife, is a man—and a father—of principle to his only son, Trey (Cuba Gooding, Jr.). In a scene on the rocks by the ocean in the prologue, he lectures his little boy on respect for women: "Any man with a dick can make a baby, but only a man can raise a child" and on the white power structure: "I went to Nam; black man got no place in the white man's army." He radiates contempt for a racist black cop. This parent is bent on instilling pride and self-worth. The little kids experience a neighborhood where corpses casually turn up in fields and where bigger kids meanly appropriate their basketball—an unsettling and somehow prophetic act.

The prologue ends with Farris arrested for theft. Cut to years later, to a party to celebrate his getting out of jail (presumably, after a later conviction). His mother is having a barbecue: the boys sit around discussing ways to get AIDS and blowjobs and such (one is reminded of the girl-talk in *Just Another Girl on the I.R.T.*). A red car cruises ominously by. Farris saves a baby left out in the street by its addict-prostitute mother. Trey has a quarrel with his girl-next-door, Brandi (Nia Long), and brings some food home to his father, who accepts it only on the condition that "you didn't bring me no swine"—not the first indication that the father is a devout Muslim.

While giving his son a haircut, Dad dishes out some counterwisdom to the macho sex code of the street: always use protection, and so forth. We see, in this tender scene, how vital it is for a growing man to get moral input from a principled—and present—father.

*Boyz* risks being preachy, like *Just Another Girl,* but so powerfully does Singleton present the forces of disintegration and the pressures to self-destruct in the hood that we assent to the necessity for a countervailing didacticism. At times, though, this didacticism can be heavy and artistically clumsy, as in a strained comment about SAT scores and in a long lecture the father, who is in the home-loan business, delivers in a vacant lot to his admiring son and awestruck locals. He addresses the evils of gentrification and the wickedness of the white man in importing guns and liquor and prostitutes into black areas because "they want us to kill ourselves." This is, of course, straight from Malcolm and from the movie *Malcolm X,* too. Trey makes it all even more explicit by worshipfully stating, "Pop is like Malcolm or Farrakhan."

Rick, Trey's best pal, has a bright future despite already being burdened with a wife and baby son, for USC wants him to come play football. In an uncomfortable scene, a USC recruiter calls and is welcomed on a plastic-covered sofa by an overanxious mother. But Rick seemingly fumbles his SATs even as Trey aces them.

That night, Trey and Rick are pulled over and tormented by a pair of cops (the black cop nastier than the white one), who just assume they are gang members. In a long, excruciating close-up, the black cop holds a gun to the throat of Trey, who cries in anger, frustration, and humiliation. At Brandi's, Trey explodes in rage at the structure of the world he sees around him. In a gesture of comfort and consolation, they have sex; it's a voluptuously, caressingly shot sequence that, like the sex in Spike Lee, shows sex as not just Eros but as freedom and release for trapped people.

Next day, Rick and Trey walk to the store, so Rick can buy milk for his baby. As they go along, Rick considers the army, since he thinks he has blown USC; Trey repeats his father's position on the armed forces. On the way back, that cruising red car—a lurking presence throughout—turns into an attack vehicle and tracks the pair through back alleys. Rick wants to split up, but the smarter (and more symbolically correct) Trey insists they stick together. Rick, insensitive to the peril, stops to urinate and to scratch a milk carton for lottery numbers and is gunned down by the red-car gang.

Trey, bloodied, goes home to get his gun; his father confronts him: "Give me the gun! Give me the motherfucking gun!" A long heart-stopping pause. It is the moment when the father's lifetime of love pays off: Trey gives him the motherfucking gun, and his dad hugs him.

But the macho code of revenge still beckons Trey, who slips out of the house that night to join Farris, also out cruising for a kill. Farris is overwhelmed with guilt for Rick's death—an irrational guilt his distraught but cruelly unfair mother has laid on him. Trey's dad stays home fingering steel balls. Rick's mother is home crying over Rick's newly arrived SAT scores. The revengers cruise.

At the penultimate moment, his father's values triumph within Trey and he cries, "Let me out!" Farris finds the three red-car killers eating burgers and fries in a dark, deserted fast-food parking lot; they're talking about ketchup and haircuts. This is one of Singleton's admirable abilities: to show the ordinary humanity in everybody. Even these guys are human beings. Farris glides up to them and avenges his brother with an Uzi, plugging one in the head as he crawls and taunting another, "Turn your punk ass over." Cut to Trey, collapsing at home on his bed, a battlefield of emotions.

The following morning is inappropriately golden and clean—a frequent Los Angeles paradox—as Trey and Farris speak in code on the stoop, that stoop where much of the film has transpired, where the texture of everyday life has been visible and audible. Farris is glad Trey got out of the car and says, "You never belonged there anyway." "J'all get 'em? . . . yeah," Trey asks and answers his own question. "I don't even know how I feel," comments the ungloating, indeed the fatalistic and tragic, Farris, who, in a poignant bit of filmic imagery, fades as he walks away.

A card informs us that Farris was killed two weeks later, that Trey went to Morehouse College in Atlanta (alma mater of Spike Lee), and that Brandi went to Spelman, also in Atlanta. "You still got one brother left" were Trey's last words to Farris, and we feel that his education will be in a sense for Farris and for Rick as well as for himself. Ice Cube's rap song "How to Survive in South Central," with its talk of a "concrete Vietnam," rises on the soundtrack.

Charles Mills's blazing images often seem to be ironically contrasting the bright possibilities of day with the lurid angers of the night. *Boyz N the Hood* excels in its performances, especially in those of the males, on which it concentrates. Larry Fishburne projects a Spencer Tracy authority, recast, of course, in a nobly African-American key. Cuba Gooding, Jr., as Trey brings force and charm to the role of the hood's golden boy; his most powerful scene occurs when he weeps in front of Brandi: "I never thought I'd be crying in front of a female." Gooding is clearly a future star. Ice Cube, as the unloved child driven into negative behaviors by constant unflattering compari-sons to a perfect sibling, is able to find the humanity within the stereotype. The film's women—Nia Long, Tyra Ferrell, and Angela Bassett as Rick's wife—are fine, but *Boyz* is essentially an examination of male codes—codes of destruction and codes of survival as they have evolved in the jungle of pleasant-seeming South Central Los An-geles.

Singleton is clearly a filmmaker with an agenda, but the urgency of his agenda is a response to what is real—how real the subsequent L.A. riots made clear. In *Boyz N the Hood,* agenda and art are one: the internal dynamics of the black family and the societal dynamics of power are not separate, but interconnected, as the film shows. Sin-gleton's subsequent film, *Poetic Justice,* set in the same milieu, focuses on a feisty young woman, a poet named Justice (Janet Jackson), and on her struggles with the men in her life and the life in her men. Singleton clearly wants to widen this *boyz*-centric perspective of his first film.

The movie takes an emotionally wounded beautician (Janet Jackson, in an uncertain film debut) and a suspicious mailman (Tupac Shakur, so powerful in *Juice*) on a journey of discovery up the scenic California coast from Los Angeles to Oakland. The pair learn to open their closed hearts through seeing both the glories (communal festivals) and pathologies of black life. Not wholly successful, especially in comparison to a movie like *Just Another Girl on the I.R.T.*, *Poetic Justice* has pleasures, above all Shakur's performance.

Another film that ends with a bright minority youth going—or at least applying—to college is *Hangin' with the Homeboys* (1991), written and directed by Joseph B. Vasquez, who had earlier made *Street Story* (1988) and *The Bronx War* (1989).

*The Bronx War* was an interesting film that, on the bloody surface, dealt with intertribal, black-versus-Hispanic drug wars, but was really a tense study of intrafamily dynamics: Tito (Joseph), though very nearly dragged down by the hospitality he extends to his treacherous, femme fatale sister-in-law, Rachel (Charmaine Cruz), returns redeemed at the end to his wife, Maria (Frances Colon). Catholic imagery (the Sacred Heart, the Virgin Mary) abounds—and its use seems more sincere than in the work of Ferrara. Himself half black and half Puerto Rican and from the Bronx, Vasquez chronicles in *Hangin'* one Friday night in the lives of four young friends from the racially mixed and racially sensitive South Bronx. Two are Puerto Rican, a supermarket clerk Johnny (John Leguizamo) and Italian wannabe-womanizer Vinny (Nestor Serrano); two are black, aspiring actor Tom (Mario Joyner) and "militant" welfare recipient Willie (Doug E. Doug). By dawn's light, it has become clear that Vinny and Willie are stuck in self-destructive ruts, while undiscourageable actor Tom and Johnny, who rejects his friends' cynicism and who has, moreover, had the luck to meet an educated and adult young woman, resolve to fight for their dreams. *Hangin'* is a winning parable, if slighter artistically than comparable films like those of Singleton, Dickerson, and Rich.

Charles Burnett was born in Mississippi and raised in Los Angeles, where he earned a Bachelor of Arts at UCLA, with a major in film. His first feature, *Killer of Sheep,* was filmed in black-and-white in 16mm in the 1970s and was shown at film festivals in 1981. His second feature was *My Brother's Wedding* in 1984. Both films are set in the middle-class, African-American Watts part of Los Angeles, a region whose poetic chronicler Burnett has become. *My Brother's Wedding* explores the textures and pressures of life there in a story of a young man working in his parents' dry cleaning store who has to decide whether to go to his yuppie brother's wedding or to the funeral of his best friend. Forces both centrifugal (class mobility, father-son conflict) and centripetal (traditions, family bonds) in the modern African-American community are subtly and powerfully shown.

In 1990, Los Angeles–based Burnett wrote and directed

*To Sleep with Anger.* He set it in one of the older parts of Watts, where the two-story houses are bigger, more rambling, and more substantial than the one-story bungalows of John Singleton's South Central. Burnett's film, also deeply African-American, has a very different feel from Singleton's; Burnett is telling a fable, a myth, a legend. Basing his screenplay on Southern folk tales he heard from his grandmother, he tells the tale of a trickster, "a man who comes to town to steal your soul." The huckster, Harry, is played by Danny Glover, who, as coexecutive producer, godfathered the movie in a spirit similar to Harvey Keitel's help on *Reservoir Dogs.*

The film's eerie blend of naturalism and the numinousness of magic is established in cinematographer Walt Lloyd's indelible opening shots of Harry sitting in a natty cream suit at what could be a Louisiana railroad station, suitcase poised alongside him. He sits on the left of the screen; to the right is a bowl of fruit on a table. Harry sits there, seemingly placid but actually full of malignant aggression, as is visualized in the tongues of flame that begin to lick, but not to burn, his fine attire and the glowing, unoffending fruit. Harry is the devil.

He is also the youngest brother of Gideon (Carl Lumbly, the fellow prisoner who introduces Malcolm to Islam in Spike Lee's *Malcolm X*), an old-time preacher and patriarch who has lived for some thirty years in Watts. Gideon has a wife (Mary Alice), two sons, Junior (Paul Butler) and Sam (Richard Brooks), two daughters-in-law (Vonetta McGee and Sheryl Lee Ralph), and a little grandson. The family's home and life-style have preserved as much of Louisiana as is possible in Los Angeles: there are chickens in cages out back, and there are birds. As so often in families, as, for example, in John Singleton's single-parent, two-son family in *Boyz,* one son is blessed with paternal approval—Junior here—and is the typecast *good* son. He and his pregnant wife are seen at Lamaze class. The little grandson is the child of Sam, a loan officer, and his wife, a real-estate broker. It is Sam and his wife who seem perpetually to be incurring Gideon's disapproval. The boy plays quietly about the house throughout, and in fact his play becomes crucial to the story.

As the day starts, Gideon mentions to his wife that he has lost his magic charm, his *toby,* which he has kept from down south. Later, it is found atop the refrigerator, when it causes a vase full of marbles to shake and fall.

Harry, unseen for thirty years, appears on the stoop, bag in hand. At once, bad vibes are felt: the boy "accidentally" touches him with a broom, a karmic no-no; the pregnant wife feels her baby kick and recoils when she is being introduced to Harry. Harry himself comes equipped with potent voodoo: a knife, a rabbit's foot, and decks of marked cards, emblems of his enthrallment to evil. After we see Harry at cards—he has unerringly chosen the disgruntled Sam to corrupt—we see Gideon at a baptizing service, standing in water and immersing a woman. It is fire versus water.

The weak and resentful Sam is soon seduced by Harry's wiles and snarls at his wife, "Don't pick up the cards; you're not in the game." It is above all the marriage unit, the family unit, that the destructive force is drawn to.

When Junior's wife explains to Harry that, on weekends, she works to feed the hungry, sometimes serving two hundred meals, Harry smoothly advises her that it is better to fatten one's stomach. For all the signs and portents surrounding Harry, we are for a while uncertain exactly what he is—a mischievous rogue bringing some forbidden fun to the house of a rigid, joyless preacher or something more malevolent and dangerous.

It is the community's verdict on Harry that makes up our minds. Hattie, a feisty old sinner now come to God, pays a visit to the house and knows right away what she is seeing in Harry, with his talk of swamproot and his flavor of the bayous. "You remind me," she says, "of all that went wrong in my life . . . you ain't worth the salt they put in greens." That night, there is a party, introduced by a delightful montage of colorfully got up guests arriving at the front door. Harry urges, but Hattie won't sing a sexy blues: "I told him I'm a different person now; I'm saved." She sings a hymn instead. Out in the kitchen, one of the guests presses Harry, who is uncomfortable, about a bloody incident in Louisiana, asking, "How exactly did those boys die?" The Harry picture begins to come clear.

Gideon, meanwhile, accuses Sam of neglecting his son. Sam reacts with rancor and resentment; it is Mother—Gideon's wife—who forces father and son to shake hands out on the lawn, so as not to sleep with anger.

Next morning, the two brothers take a walk on the railroad tracks and discuss family memories. We see, in soft-focus shots evoking history and memory, workers laying the track.

At home, Harry, sitting smugly in the kitchen, takes his knife to an apple, while upstairs Gideon has sickened and taken to his bed. Harry brings him soup; it is not, we suspect, a healing soup. Spiritual power in the household can be felt to be passing from Gideon to Harry. Harry begins to don the mantle of the weakening patriarch: he demands a clean bath, he cuts his nails downstairs, he develops a few mimic symptoms of illness himself. The balance shifts a bit when the community, Gideon's congregation, visits their sick pastor, whose wife feels that both Christian prayer and "old-fashioned remedies" like charms can be useful. Harry's induction of Sam into his dark mysteries continues.

When Junior criticizes Harry, his electric lights suddenly go out. Harry's strong powers are also visible in the disintegration of Sam's marriage. Sam's wife is reduced to a humiliated and weeping servant, standing and doling out food to a tableful of Harry's cronies. When she retreats from this abasement to the kitchen, Sam pursues and smacks her. She moves out, taking her son and going to Junior's house where the older brother shows only contempt for his younger brother.

The little boy cries, "I want my daddy," but the satanic Harry has gotten possession of his daddy, taking him walking by a stream in a diabolic echo of God's walk with Adam. Sam hears, magically, his little son's voice calling, but he is powerless to respond.

In a comic interlude, an old geezer proposes to the very unamused not-yet-widow of Gideon.

Sam, in torment, drives up to Junior's house and sits glumly in his car. Junior goes out to the car, yelling at his brother to roll down the window and talk, but he does not—cannot. He just sits there, shot from both outside (Junior's point of view) and inside (compassionate narrator's point of view).

Hattie gives Mother the lowdown, saying Harry is dangerous: "You can't keep a *wild* thing around children." "What must I do?" pleads Ma. "If it was left to me, I'd poison him." Harry glares balefully at what he intuits will be his nemesis, the little boy sweeping up. And we recall that, in the mythic cosmos of *To Sleep with Anger,* a broom is a prophylactic against evil, like garlic or a crucifix against Dracula.

Mother is beginning to see the light and gravely wonders, "Are you a good man; are you a friend, Harry?" Harry and his cronies have taken possession of Sam's house, now abandoned by his wife. Harry now feels free to air his philosophy of human relationships: "Never treat a woman as an equal. Come with me, Sam. We'll show you steamin' hot joints and some steamin' hot women." What Burnett succeeds in doing here is harder than it looks; he paints the face of evil in everyday life. He eschews the fire imagery of the film's prologue; still less does he indulge in the flamboyant theatrics of the apocalyptic climax of *Barton Fink*. It all looks very homely, very simple.

A rainy night. Sam pays a visit to his ailing father's house to announce, "I'm going back home with Harry." It seems Mephistopheles has captured Faust. But redemptive domestic details intrude: Gideon's bed has to be moved to get it out from under a leak in the roof. Junior, incensed at Sam's refusal to help, calls him "boy." This is inflammatory. The brothers fight. Sam has been holding a knife (Harry's diabolic armory) and brings it into play. He is about to stab Junior when their mother interposes and takes a deep wound in her hand. Her sacrificial intervention instantly clears and sobers the situation. Junior *and* Sam rush her to the Emergency Room; Junior asks a (white) nurse why it's so crowded. "Friday Night, full moon," she replies.

The next images, after those of the hospital, are of wet corn and bedewed flowers; it is as though nature, life, goodness are starting to reassert their strengths. In slow motion, Mother is helped up the steps of the home. Harry pays a visit, supposedly of farewell, but he is yet to be exorcised. The exorcism proves child's play. Harry slips on the boy's marbles, accidentally—or perhaps accidentally on purpose—left lying on the kitchen floor. Sprawled on the floor, he has what looks like a heart attack and dies. It is more as if the household and the community had collectively *willed* him dead.

A white paramedic refuses to remove the body on the grounds that the death did not occur while Harry was in his care. The corpse in the kitchen becomes grievance and annoyance and joke for the rest of the film. Laughter has returned to the world. The irrepressible Hattie arrives, bends over the body, and declares, "I never noticed how big his eyes were." Food is brought by all. It is a kind of wake.

Gideon awakens, rises from his bed, and makes his

gingerly way downstairs to the amazement of all. The spell on him has passed now that its source is gone. Gideon has learned a little something, it appears, for he addresses Sam, who happens to be wearing one of his father's shirts, with something resembling affection; Sam gently sasses him back; an old familial wound is beginning to heal. Sam later explains to his wife that he was in hell: "There was a struggle inside me." "What lessons have you learned, Samuel?" she lovingly asks as their little boy looks on contentedly.

When Gideon attempts to tell a preacherly joke about hell, his wife sternly intervenes and stops him. She brandishes her bandaged hand in earnest of her own recent and very unfunny experience in hell.

Next day, the body is still there. The municipal ambulance will not come into the neighborhood. A mild earthquake upsets the gathered folk (they are not exactly mourners), but only for a moment. All troop out to a neighbor's picnic, leaving the sheeted body still on the kitchen floor. A kid down the block cacophonously practices the trumpet—this has been a running irritant throughout.

Burnett's mix of religious fable and sociological naturalism is a delicate and moving accomplishment. Aided by a rich and subtle gallery of performances—in particular by Danny Glover's smoothly suckering bonhomie as Harry and by Mary Alice's quiet iron as Mother—he has brought the universe of juju and toby and old-time religion into a contemporary African-American context and shown its pertinence. Telling of a trickster fishing for a soul, Burnett makes some of the same points as Singleton in *Boyz*, where also, we recall, the strongest character grounded his values in a religious code, that of Islam. Burnett's film is about a devil and about the virtues of family love and transgenerational solidarity, even as the African-American family changes from preacher-centered, patriarchal ways to a time of loan officers and career women. Burnett's touch on both the supernatural and the sociological is light, light but serious. He is a tactful artist, never showing more of hell or of heaven that we need to get the message. There is, finally, a feminist perspective in *To Sleep with Anger*, in which hell means the humiliation and marginalization of women, while, conversely, heaven is made possible by the redemptive gesture of a woman.

$G$regg Araki, born in Los Angeles in 1962, took a B.A. in film studies at UC Santa Barbara in 1982 and an M.A. in film production from USC in L.A. in 1984. His biggest influences have been Jean-Luc Godard, Rainer Werner Fassbinder, Terrence Malick, and other usual suspects. In 1987, he made his first feature, *Three Bewildered People in the Night*, and in 1989 his second, *The Long Weekend o' Despair* both in black-and-white and costing about $5,000. In 1990, he met Jon Jost, a veteran of the American independent film scene. Jost liked Araki's work, gave him some Fuji film stock, and lent him sync-sound equipment, thus enabling him to make *The Living End*, his third film, in the fall and winter of 1990–1991 in color and with sync sound, although the actual filming "in the boondocks of L.A." was, says the filmmaker, "still done very much guerrilla-style, without permits, utilizing a minimal crew." Araki was his own cameraman and editor. A loan from a relative got things rolling, and, well into postproduction, there came a $20,000 grant from the American Film Institute to finish up.

Araki wrote *The Living End* in 1988 as a tragedy about two HIV-positive gay lovers who die together in a blazing Liebestod; it was then called *Fuck the World*. But he found himself shying away from making a despairing statement, turned to another project, and only later returned to a rethought *Living End*. Rethought, but not defanged. The picture is still an angry, violent road movie about two doomed (seropositive) gay lovers rocketing around mallscapes, landscapes, and, finally seascapes in California. It both fits into and stretches the set boundaries of a genre that boasts Fritz Lang's *You Only Live Once*, Nicholas Ray's *They Live by Night*, Joseph H. Lewis's *Gun Crazy*, Arthur Penn's *Bonnie and Clyde*, Malick's *Badlands*, and Godard's *Pierrot le fou* (a pervasively seminal work for filmmakers today, full as it is of picturesque alienation).

The plot is disarmingly simple; the narrative energy is compounded of high anger and low humor. The film's first image is a spray-painted slogan: FUCK THE WORLD. Luke (Mike Dytri) is a loose cannon, a tattooed outlaw, a hustler, bursting with in-your-face hostility. Hitchhiking in the outskirts of L.A., he is picked up by two lesbian serial killers (Johanna Went and Mary Woronov), but spared. Luke finds himself becoming a serial killer of sorts himself, offing some gay-bashing skinheads (this is shot for laughs) and a cop. This begins to look like deep John Waters, but things change tone with the introduction of Jon (Craig Gilmore), a timid, middle-class movie critic who keeps meaning to write the definitive piece on "The Death of Cinema." Jon has just gotten the news about his HIV status and is in shock when he bumps into Luke. They click erotically in Jon's poster-littered apartment. When Jon conscientiously tells Luke the news, Luke, far from recoiling in horror, says he is seropositive, too: "Don't worry about it. No big deal. So we're both going to die, maybe in ten years, maybe next week. We're victims of the sexual revolution. We have nothing to lose. We can say fuck the system, fuck everything. We're totally free."

Fortified by Luke's paradoxical exultation, the prim Jon casts his lot with his new lover. Luke uses Jon's bewildered attraction, his disorientation, his deracination by sexual attraction and disease to cast him as his road buddy in a spree flick. The dynamic and humor of *The Living End* stem from Jon's increasingly feeble attempts to maintain bourgeois Apollonian sobriety as Luke drags him screaming into a Dionysiac abyss. This very odd couple has lunar echoes, then, of Martin and Lewis, Ricky and Lucy, George and Gracie.

They hit San Francisco, where a respectable gay friend of Luke's slams the door in their faces. They cruise through a bleak, neon-and-asphalt cosmos of gas stations and parking lots, junk-food places, and cash machines—all symbolic of the uncaring America in which the pair are internal exiles. Says Luke, "If Bush got injected with the virus, I bet there'd be a cure found tomorrow."

Jon tries to keep in touch with his ordered past life by calling, collect, from public phones, his good friend Darcy (Darcy Marta), who, back in L.A., is crazy with worry about him. (They are by now hunted cop killers.) Darcy's boyfriend tries to calm her down by saying, "You're not talking about the most well-adjusted person in the world to begin with." Jon also tries to maintain his Apollonian cleanliness: "All I know is that if I don't brush my teeth in two minutes I'm going to kill myself. I'm a fag, okay? I can't stand feeling dirty."

The couple's directionless odyssey acquires a neurotic pattern of repetition: Luke will commit some outrage, like shooting up a cash machine; Jon will announce he's had enough; Luke will then draw him back into complicity by the power of his frank sexuality. Finally, after Luke goes on an unusually out-of-control shooting spree, Jon tries to split (again) and the berserk Luke sticks a gun into Jon's mouth. He has put the gun into his own mouth before and is clearly capable of pulling any trigger. We are on a deserted, surf-pounded Southern California beach at dawn. The film's conclusion becomes, in this tense and sexy showdown, a living end; the gun loses its gun-ness and behaves as a phallus, an instrument not of Thanatos but of Eros. For a moment, life and love go on, precariously.

Araki calls *The Living End* "easily my most desperate picture to date," as well as "the most frankly gay," but insists equally on its romantic aspect, its valorization of the "irrationality of love" and "the possibility of romantic redemption." It is indeed the abrasive, explosive copresence of rage and romance that gives the film its distinctive color. It *is* sexy. Araki has, however, a way to go before he finds cinematic shapes that express his character, concerns, and sensibility as richly and convincingly as those that, say, Hartley or Van Sant have worked out for themselves. There is still much artistic roughage in the Araki diet: verbal rage needs variety, and it needs narrative inventiveness to work. But *The Living End* does have life, and that is basic.

Craig Gilmore, a veteran of soaps, makes a sympathetic Jon, and Mike Dytri is a believably loco Luke. Both actors make a point, in their publicity material, of being openly gay. (Is it an accident that this unevangelical pair, Jon and Luke, have evangelists' names?) Darcy Marta, who was in Araki's *Three Bewildered People,* is a very likable listening post here. One name that should be singled out is that of Mary Woronov, as lesbian killer Daisy. Woronov, a star of independent cinema from the days of Warhol through Paul Bartel, is the beautiful Pallas Athena of the avant-garde, coolly alluring and dismissive at once.

*The Living End* is grittily soundtracked with "alternative/industrial" rock cuts. Sample title: "Reactionary Lesbos with Gun," as performed by Cambodia and published by Braindead Musick.

Araki's next film, described as an investigation of gay and lesbian teens, is called *Totally Fucked Up.* No surprise there.

*T*wo filmmakers whose work, while confrontational, is more overtly theoretical and formally subversive than

Araki's are Todd Haynes and Tom Kalin. Haynes, raised in Encino, California, graduated from Brown University in Providence, Rhode Island, with a B.A. in semiotics. His first 16mm films were *Assassins: A Film Concerning Rimbaud* (1985) and *Superstar: The Karen Carpenter Story* (1987). The former deals with the cult of the French *poète maudit;* the latter uses a mélange of Barbie-like dolls, miniatures, and documentary footage to examine the life of the tragically anorexic singer, whose survivors have succeeded in having the film pulled from distribution. Both *Assassins* and *Superstar* ran forty-three minutes.

In 1989, Haynes began filming *Poison,* a 16mm, eighty-five-minute film he wrote himself. It has three separate but interlocking tales: *Hero,* a tabloid-TV-like mock investigation of a suburban tot who slew his father ("He seemed like such a nice boy," purr neighbors), *Horror,* a black-and-white sci-fi-ish story of a scientist investigating and catching a deadly sex virus and thus joining the ranks of its shunned and persecuted victims (parallels to AIDS abound), and *Homo,* a color episode about male inmates in love that explicitly evokes the ethos of Jean Genet's writings and his short film *Chant d'amour.*

*Poison* was filmed in six weeks in Brooklyn and in Castle William on Governors Island off Lower Manhattan for a budget of $250,000, of which some $75,000 came from the New York State Council on the Arts and from the NEA. It is a film whose didacticism—about, say, the deceptiveness of suburban normality—is never subtle or particularly surprising.

Tom Kalin made *Swoon,* his first feature, in 1991, though he had earlier written and directed shorts and videos and had been a producer for the educational film company AIDSFILMS. *Swoon* takes a revisionist look at the famous 1924 kidnapping and murder of a child by rich Chicago homosexuals Nathan Leopold, Jr., and Richard Loeb, as well as their subsequent trial. At that trial, defense attorney Clarence Darrow used psychiatrists to convince the jury that the pair's homosexuality was itself pathological and proof of insanity and hence grounds for sparing their lives.

These events had been lightly fictionalized in the 1940s in the Patrick Hamilton play and the Hitchcock film *Rope*—and in the 1950s in the book and movie *Compulsion*. But Kalin is not after sympathy. His is a cinema of cultural deconstruction, of bullying theory. He wants us to take notes, and not to argue back.

The works of Araki, Haynes, and Kalin do show a modernist edge and shape conspicuously missing in the two quasi-mainstream, AIDS-themed films written by Craig Lucas and directed by Norman René: the moving ensemble drama *Longtime Companion* and the weakly allegorical *Prelude to a Kiss*.

Quentin Tarantino was born in 1963 in Knoxville, Tennessee, but came to Los Angeles with his divorced mother two years later. He lived as a kid in the grimy, sooty, factory-ridden South Bay section, which abuts the South Central area of *Boyz N the Hood* and has been described as a mixed, white-trash extension of South Central. We are talking about *mean* streets. On the *other* side of South Bay is the Pacific, both the posh Pacific of

Malibu and the prole Pacific of Manhattan Beach.

Tarantino boasts of *not* being a graduate of film school, bragging in interviews, ''I didn't go to film school. I went to films.'' He haunted local movie houses for karate and slasher flicks and got a formative job in a Manhattan Beach video store, which in essence served him as a library of film history. In his early twenties, he turned to a career in acting, landing small roles on TV and in the odd feature, such as Godard's *King Lear*.

In the late 1980s he started writing scripts; in October 1990 he wrote *Reservoir Dogs* with the idea of directing it himself—''guerrilla-style'' (a Sixties-radical idiom used by many independent filmmakers, especially early on in their careers)—in 16mm, black-and-white, on the familiar streets of Los Angeles, with himself as Mr. Pink and his partner-producer Lawrence Bender as Nice Guy Eddie, with assorted pals filling out the cast.

Through an acting-school connection of Tarantino's, the script got to Harvey Keitel, who had already been Tarantino's dream choice for the lead, Mr. White. Keitel, enthused by what he read, signed on at once as star and coproducer with casting approval. It was a memorable moment in independent cinema when the powerhouse presence of *Mean Streets, Mortal Thoughts,* and *Bad Lieutenant* midwived an exciting new project. (The actual financing came from the video division of LIVE Entertainment, which also contributed to the financing of Ferrara's *Bad Lieutenant,* also with Keitel.) The final cast proved one of the tightest, tensest ensembles in recent cinema.

In essence, *Reservoir Dogs* is a bungled-heist flick in the tradition of Stanley Kubrick's *The Killing*, John Huston's *Asphalt Jungle*, Robert Siodmak's *Criss Cross*, and Raoul Walsh's *White Heat*. (That title: in one of his elusive explanations of it, Tarantino said it was his garbled pronunciation of a film he often recommended in that video store: *Au revoir, les enfants*.) "It is," he says, "the pulp novel I always wanted to write. Although the story is very much present-day, it has a Fifties look, and I consciously used music from the past."

The Sundance Institute Directors Workshop and Lab gave Tarantino a preproduction and rehearsal grant. *Reservoir Dogs* was shot in five weeks, largely in the rundown, low-rise commercial and residential streets and buildings of East Los Angeles, old Los Angeles, lost Los Angeles. A warehouse where much of the film transpires—the heist is planned there and the crooks repair there afterward—was a former mortuary at Figueroa and Fifty-ninth; one of its old embalming rooms upstairs became the apartment of Mr. Orange, the only crook given a private life, and that only because his private identity is not in harmony with his assumed persona. Like Edmond O'Brien in *White Heat*, he is an undercover cop.

The evenly, boldly lit sets are shot in very deep focus and long-held mastershots by Polish-born cinematographer Andrzej Sekula. Tarantino's is a Bazinian cinema of lengthy takes and minimal montage.

The story of *Dogs* is told in shuffled chunks of time, each labeled with the name of the character who is being backgrounded. We do not see the heist of Israeli diamonds itself, only its preparation and its aftermath. But this oblique and postmodern style is perfect for the material.

The crooks are assembled and coached by a gruff, small-time, Teamsterish hood called Joe Cabot (Lawrence Tierney), assisted by his hulking son, Nice Guy Eddie (Chris Penn). The oldest, hippest, and steadiest crook is Mr. White (Harvey Keitel), who pairs off naturally with the bright young Mr. Orange, the secret cop, who seems a cut above the others intellectually (Tim Roth). Mr. Blonde (Michael Madsen) is an ex-con who has just done time for Joe. Mr. Pink (Steve Buscemi) is a whiner and complainer. Lesser lights are Mr. Brown (Tarantino himself) and Mr. Blue (Eddie Bunker, a quondam con whose criminal experiences served as the basis for the film *Straight Time*). Joe insists on the quaint color names to depersonalize the robbers; if one is caught, he will know nothing, not even the real names, of the others. The men dress exactly alike to further this homogenization, in black suits, white shirts, narrow black ties, shades—like hired pallbearers or members of the secret service. This is a stylized caper inside a stylized caper movie.

*Dogs'* verbal wit is a match for its visual bravura. A precredit sequence illustrates: as the gang sit in a greasy spoon, Brown indulges in an appropriately steamy *explication de texte* about the Madonna lyric "Like a Virgin": "It's about this girl who digs a guy with a big dick. The entire song, it's a metaphor for big dicks. It hurts, it hurts her. The pain of reminding a fuck machine what it was once like to be a virgin, *like* a virgin." This is both funny and plausible. Stingy Pink next launches into a long and clever justification of his refusal to tip waitresses. That settled, all the crooks march out in slomo. K-Billy radio station is having a Seventies nostalgia festival; introduced by the laconic, affectless DJ-voice of comic Steven Wright, the kitsch sounds of that decade will counterpoint the action.

After the credits, we are at once in the movie's present tense, just postheist. Orange's stomach is gushing blood over his shirt and over the whole rear seat of a car being driven by White. He's been shot and begs White to take him to a hospital, but White sticks to the plan and heads for the warehouse. White does, though, offer encouragement, a comradely cheering-up to the terrified, sopping younger man. The contact these two men make is the only human relationship in the film; there are no women present at all.

Back in the warehouse, Orange and White exchange their real names as an earnest of friendship *and* because White clearly thinks Orange is a goner. Orange lies virtually insensible while White and Pink bicker acrimoniously about what to do and what went wrong ("People were killed." "Real people?" "No, just cops.") Blonde arrives with a surprise: he has a cop (Kirk Baltz) in the trunk of his car; he spits on the cop and ties him to a chair.

Now is where we get a flashback about Blonde's induction into the gang: just out of jail, in Joe's office, which is adorned with symmetrical elephant tusks and a painting of a punctured Saint Sebastian, Blonde engages in a mock-hostile insult bout with Nice Guy Eddie about prison sodomy and blacks. It is another of Tarantino's vertiginous verbal cadenzas that manage to shock the political left and right alike in their heightening and tightening of macho rooster rhetoric and in their hilarious and unashamed exploitation of street sexism and racism. One feminist accused the film, and not just its characters, of a "paranoid homophobic fear of the other that explodes in hate speech"; she was also less than pleased with the film's one-gendered cast. Another critic spoke of the film's "excessive violence and self-loathing and insufficient catharsis and redemption," as if rating a chili recipe.

Quentin Tarantino displeases some precisely because he clearly has a sense of humor. We think, after this flashback, that we know Blonde for a loyal goombah. We are wrong, for, back in the present tense, he proceeds viciously, sadistically (taking up that throwaway hint in the Saint Sebastian image), and sarcastically to torture and maim the helpless cop: "It's amusing to me to torture a cop. . . . Was that as good for you as it was for me?" He slices off an ear as the radio croons, "Stuck in the Middle with You." Pouring kerosene over the pleading cop, he is about to torch his victim when he is shot by the supine, bleeding Orange, who can barely raise his gun. Orange grunts, "I'm a cop" to the other cop, who says, "I know. I met you."

The camera, which has been circling and dancing around the victim in seeming kinetic complicity with

Blonde (this camera movement is the film's only morally indefensible moment), now gives us close-ups of the two wretched cops: "How do I look? I'm fuckin' deformed," says one. "I'm fuckin' dyin'," says the other. Then a long wide shot with Orange on the left and the uniformed cop on the right. The film seems to have righted itself morally because it's sympathizing not necessarily with cops, but with pain.

Then comes the in-depth Orange flashback, for we have just found out his secret. In a diner he boasted to his superior that he could convince the hoods he is a drug dealer. He "rehearses" his "script" on a roof and in his blue apartment, which is decorated with a poster of the comic-book hero Silver Surfer and a cross. To gull the hoods, he tells them a scary story of cops and blood-hounds in a men's room; we *see* his lie enacted on screen and then we see him step out of the lie while the camera (a surrogate for the hoods) stays inside the lie. (It actually gets even trickier, as the cops inside his story read *his* lines.) This formalist playfulness and dazzle trumps Hitchcock's visual mendacity in *Stage Fright*.

Back in his apartment after convincing the hoods, Orange cheers himself up: "Don't pussy out on me; you're fuckin' Baretta; they believe every word." That cross on the wall is a portent of his coming agony. As the guys drive to "crime school," they discuss Pam Grier and was she or was she not in *Get Christie Love!* to the radio's pounding repetitions of the word *ungachaka* from "Hooked on a Feeling." Heist preparations begin with the grotesquely schoolmasterly Joe standing at a blackboard with a pointer. Pink bitches about his allotted name's effeminate connotations. White and Orange pair off for the on-site run-throughs, and suddenly we are in postheist time as a scared woman shoots Orange while he is trying to commandeer her car. The killing irony is, of course, that the (perfectly justified) woman shoots the one crook who is not a crook.

Back in the present tense for the final time, Nice Guy Eddie arrives in the bare warehouse and does not buy Orange's cover story about how he shot Blonde to prevent him from stealing the loot. Instead, Nice Guy blows away the tied-up cop. Daddy Joe arrives. A standoff forms: father and son versus White and Orange. (Pink has scampered off.) The four gun-holding men draw on each other in a samurailike four-sided parallelogram of force.

Results: father and son killed in a quick exchange with White and Orange; White hit; Orange still gushing from the stomach. It is violence as geometry, with the horror of the content almost neutralized by the formalist brio of the doing. But formalism yields to feeling as White, in a pietà pose, cradles Orange, red-slicked in his own blood. Orange, in gratitude to White for "saving" his life from the suspicious father and son, confesses: "I'm a cop, I'm sorry." White wails with grief—either at the loss of Orange or at the loss of trust. (For, of course, Orange had betrayed the whole setup.) It is a wild moment of Keitelian excess in what had been, in comparison to his unharnessed extravagance in *Bad Lieutenant,* a quiet performance. He puts his gun to Orange's head. Pity? Anger? As cops break into the warehouse, a shot rings out, but we do not know who fires or where, for the camera stays on the conflicted, pained face of White. Coup de grâce? Suicide? Tim Roth told me only he and Keitel and Tarantino know exactly what occurs at the end. Perhaps a sequel will clarify everything.

In one sense the time of the movie has been the time it takes Orange to bleed to death. And from this angle *Reservoir Dogs* is the most antiviolence movie ever made, for we spend much of ninety-nine minutes looking right at the results of one gunshot wound.

The cast is a miracle of repellent macho. Besides Keitel, Roth excels as the blood-red Orange; he is an amazing London actor who has been around since Stephen Frears's *The Hit* in 1984 and is far closer in street grit and ferocious energy to Cagney than is the Brit Cagney-lookalike, Kenneth Branagh. *Reservoir Dogs* belongs to Roth, but also memorable are, as the evil Blonde, Michael Madsen (Louise's boyfriend in *Thelma and Louise*), Steve Buscemi as the complaining Pink, Chris Penn as the powder-keg Nice Guy Eddie, and Kirk Baltz as the victimized cop. A special word is due massive, gruff, nononsense Lawrence Tierney as Joe; he has been haunting B movies since *The Ghost Ship,* in 1943, and he has been staging robberies since *Dillinger* in 1945.

Tarantino has reportedly signed multimillion-dollar deals with studios, some for screenplays alone, some for directing as well as writing. One title mentioned is *Pulp Fiction,* a tribute to the world of the crime magazines of the 1930s. Sounds juicy. Tarantino is confident he can remain Tarantino in a studio context. The eccentricity and the authority he manifests in *Reservoir Dogs* give some reason to believe him.

A Tarantino script, *True Romance* (1993), was filmed by mainstream director Tony Scott. Two low-rent lovers (a smooth Christian Slater and a sensationally sexy Patricia Arquette) take to the road, fleeing a messily violent Detroit for a choreographically violent Los Angeles. Popping up are Dennis Hopper, Gary Oldman, Christopher Walken, Saul Rubinek, Bronson Pinchot, Chris Penn—and Val Kilmer as Slater's guardian angel, Elvis (see *Mystery Train*). It is Tarantino Lite, but it is brilliantly funny.

Carl Franklin's *One False Move* is a twisty and surprising thriller that moves from South Central Los Angeles to Star City, a fictional town in Arkansas. It was written by Billy Bob Thornton and Tom Epperson, who grew up buddies in the small Arkansas town of Hot Springs and know in their bones all the canny ways and detours human nature can take in small Southern towns. The two wound up in Los Angeles, where Thonton became an actor but also wrote and sold scripts. *One False Move* is the first of their scripts to be produced.

As their director, producers Jesse Beaton and Ben Myron hired an unusual talent. Reared in a rough part of Northern California, Carl Franklin, now in his mid-forties, started acting at UC Berkeley in the late 1960s, then became a moderately successful stage actor in New York and a regular on TV in L.A. until he hit it big on *The A-Team*. But his reaction to TV serial stardom was to start working, in 1986, toward an M.F.A. in directing at the

AFI. He cites as among his favorite filmmakers Kurosawa, Scorsese, Coppola, Renoir, and Charles Burnett.

While a student at AFI, Roger Corman's Concorde films hired him to direct low-budget movies, among them *Nowhere to Run* (1989), in which Jason Priestley of *Beverly Hills, 90210* and five other high school seniors in a small Texas town get involved with sex, municipal corruption, and a crazed revenge killer. The versatile Franklin also directed *Full Fathom Five,* a submarine technothriller. But *One False Move,* filmed in Los Angeles and in Cotton Plant, Arkansas, in 1990 but released in 1992, was Franklin's first solid at-bat in the artistic majors. He hit a homer.

*One False Move* opens at night on a bungalowed street in South Central L.A., the locale of *Boyz N the Hood*. A car pulls up and Fantasia (Cynda Williams), a coke slut/femme fatale, puts her long legs out to join a birthday party, a party its happy celebrants are videotaping. But Fantasia's treacherous role is to admit her two cohorts, Ray (Billy Bob Thornton, the real-life husband of Cynda Williams), a frazzled but lethal piece of white trash, and black Pluto (Michael Beach), a glacially impassive sadistic killer. Pluto leaves the video camera running as he gags, smothers, chloroforms, and stabs the three partygoers. Ray kills three more at another house. It is all about drugs and cash.

The evil trio take their cash and coke and head east—to sell it in Houston and then to make a stop in Star City. Beautiful Fantasia, a wispy, sad soul, half white and half black, the lover and accomplice of Ray but somehow a limp victim of Ray's, too, seems to perform all her awful actions in a dreamlike, remorseful trance. Ray orders Fantasia upstairs to kill the household's little boy, whom she dolefully hunts in the shower and the bedroom and finds cowering and crying in a clearly lit closet. (All of James L. Carter's interior shots in this movie are luminously, smoothly lit in dry colors.)

*One False Move* is hypnotized by symmetries and by differences. It is a rarity in recent American movies in being about relations *between* the races. One expression of the film's symmetry is its matching pair of human triangles. Just as Fantasia's glance falls compassionately on the little black boy in Los Angeles, we cut to a white father (Bill Paxton) in Star City rushing into his little daughter's bedroom to comfort her after a bad dream. Pensively, he pulls down the lamp chain in her room.

Tom Epperson's favorite film is *High Noon,* and he here plays some ironic variations on that classic. In L.A. next morning, two homicide cops, one white (Jim Metzler) and one black (Earl Billings), survey the crime scenes; when the videotape yields a mention of Star City, it is clear they'll have to go there and a call is placed to L.A. by hotshot, eager-beaver, good-ole-boy Sheriff Dale Dixon, nicknamed Hurricane. Dale is the father of the little girl, who sits on his lap in his office as he talks to the condescending big shots in L.A.

Meanwhile, the three criminals are heading grimly eastward toward some kind of rendezvous in Star City. Coiled up like three rattlers in their car, they drive through New Mexico and Texas. Pluto hates the road, hates the idea of going to Star City, and wants to go home to Chicago. He is a city rat. In a lurid New Mexico hotel, the trio snarl and fight; Ray eats take-out chicken, Fantasia snorts a line of coke, and Pluto reads a newspaper and gazes with disgust as the lovers cuddle.

By contrast, Arkansas offers tableaux of hospitality and feasting. The two L.A. cops land in Little Rock and drive toward Star City (the white cop, Dud, sarcastically says, "I'm a country boy. I was born in Malibu"). Dale intercepts them and takes them to lunch in a café. He exudes a puppyish eagerness to please. But, for all his deference to the city cops, he knows a lot they do not. He knows his town, and we see his easy knowledge: the waitress's husband's gall bladder, the bridge he scarred when he was fourteen, how to calm down a drunken husband with an ax (Dud, by contrast, draws his gun and scares everybody).

Dale and his wife, Cheryl Ann (Natalie Canerday), have a barbecue on the lawn for the visitors. It proves an evening full of down-home goodwill, despite Dale's thoughtless reference to the approaching trio as "that piece of white trash and them two niggers." The film treats Cheryl Ann with respect, despite her cookie-baking and her slight pretentiousness ("I read nonfiction"); temptations to condescend to her are mostly resisted. Toward the end of the evening, Cheryl Ann pleads with Dud to keep her husband from hot-dogging it.

Out on the porch, to a chorus of crickets, Dud tells Dale how lucky he is: "nice house, nice family." But Dale is deaf to nuance and cheerily boasts, "Yeah, I hardly ever lose a coin toss. My ma told me I was born under a lucky star." His luck, we suspect, is about to be severely tested.

Cut to the antithetical trio: a cop in a Texas convenience store smells something fishy, follows the trio's new-bought car along a stretch of night road lit only by their four headlights, pulls them over, orders them out of the car, and gets shot by Fantasia because Ray, despite Pluto's urgent plea, lost his cool and got snotty to the cop. Fantasia had been sweetly friendly to the cop in the store and at the car window ("Hi, it's you again"); she can scarcely believe what she had done: "Did I kill that man back there? I think I killed that man." This whole whispered, stark, minimalist sequence, full of ticking menace, deserves to be a film-noir classic, worthy of *Detour*. And Cynda Williams is a marvel of screen acting; her unfocused, vague dreaminess creates a frightened and whipped creature, responsible and not responsible for what she does. By now, Ray and Pluto know and resent that she spared the kid in L.A.

Next morning in Arkansas, snobbery and insincerity strain the good trio's coherence. Dale shyly asks Dud if he might be welcome to come to L.A. and join the force there; Dud patronizingly agrees but later mocks and derides Dale to his partner, McFeely, who likes Dale more than Dud does, actually—symmetries again. Dale overhears, mortified, behind the candy counter in the diner—slow dolly into his face, registering shame and resentment. In that long, tight moment he surrenders his L.A. dreams, as Fantasia had to.

But the smartass Angelenos mocked too soon. The next scene is in Dale's office, where a picture of the three desperadoes taken by the convenience-store camera has come through. The men's pictures have been in the papers; Fantasia's not. Dale sits somberly drinking coffee by his window and remarks, "Her name is not Fantasia; it's Lila Walker." How he knows this is the film's very heart. What he intends to do about it is the film's denouement.

This is the moment of the movie's peripeteia. Lila was a local girl who left town some five years back. That night Dale takes the L.A. cops to the Walker house, where live her mother, brother, and five-year-old son, "good people, Christian people," as Dale says. He explains to a nosy McFeely that he once arrested Lila for shoplifting: "It wasn't but ten bucks, lipstick and that shit they put on their eyes." McFeely remarks that Lila seems to have graduated from shoplifting; Dale insists: "I don't believe she killed anybody." And he rejects McFeely's insinuations about a personal relationship. Back home, Dale strokes his sleeping wife and gazes at his sleeping daughter, as if to ground himself before setting out for his fate.

Lila, having lifted their money and left the two men in Houston (where they will murder three more drug dealers), gets off a bus at a rural crossing and is met by her brother. Franklin here mixes long, fatal, high-angle shots with close-ups in the car full of hope and life. Her brother takes her to a deserted house on the outskirts of town, that classic noir setting. Night falls; Lila's brother and little son leave her after a visit; Dale enters the kitchen. She is at the sink. He frisks her—their touch is electric. They move to the living room. She wants him to let her go; he says he doesn't have the legal authority. Her come-back articulates what we have come to suspect: "You didn't have the legal authority to fuck me when I was seventeen. Byron is your son. He's nearly as white as you." It is the moment when the two triangles intersect. This is why Lila spared the kid in L.A.; this is why Dale awoke in the night at that very minute.

The two sit in the dark. He rejects her offer of sex (she gropes him) and is uncomfortable at her ironic inquiries about his wife and daughter. There is a classic noir confrontation about cigarettes and guns when she goes to her purse for her menthols. He grabs her first and pulls out a gun. Innocence! Surprise! "I forgot that thing was even in there. I don't know how it works." "You pull the damn trigger." But, a bit mollified, he throws her the pack and gives her a light. He has refused a piece of "our son's" birthday cake, but he begins to accept her truths and to believe her when she says, "I never meant you any trouble. I still don't."

Morning light is beginning to slant horizontally into the peach-colored room. Dale draws all the shades. The two onetime lovers sit smoking at opposite corners as the morning breaks outside. It is a moment that might recall the end of *Criss Cross* where doomed, betraying lovers await the dawn, but the configuration is fraught with new meaning here; the morning might actually change something. "I'll start giving your mother money for him," promises Dale. "Why don't you just say, 'Byron, I'm your daddy'?" she presses him. She kneels at his feet and pleads with him to let her go.

Ray telephones. Lila gives him directions, but cooperates with Dale in setting up an ambush. "And then you'll let me go?" "I'll let you go." Soon the players for the final face-off are in place—or, in the case of the L.A. cops, *out* of place, for little Byron has mischievously misled them about the location of the deserted house he had visited the previous night. (Cheryl Ann is seen at home pouring cereal for her daughter's breakfast; the day can bring her little good.)

Dale's scheme works at first; he surprises Ray and Pluto and orders them onto the floor. But he is distracted by Lila's confused, anguished reply to Ray's charge of betrayal and gets stabbed by Pluto. In quick succession, Dale shoots Pluto and is winged by Ray. Out on the porch, Lila is shot in the head by Ray, who was aiming at Dale, who savagely pours bullets into Ray. Pluto, in a last spasm of malice, staggers outside to die. It is a tragicomic, bloody mess: three dead, one gravely wounded and curled on the ground.

The L.A. pair, with little Byron, roar up too late, guns drawn uselessly again. "That son of a bitch nailed 'em" is McFeely's impressed tribute.

A high-angle shot takes in all the carnage in the dewy front yard. Then we go down in the dirt for a long, low-angled final shot. Dale lies supine in front of the cop car, whose radio squawks that an ambulance is on the way. Little Byron comes up to Dale, asking, "Mister, are you dead?" He starts to go looking for the "pretty lady," but Dale, in a weak voice, tells him to stay and engages the child in small talk about keys and the boy's exact age. Dolly in slowly to a close-up as Dale reaches up tenderly to grasp the boy's arm. The end. He has publicly embraced his son. Too late? The exact fate of this father and son must stay unknown, like that of the similar relationship at the finale of *Reservoir Dogs*. But the final pairing of white father and black son—half-fortuitous, half-fated, and amid so much tragedy—is profoundly moving.

Many streams contribute to the excellence of *One False Move*. There is the film-noir element. The script has been described as "in the gritty, white-trash tradition of such authors as Jim Thompson." Bill Paxton says he was drawn to the script because it reminded him of a Jim Thompson novel. Carl Franklin stresses rather the moral side, saying, "The whole movie is about atonement. It's about reaping what you sow. The original script was called *Hurricane,* and that character, the sheriff that Bill Paxton plays so well, is absolutely the center of the story. In a sense he brings it all on himself."

And just as Epperson's favorite film is *High Noon,* so Billy Bob Thornton is drawn to the Horton Foote of *Tender Mercies*. All the ingredients make a fresh whole: the noir obsession with the destructive grip of the past, Carl Franklin's African-American feeling for the fact that America's past is inescapably a story of racial interactions, the *High Noon* narrative energy that brings the two groups into collision, the redemptive Southern humanism of a Horton Foote. Thornton and Epperson know the South. Epperson maintains that "the South gets a bad rap in race relations; real people aren't driven by the anger we often see in films." *One False Move* brings a knowledge of lived lives to its agenda; it is not, like the Coens' *Blood Simple,* a film-school thesis on noir.

Carl Franklin knows just how to let the story unfold in

its own rhythms. He is especially good at letting character ripen and flower on the screen. He is a miraculous elicitor of minimalist cinema behavior; the tiniest verbal and gestural details are telling. All the actors excel, from small parts like Kevin Hunter's as Lila/Fantasia's brother through cops Jim Metzler and Earl Billings and bad guys Billy Bob Thornton and (especially) Michael Beach as Pluto. Natalie Canerday makes much of little in the role of the Sheriff's wife.

The outstanding jobs are by Bill Paxton as Dale and Cynda Williams as Fantasia/Lila. Paxton, a Texan, has been working in genre pictures for over a decade and is perhaps best remembered as the obnoxious coward in James Cameron's *Aliens* or as a vampire in Kathryn Bigelow's superbly moody *Near Dark*. His finest hour is in *One False Move* as he slowly and skillfully expands the stereotype of the bubba/good ole boy into a complex and ennobled human being. Cynda Williams, born in Chicago to a white mother and a black father, was able to empathize with at least that aspect of Fantasia. A singer by training, she first registered strongly as torch singer Clarke Betancourt in Spike Lee's *Mo' Better Blues,* a drama about musicians. (Spike Lee is an extraordinary director of women, perhaps even more than of men—Rosie Perez, Angela Bassett, Cynda.) Here she gives a great movie performance, letting us see in the smallest gestures the little girl in the depraved woman and vice versa. The scenes Paxton and Williams have together are redolent with the perfume of past sex.

It is, finally, race, the erotic and social collisions of

white and black in a small Southern town, the necessity of simply telling the truth about race, that give *One False Move* its gravity and beauty. The phrase *film noir*, in the gifted hands of African-American director Franklin, has a new significance. The last film noir of any quality, Stephen Frears's 1990 film of Jim Thompson's *The Grifters*, ended with the destruction of a child by a parent. *One False Move* ends with a (white) parent acknowledging, in a fashion, a (black) child. Faulkner's supreme novel *Absalom, Absalom* dealt with this very theme; *One False Move* is not *Absalom, Absalom*, but it is a very welcome and overdue step in that direction.

An earlier attempt to bring Jim Thompson to the American screen was James Foley's *After Dark, My Sweet* (1990). Thompson was an heir to the James M. Cain tradition of noir, in which a male sucker falls for a femme fatale. Here Jason Patric is the classically bestubbled drifter (plus ex-con plus ex-boxer plus mentally shaky) who stumbles into a bar in a hot Arizona town and bumps into alcoholic, widowed seductress Rachel Ward. Before you can say "gas chamber," he is the gardener on her derelict estate. At this point, as if more sleaze were wanted, up pops Uncle Bud (Bruce Dern), who masterminds a harebrained scheme to kidnap a diabetic rich kid. The sucker hesitates but is soon in on the caper, saying, "I'd been set in a rut and had to follow it out to the end." He loves Ward, asking, "Can there be a you and me?" He dimly intuits that he is being set up, but then a roll in the hay suffices to convince him of Ward's basic decency all over again. He calls her "basically as good a person could be and hating herself for not being better''—this after she has tried to kill a sick child. The dead and laughable clichés of this script, by Foley and Robert Radlin, are exactly the sort of thing *One False Move* leaves decisively behind.

*I*n 1984 Joel and Ethan Coen, the sons of Midwest academics, made *Blood Simple*, a shoestring parody/salute to noir. Joel gets director credit in this pair's outings, but both write the scripts. In fact, the distinctions in credits are artificial, for both brothers are on the set and in active collaboration throughout shooting. *Blood Simple* took a classic premise—bar owner husband (Dan Hedaya) hires a sleazy private eye (M. Emmet Walsh) to check out his possibly adulterous wife (Frances McDormand)—and gave the old screw some new turns, especially in the monumental corruptness of the Private Investigator. Betrayals and deceits mount, and the style of the piece keeps pace with its ethics—showy, flamboyant, lots of dark angles. It is an inventive exercise in genre deconstruction, if little more.

*Raising Arizona* (1987), the Coens' sophomore outing, is a mobile-home, down-market screwball comedy about a convenience-store robber (Nicolas Cage) and his police-woman wife (Holly Hunter) and their scheme to remedy their childlessness by kidnapping one of a batch of quintuplets from a rich nursery. The zany flirts with the desperate in the film's tone; in this, it remembers much recent independent cinema. Its signature image is a baby sitting happily in the center lane of a highway as cars whiz by.

The Coens' 1990 feature, *Miller's Crossing,* offered a lugubriously stylized take, set in 1929, on the gangster/ betrayal story—sort of *Scarface* crossed with *Last Year at Marienbad.* The not terribly complex saga of seemingly switched allegiances stars Albert Finney and Gabriel Byrne, but the star turn is by John Turturro as an effeminate and frankly cowardly hoodlum begging for mercy in a forest. Barry Sonnefeld's cinematography excels at pale and washed-out hues.

John Turturro plays the title role in the Coens' 1991 *Barton Fink,* that of a successful New York playwright of the 1930s brought out to and profoundly changed by Hollywood, seen as a locus of evil, as the essence of America, as hell. Fink's Broadway success had been a Clifford Odetsian tenement-socialist play, improbably called *Bare Ruined Choirs,* which is a phrase from a Shakespeare sonnet. The play was a phony idealization of the working-class hero, the revolutionary, the common man—all realities unknown to the shy and bookish Fink. In Hollywood, he is assigned to a "Wallace Beery wrestling picture" by a sadistic and megalomanical studio head (Michael Lerner, over the top); he is housed in a cavernously empty hotel where the walls sweat and the only visible humans are chipper clerk Chet (the ubiquitous Steve Buscemi), a wizened elevator operator, and a friendly salesman named Charlie Meadows (John Goodman in a terrific performance). Meadows turns out to be serial killer Karl Mundt.

The only writer Fink meets (in a studio urinal) is a Faulkner-type (John Mahoney) who turns out to be a mean, drunken fraud, verbally abusive and violent to his

Muse cum ghost Audrey (the brilliant and acid Judy
Davis, who actually convinces one she is a Southerner, a
woman of the Thirties, and a writer). It is Audrey who
has actually written his late, acclaimed novels, including
*Nebuchadnezzar* (note that the Hitlerian destroyer of Jeru-
salem replaces the tortured Absalom, used by the real
Faulkner for a biblical title).

"Turns out to be" is a key phrase in discussing the
Coens. Systematic belittling runs through *Barton Fink*.
Since Fink *is* virtually Odets (insofar as he exists at all),
it is fair to observe that Odets's New York plays like *Awake
and Sing* and his Hollywood scripts, including the superior anti-Hollywood script *The Big Knife* and his brutal
New York piece *Sweet Smell of Success,* much transcend
Wallace Beery wrestling pictures. So did Wallace Beery
pictures, by the way.

When Fink meets the Common Man he idealized, he
turns out to be not Willy Loman but Hitler. (Karl Mundt,
by the way, was the name of a McCarthyite senator.)
Mundt likely goes, to be consummately nasty, to Brooklyn to wipe out Fink's family, whose telephone does not
answer.

Sex in *Barton Fink* is death. On waking up next to
Audrey, who came to help him with his writer's block
and stayed to make love, he swats a mosquito on her flesh
and finds her slashed to death. Charlie assists in dispos-
ing of the inconvenient remains: shots of the swirling
vortex of the toilet (in the brilliant chromaticism of Roger
Deakins's photography). Her head awkwardly survives,
however, it can be assumed, in a neat box Charlie gives

Fink for safekeeping. Audrey's death, her blood—whether shed by Charlie or by Fink—seem to unlock Fink's dried-up creative juices. In his sweaty room, with the wet walls decomposing, he begins tapping out a script. The typewriter takes on a compository will of its own, combining texts. Next to the typewriter is the neat box; on the wall above the typewriter is a calendar-art lithograph of a pretty girl posing at the shore, with a snap of Charlie stuck in the corner. These are Fink's Muses now.

His script is predictably rejected with venom and contempt by the studio head, now garbed as an officer, for World War II has broken out. He snarls, "I can get that Barton Fink touch from twenty writers." Fink glumly returns to the hotel, which is consumed in a holocaust by a cackling, overtly Hitlerian Mundt/Meadows. Nothing is left unsaid in the Coens' eagerness to make their points.

After the hotel holocaust, Fink sits dazedly by the Pacific, clutching his box. The pretty girl from the litho walks by. "Are you in pictures?" he, almost punningly, asks. She assumes the very pose from the picture and says, "Don't be silly."

. It is safe then to say that you cannot win in the universe of *Barton Fink*. The Coens' cerebral gymnastics systematically annihilate, one by one, the possibilities of creativity or contact. And Turturro's one-note bewildered stupor does not enliven matters. Only Judy Davis's intelligence and John Goodman's edgy bonhomie work among the performances. Finally, with its Chinese boxes of nihilistic bravura, *Barton Fink* is much less convincing than

Nicholas Ray's *In a Lonely Place* as a Dantesque descent into Hollywood as writer-hell.

The Coens' 1994 film is *The Hudsucker Proxy*, with Tim Robbins, Jennifer Jason Leigh, Paul Newman, Peter Gallagher, and Steve Buscemi. Based on a script the Coens and Sam Raimi have had around for a while, it is a farce on the order of, supposedly, *His Girl Friday*, set in the business world of the 1950s. The invention of the Hula Hoop plays a part. A lighter work, doubtless, than *Barton Fink*.

The Coen brothers' leading man, Tim Robbins, made his own debut as writer-director in 1992 with *Bob Roberts*, a smug *faux* documentary about a folk-singing demagogue. Elia Kazan hit the same targets in 1957 in *A Face in the Crowd*.

A more vivid directorial debut came from Allen and Albert Hughes, twins born in Detroit in 1973 who started making home videos at the age of twelve. They were soon creating hip-hop videos for, among other singers, Tupac Shakur. Tyger Williams, a Californian of twenty-three, gave them the script for *Menace II Society* (1993), a relentless and desperate picture of black youth in Watts.

Opening with the murder by young O-Dog (Larenz Tate) of a Korean grocer and his wife, *Menace II Society*, in a totally unsentimental way, looks at the efforts of O-Dog's decent friend Caine (Tyrin Turner) to rise above the legacy of his family and the enticements of his environment. The film has been called a grimmer, more honest *Boyz N the Hood*, but in fact more resembles a West Coast cousin to Dickerson's *Juice*.

## CHAPTER FIVE

# *F*rom the Heartland

*T*he heartland of America has served as inspiration, stimulus, and backdrop for as much innovative cinema as either coast. In many respects, films set outside the New York or Los Angeles areas have been more radical than work emanating from the cultural centers. One of the most striking takes on small-town America was a 1989 high-school comedy called *Heathers,* the first film for director Michael Lehmann and writer Daniel Waters. Dubbed the *Blue Velvet* of teen sagas, *Heathers* turned upside down every imaginable convention of the alienated-youth flick. Although it preceded *Beverly Hills, 90210,* it could pass today for a savage parody of that teen-catering show.

There are three girls named Heather who constitute the dominant clique in Westerburg High School in Sherwood, Ohio, where they tyrannize over the styles and attitudes of their classmates. (Waters admits to basing *Heathers* on his own experiences at Riley High School in

South Bend, Indiana. The town and the school in the movie doubtless allude to *Winesburg, Ohio,* Sherwood Anderson's classic 1919 collection of short stories that amounted to a mosaic of lonely, unhappy lives in a paradigmatic small town.)

The central figures in *Heathers* are Veronica (Winona Ryder), a junior who is just being taken up by the exclusive Heathers and forced to drop her earlier, sweeter, but less hip best friend, and the biker J.D. (Christian Slater), an exotic, surly, wisecracking transfer student. The name J.D. evokes both James Dean, godfather of teen rebellion, and the old scare-label *juvenile delinquent*. Veronica is ambivalent about subscribing to Heather values. She is compelled by them to participate in a cruel prank aimed at humiliating Martha, the class fatso. She gravitates, by instinct, toward the seductively alienated biker and is soon having an affair with him as an antidote to Heatherness.

But J.D. proves no sensitive-sweetheart-behind-the-denim, à la Dean, say, in *Rebel* or Luke Perry's Dylan in *90210,* but a homicidal nihilist. When Veronica is threatened with public disgrace by Heather #1 (Kim Walker) for vomiting at a college frat party, she wishes Heather dead. J.D. cheerfully obliges; they put Drāno in her diet soda and take it up to her pastel-princess bedroom, where the haughty beauty drinks it and crashes, in slomo, through a glass-topped table. Veronica finds the results horrifying (''I just killed my best friend; they'll have to send my SATs to San Quentin'') but intoxicating. She agrees to forge a suicide note.

The school authority figures take Heather's death with solemn fatuousness, but Heathers #2 (Shannen Doherty of *90210*) and #3 (Lisanne Falk) are concerned only with the brevity of the commemorative break: "It's not fair we only get a half day."

This tone of deliberate and impudent heartlessness runs throughout *Heathers* and is mostly brilliantly funny. When two abusive jocks insult Veronica, she and J.D. lure them, on a pretext of sex, to a remote spot in the park, have them disrobe, and shoot them, leaving notes that will make their deaths seem like a gay suicide pact. Sneers J.D.: "Good riddance. All they were good for, after football season, was date rape and AIDS jokes."

School authorities fret. Teenage suicide—not to mention a number-one song by that title, sung by Big Fun—becomes the rage. Heather #1 makes a posthumous appearance at the jocks' memorial service and complains to Veronica in the baptistery that "the afterlife is so boring; if I have to sing 'Kumbaya' one more time . . ." In an attempt to be with it, Martha attempts suicide by walking into traffic but succeeds only in crippling herself.

J.D. is proud of his three murders, boasting that "suicide gave Heather depth, Kurt a soul, and Ram a brain." He plans an apocalyptic demolition, again disguised as suicide, of the entire student body during a pep rally in the gym. At this point, Veronica calls a halt and determines to stop her psychopathic puppy. She intervenes to save the school. J.D. blows himself up colorfully in front of the school in yet another reference to *Pierrot le fou*, in which Jean-Paul Belmondo did something similar.

*Heathers'* narrative is a mere pretext for inventive and scathing satire, adding up to the most exuberantly nihilistic slice of Americana since Russ Meyer's *Beyond the Valley of the Dolls* or John Waters's *Pink Flamingos*. If Meyer, whose title *Faster Pussycat! Kill! Kill!* says it all, is a hedonist who delights in mocking his own megalomaniacal fetishes, Waters is a genuine American dadaist, importing the logic of nonsense and nightmare into the streets and outskirts of Baltimore, whose laureate he is. In uncompromising early films like *Pink Flamingos* (1972) and *Female Trouble* (1973) he thoroughly upends bourgeois virtues in the best Buñuel spirit. And Waters had the commanding presence of the obese transvestite actor Divine to incarnate his intentions. Divine, a gifted and audacious comedian, represented a far more radical critique of the mainstream notion of glamour than the "superstars" of the Warhol Factory. In *Pink Flamingos* Babs Johnson (Divine) wars with rivals for the title of "the filthiest person alive"—a title Divine clinches in a climactic scene involving canine defecation. In *Female Trouble* Dawn Davenport (Divine) goes from pouting teen princess to mass slayer proud to be grilled in the chair.

With a truly Swiftian rigor, Waters pursues in these films the reversing of such conventional antitheses as beauty/ugliness, cleanliness/filth, and crime/goodness. And he goes about this potentially gloomy task in scenarios that bristle with good humor and a paradoxical sweetness. Later Waters films like *Hairspray* (1988) and *Cry-Baby* (1990), both costume musicals about the early shock of rock in Baltimore, are too sweet; they blur satire into nostalgia. His next project, entitled *Serial Mom,* could be a return to form.

*Heathers* aims at everything: parents (Veronica's are sitcom Pollyannas; J.D.'s dad is a demolitions fanatic who once blew up J.D.'s mother); teachers ("Whether or not to commit suicide is one of the most important decisions of a teenager's life"); TV news; preachers. But the movie's laser wit does not spare teen angst or pretentiousness: when Veronica, guilty and anguished at her numerous misdeeds, burns herself with a car's cigarette lighter, J.D. deftly lights his cigarette on her flesh. A soulful diary entry reads, "If you want to fuck with eagles, learn to fly." *Moby Dick* is used as a suicide text. Mineral water is a sign of gayness in Ohio. *Heathers* is fearless and freeform in its choice of targets.

Back in 1976, there was a somber and humorless movie about high-school fascism, Renee Daalder's *Massacre at Central High,* a little-seen gem. *Heathers* wed the theme of *Massacre* to the flip, *épater* sarcasm of *Beyond the Valley,* which was written, incidentally, by Roger Ebert. Indeed, *Heathers'* final scene, with crippled Martha circling her wheelchair around Veronica, almost seems a reference to *Beyond*'s late shot of a cripple attempting to walk with crutches on a log above a stream. Works like these erect bad taste into a principle of self-aware humor. And in a sense, by making its parents and all its authority figures such nincompoops and by not sparing its teens, *Heathers* goes beyond the blame-the-society game played in films at least since *Rebel Without a Cause.* True, there are moments toward the end that can be viewed as

Veronica's growth into moral responsibility, but even these are quickly toppled into the absurd (by, for instance, that wheelchair). Satire this perverse is finally anarchic.

Lehmann's direction is cool, remote, never intrusive upon the pastel absurdities of the script or the decor. The script's epigrammatic brio is a marvel.

The roles call for caricature. Kim Walker's head Heather, mercilessly blonde and mercilessly nasty, excels. As Veronica, Ryder has the difficult task of occasionally having to shade in a third dimension amidst the film's cartoons; she does so without becoming earnestly boring. As J.D., Slater has the look of a demented Ohio replica of Dean, but he was allowed to pitch his characterization on a one-note imitation of Jack Nicholson. It might have seemed an amusing idea, but, despite Slater's nasal charm, in the long run it proves an irritant. (Ironically, Slater gave a much better, more rounded performance in 1990's *Pump Up the Volume,* an Allan Moyle film, in which he costarred with the wonderful Samantha Mathis and which was in many respects a white-bread, decaf *Heathers.*) *Heathers,* though, remains a gem of Midwestern satire, in the misanthropic tradition of Ambrose Bierce and late Mark Twain.

It is sad to report that Michael Lehmann's promise remains as yet unfulfilled. His next film, *Meet the Applegates,* released in 1991, he wrote with Redbeard Simmons; it was a witless fable about a family of Brazilian beetles who transform themselves into a typical suburban American family in order to save their environment.

Don't ask. In 1991, he directed *Hudson Hawk*, a moronic and hugely expensive Bruce Willis caper flick that proved to an object lesson in what *can* happen to be an independent director caught in the maw of Hollywood.

*A*nother unforgettable 1989 debut was that of filmmaker Steven Soderbergh with *Sex, Lies and Videotape*, which he wrote and directed. *Sex, Lies and Videotape* is a movie as quietly provocative as its title. It's that *lies* which lends the real piquancy; with just sex and videotape, we'd expect either tabloid TV or a high-minded meditation on the interrelationship of technology and erotic fulfillment today. But the movie proves as subversive of expectation as its title.

Steven Soderbergh was born in Georgia in 1963 and, after a peripatetic childhood in Texas, Pennsylvania, and Virginia, found himself settled in Baton Rouge, Louisiana. At the age of thirteen, he was making short films there. Fresh from high school, he was off to Los Angeles, but, after some disillusioning show-business letdowns, he returned to Baton Rouge. Home seemed a better nursery of his cinematic talent than Hollywood. He worked his way up from such jobs as coin attendant at a video arcade to shooting commercials for local TV and then to cutting programs for Showtime cable. The whole while, he went on writing film scripts. Showtime recommended Steven to the rock band Yes as the man to shoot a documentary. This led to Soderbergh's shooting a feature-length concert movie for Yes for MTV in 1986 that was nominated for a Grammy. On the strength of that, he got an agent and a connection to Outlaw Productions, which greenlighted his *Sex* script in 1988, when Steven was twenty-five. After premiering at, and becoming the sensation of, the Sundance Film Festival, *Sex* won the Palme d'Or, the highest award at the Cannes Film Festival. At twenty-six, Soderbergh was a star.

*Sex, Lies and Videotape* is set in Baton Rouge and conveys some flavor of life in that relatively small Louisiana capital, but it is not in essence a public or societal film at all. It is, from the start, a nosy invasion of the privacy of its characters, a soft insinuation into intimate parts. Graham (James Spader), a college buddy of yuppie lawyer John (Peter Gallagher), is driving back into town after a nine-year absence and is going to stay for a bit with John and his beautiful, restless wife Ann (Andie MacDowell). John is having an affair with Ann's witty, sexy sister Cynthia (Laura San Giacomo).

The film opens with a cross-cut mosaic of the activities of the central quartet: vain Graham changing clothes in a bathroom, John boasting of his sexual magnetism to office colleagues, Ann sitting awkwardly on a couch at her shrink's talking of her sexual unsatisfiedness; as she confesses her inability to experience an orgasm and her hatred of sex, John and Cynthia have it off at Cynthia's place. ("I only get one today?" he piggishly asks.)

The pieces are thus neatly and perhaps predictably in place: handsome stranger, unfulfilled wife, philandering husband, witty adulteress. But *Sex* will surprise, not least in its quiet refusal to hurry or to shout. When Graham drives up to John and Ann's coldly polished and bare house, only Ann is home. They have a stiff exchange about smoking (Ann says no) and strawberries (he's brought some) and where is the bathroom. Dinner later is a guy ritual, with John patronizing Ann about her cooking. An overhead shot of the two men at the table eating strawberries emphasizes the wrongness and lifelessness of this domestic setting. Graham offers little explanation of himself, saying merely that he likes a nomadic life; John boasts of his yuppie life-style, and Graham counters that lawyers are inferior only to liars.

Next day, while Cynthia and John are having sex at John's (flowerpot over his crotch; she drops an earring), Graham and Ann perch on stools in the window of a coffee shop and exchange sexual secrets. (She cannot orgasm, as we know; as for him, "I'm impotent. I can't get an erection in the presence of another person.") Soderbergh allows the voices of one pair to overlap into images of the other pair—easy but cheating sex and strained but honest sex-blockage interpenetrate each other. This is more than clever technique; it is expressive of a conviction of the moral interrelatedness of things. In this sense especially, Soderbergh is akin to Eric Rohmer, the French filmer of moral studies to whom the American has often been likened.

The married couple is seen rigid in bed together, an icon of frozenness. We get to see the sisters together. It is a relationship we've been wondering about. At Cynthia's warm, plant-filled, ground-floor apartment in a wooden house, Ann wanders curiously around fiddling with things, putting out Cynthia's cigarettes, and deciding what to get their mother for her fiftieth birthday. Cynthia gets dressed for her job as a bartender and makes sarcastic cracks about the new guy in town, "Zen master" Graham.

We've seen the sex. We've seen the lies. What about the videotapes? Graham, the purring iconoclast, has gotten himself a scruffy but sunny pad, the antithesis of John's gleaming place. In it, a woman is talking about masturbating on a plane. It is not live; we see a camera, then tapes. Graham, nude, is watching the tape and stroking his chest. Ann's arrival interrupts this masturbatory ritual. He explains that the tapes are a "personal project." Then, in a long-held medium shot of the kitchen, Zen master Graham makes her some iced tea. It is a formal offering, somehow emblematic of his watered-down Dionysiac promise. The camera slowly dollies into each face. She drinks and splits. She is hovering in uncertainty about Graham.

Cynthia, her interest piqued by Ann's mysterious friend, pays him a visit herself. She gets some iced tea, too, but without lemon. Graham, sensing Ann is a different being, brings up the tapes, saying they are "what got Ann so spooked," and, next thing, Cynthia is making a video for Graham. His direction is soft-spoken, soothing: "Sit on the couch, speak in a normal voice. When did you first see a penis?" He teases out accounts of her early sexual experiences, while he sprawls on the floor and she unfurls on the couch and starts masturbating as she talks. Cynthia's solitary exhibitionism and Graham's solitary receptivity seem matched: the two, never touching, form a tableau of alienated sexuality. Graham later gets off listening to the tape, just as later Cynthia writhes atop a sweating John—both seem to be having sex in the head. Cynthia then throws John out.

Life goes on for Ann, who brings their mother's birthday present, a dress, into the bar where Cynthia works. There is a very funny, seemingly permanent drunk, played by Steven Brill, in this bar. Back home, the anal Ann, while polishing and vacuuming, finds Cynthia's earring and gets the picture. Her immediate instinctive reaction is to go to Graham's and make a tape. This is the key sequence in the film. Videotape, used by Graham as prop for his masturbatory solipsism, has turned in Ann's mind into an instrument of sexual unblocking and liberation. If her hedonistic sister could do it so effortlessly, why then she will, too. The unsuspecting Graham is in the kitchen: "Sorry, no iced tea. Mineral water?" She cuts to the chase: "Let's make a videotape." Soderbergh then cuts right to a later time as Graham, clothed, hovers over Ann in close-up. We have no idea what has gone on.

Cut to Ann at home with John. She declares, "I want out of this marriage." John intuits what has gone on, demands, "Did you make one of those videotapes?" and storms over to Graham, whom he beats up and ejects from his own apartment. John then settles down in Graham's empty living room to watch the tape.

There follows a sequence whose formal complexity and chronological play rival *Reservoir Dogs'* audacious stunts. As John smolderingly watches the tape we have not yet seen, the taped Ann confesses, "Orgasms? I'm

not sure, so I guess I've never had one." Graham asks if
she has had sex with anyone other than her husband. At
this exact point, we go back—live—to the moment of the
taping. We'll get to see some of what we missed. Graham
says, "I've thought of you having an orgasm." She asks
*him* to masturbate; he shies off, admitting, "I was—
*am*—a pathological liar, and I often expressed my feelings nonverbally." Then Ann takes the initiative sexually
and artistically; becoming the director, she turns the camera on Graham, who complains, "I don't find this turn-
ing-the-tables thing very interesting." "I do," she calmly
responds. "I've got a lot of problems," he pleads. She
persists, saying, "I'm leaving my husband, in part because of you." Still uncomfortable at losing control, at the
subversion of his accustomed scenario, he whines, "This
isn't supposed to happen."

Taking control, Ann goes to the couch, laying his head
on her lap in extreme close-up. He palpates her face. She
is the aggressor. They kiss. She gets up and turns off the
camera. This turning off of the recording instrument is
the sign of the possibility of mutual Eros. The shy, long-
suffering Ann has seized power to put an end to John's
sexual exploitation of her and to Graham's technosexual
exploitation of women. The lies each had been telling
themselves were necessitated by a fear of the other, a fear
now surmounted.

Back in present time, the camera closely circles John,
glumly staring at a blank screen. After John splits with a
few belittling remarks, Graham, who has been crouching,
battered, on the dark porch outside, goes inside, wrecks

his tapes with a hammer, puts them in a big carton, and tosses them into the blue night.

In a few quick scenes, the characters' fates are then settled: John's career, as well as his marriage, is in ruins (poor John is totally unsympathetically caricatured and punished by Soderbergh—an artistic mistake); Ann goes to Cynthia's bar for a gesture of sisterly reconciliation; in the last scene, Ann and Graham tenderly hold hands on his wooden porch in the rain. The rain and the outdoors—or rather, the porch, that halfway house between interior and exterior—symbolize the lovers' unstoppered emotions. Cinematographer Walt Lloyd's bright colors yield to softer and warmer tones.

*Sex, Lies and Videotape* has the delicate wisdom and sneakily unassertive charm of a Shakespearean romantic comedy—let us say *Love's Labour's Lost,* if not quite *As You Like It.* In *Sex,* two complementary erotic and emotional deformations meet and magically transform each other. Soderbergh does not have Hal Hartley's surreal streak, but he does manifest a similar eye for unlikely romantic possibilities in American life. The performances in *Sex* are perfectly judged. James Spader's purring smartness has never again seemed so fresh, appealing, and uncloying. The amazingly sensitive and attractive Andie MacDowell makes Ann's subtle, slow awakening a victory for minimalist playing. Laura San Giacomo brings a Patricia Neal throaty sexiness and wit to cynical, but ultimately lovable, Cynthia. Peter Gallagher as the unmitigated heavy, John, doles out the sleaze with a likably professional warmth.

Soderbergh's second movie, the 1991 *Kafka,* was written not by him but by Lem Dobbs, a young Englishman who had finished the script some ten years back. The setting was the Prague of 1919, for which the Prague of today, exquisitely filmed in black-and-white by Walt Lloyd, did duty. The far-fetched conceit was this: a clerk called Kafka (Jeremy Irons, phoning it in) by day works in a rigidly bureaucratized insurance office and by night writes weird stories ("I'm working on a story about a man who turns into a giant insect") and an endless letter to his unapproachable father. This Kafka is questioned by police investigating a coworker's mysterious disappearance and soon gets involved with a gang of anarchists who take him to a café and assure him that a "cover-up of monumental proportions" is operating and that his colleague was in fact abducted and taken to the Castle that looms over the town. Abducted for what nefarious purposes, Kafka must enter the Castle to find out. (That un-ironic use of the word *cover-up*—supposedly in 1919—is typical of this film's clumsiness.)

Kafka proceeds to crawl through a succession of womb-like openings—file cabinets, elevators, tombstones, underground tunnels—and emerges into a (suddenly) red-hued laboratory atop the Castle. There a mad scientist named Dr. Murnau (a pointless allusion to the great director) is conducting experiments on live people in an attempt to create "a more efficient person," that is, a new race of supinely obedient helots. Cackles Murnau: "The modern . . . you write it, I embrace it." Ripostes Kafka: "I write nightmares; you build them." This is Dobbs's notion of wit. Then, taking a leaf from Indiana "Nazis—I hate Nazis" Jones, Kafka blows up the lab real good, although everything will be subsequently "covered up" by the powers that be. Kafka is last seen coughing blood onto his typewriter as he types up his paranoid intuitions of the future.

Lloyd's atmospheric camerawork and Soderbergh's sensitive direction are wasted on this embarrassingly reductivist silliness, which sets out to chart a boyish adventure as the source of Kafka's dark vision. Dobbs's notion of evil is, however, on the level of Fu Manchu and Ming the Merciless. Nor does *Kafka* seem in control of its wobbly Freudian subtext: Kafka is made to reenter and explode a womb; mother fixation was not Kafka's problem at all. The filmmakers cited the influence of *The Third Man,* shot in nearby Vienna, for their subterranean delvings in Prague, but *The Third Man* was a work of adult and sophisticated wit—like *Sex, Lies and Videotape* and unlike *Kafka.* Perhaps, as with Lehmann, a sophomore jinx was at work here.

Soderbergh's next film, *King of the Hill,* is one he has written and directed himself. Adapted from the memoirs of writer A. E. Hotchner, it is the story of Aaron, a precocious twelve-year-old struggling to survive with his family in a transient hotel in the St. Louis of the 1930s. St. Louis is, happily, much closer to Baton Rouge than to Prague.

And *King of the Hill* is, at the very least, a much more credible account of the psychogenesis of a writer than *Kafka.* It communicates the terror of all growing up through the specific case of a virtually parentless boy (mother in a sanitarium, father a traveling salesman) in a depressed country. Hungry and poor and ostracized, his only companions are fellow eccentrics and lost souls in the hotel that is his world. His absent family is not at all evil, just beaten and desperate. And the movie truly earns its extraordinarily blissful ending as a reunited family walks into a big brown, empty apartment that is to be theirs. Although no single performance in *King of the Hill* is so strong as that of young Leonardo DiCaprio in Michael Caton-Jones's *This Boy's Life*, another 1993 film about a young writer's tough seedtime in an earlier America (there, it was Washington State in the 1950s), Soderbergh's is a wiser and deeper film. He possesses an unassertive and tender sensibility that remind me of the writer Vikram Seth, whose verse novel of California life, *The Golden Gate*, Soderbergh might consider filming.

*R*ichard Linklater, born in Houston, Texas, was studying literature in college when he left to work on an offshore oil rig in the Gulf of Mexico. He later moved to laid-back Austin, site of the huge University of Texas and magnet for a wide variety of marginalized and eccentric folk. There Linklater founded a film society, where he himself grew to love stylized masters like Bresson, Ozu, Oshima, and Von Sternberg. He made his first film, *You Can't Learn to Plow from Reading Books*, in 1987.

In 1990, he wrote, produced, and directed *Slacker* for $23,000 under the banner of Detour Films (the name is a homage to the 1945 Edgar G. Ulmer road/sucker/femme fatale cheapie to end cheapies). When Orion Classics distributed the film, they blew the original 16mm print up to 35mm. The word *slacker*—in the new sense invented by the filmmakers—connotes neobeatniks, anarchists, drifters, crazies, lazies. *Slacker* is a dazzling and wildly original rondo of a film that winds its way through one hot day in the life of Austin, whose leafy streets, ramshackle houses, little stores, and funky bars it celebrates. The movie's structural principle is to follow one pair or group for a bit until they bump into somebody else and then we swerve off and stay with that new group for a bit until . . .

*Slacker* is formally and thematically a dialectic between the polar principles of entropy and conspiracy: entropy affirms the random and meaningless nature of collisions in the universe, while conspiracy (*Slacker* is jammed with conspiracy theorists) affirms the hidden presence of a secret, if malign, master plan.

Lee Daniel's virtuoso camera tracks like the eye of a curious but detached god along the byways of a humid Austin as the demented and the depressed and the deranged weave a crazy quilt of humanity. A few of the ninety-some persons on screen are acting; many are, eccentrically, themselves. There is not a plot, exactly, but a succession of plotlets handing off the baton of the film to one another.

We open in the early morning with a face (Richard Linklater's) in a bus window. Newly arrived in town, he tells a fat cabbie about a dream he had until the cab comes upon a woman with a shopping bag hit and killed by a car driven, it quickly turns out, by her son, wearing a BE ALL

THAT YOU CAN BE military-recruiting T-shirt. The son goes to his apartment, where there is a candlelit altar, and begins to razor pictures out of a yearbook. He is arrested. Thus far, we might be in a Buñuel farce. The tone gets lighter, if not, perhaps, less Buñuelian. A street guitarist collects coins; two guys stroll the dewy streets rapping about how the moon landings are a CIA fraud (long tracking shot switching from front to rear POV); five roommates in a dirty pad denounce Bush; a member of the band Ultimate Losers and a woman meet, on the street, a girl trying to sell Madonna's pap smear (a bizarre fixation with Madonna figures also in Tarantino); a black guy selling Nelson Mandela shirts rants about guns; a guy tries unsuccessfully to buy *USA Today* from a machine but another guy in a bathrobe grabs his copy and takes it home to read in bed but his woman wants to go out instead.

*Slacker* swings back and forth between indoors and outdoors. Outdoors seems even screwier than indoors. A guy throws a tent and a typewriter into the river to spite his girlfriend while a sympathetic pal reads from *Ulysses* about Leopold Bloom's jealousy. A guy berates a woman for giving a quarter to a beggar and cites Freud, Dylan, and Nietzsche—well, Austin *is* a university town and Linklater did do *some* time in college. Late for a movie, this woman goes into a small bookstore and is buttonholed by a JFK conspiracy buff, who soon leaves her to talk to somebody fixing a car. These two drive around with some grimy pals, one of whom says he's glad his stepfather is dead, then gets out of the car, bums tobacco,

is interviewed in the street by a mobile-camera crew, and
goes to a supermarket to talk to his friend, the security
guard there.

This guard interrupts his video game to nab a thief.
Outside the store, an oldster remarks to his daughter, "I
know her [the thief] from my ethics class." This man (an
actual, and beloved, professor of philosophy at Austin)
we stay with for a while; in him Linklater tips his hat half
affectionately, half humorously, to classical anarchism.
Surprised in his home by a Polish robber with a gun, he
befriends the robber and praises the Polish anarchist who
assassinated McKinley. The two go for a walk, and the
professor of ethics points nostalgically to the tower
whence Charles Whitman shot randomly some years ago.
"Just my luck to have been out of town," he laments. He
claims to have fought for anarchism with Orwell in Cata-
lonia, but his daughter later gives the lie to that and
returns the robber's gun.

The gunman joins some criminal pals. One of them
slues off to visit a cripple in a room full of TVs all showing either the *Challenger* explosion or the tape of a disgruntled student who shot his thesis committee. He then
visits a sort of feminist garage, where a woman raps
about chaos and the nonexistence of time.

By now it is late afternoon. In a bar decorated with an
LBJ plaque, two dudes discuss the politically repressive
nature of cartoons, while three women talk about the
difficulties of relationships. An Elvis fanatic invites the
women to come with him in his van to hear a band at a
club where his name is supposed to be on the list at the

door. Of course, it isn't. His reaction: "The universe is out of hand."

It is night now. The women calmly bicycle away, running into a guy at a gas pump (shades of Hal Hartley) who gives them a fake entry stamp, which gets them into a disco. The disco is closing, but on screen is a video in which somebody is idolizing the Manson gang ("Put Squeaky Fromme on the one-dollar bill")—still more half-assed anarchism. The bouncer tells an English woman photographer ("I'm an antiartist," she insists) that he wants to get home by four A.M. to see *Blowup* ("Mimes, tennis"). On his way home, a loitering woman gets in his car, in long shot.

Dawn again. The woman dresses and splits from the bouncer's digs. She encounters an old guy talking into a mike about women. The guy *holding* the mike goes on about shooting and death. Then *Slacker* self-consciously becomes *about* "shooting" and shooting. A filmmaker (Linklater, again) is seen holding a jerky, 8mm camera/ gun and "shooting" with it. In the company of three women, the filmmaker goes up on a hilltop and tosses the camera off the hillside. We see, from the camera's point of view, jagged and scratchy images of falling. Paul Goodman's classic indictment of the unexamined life, *Growing Up Absurd,* can be glimpsed on the ground before the camera goes hurtling.

Richard Linklater is obviously half in love with the rhetoric, the hagiography, the mystique of anarchism. *Slacker*'s anarchists, pseudoanarchists, and anarchist wannabes are treated with a bemused affection. But the movie itself is about as anarchistic as a sonnet. True, Linklater's *La Ronde* does not sport a conventional narrative shape, but there are discernible artistic strategies at work. From the matricide at the start to the cameracide at the end there is wit and balance. Actually, that matricide is the film's only violent and truly nasty incident; Buñuel would surely have capped it again and again.

*Slacker* talks a good anarchist game, but at heart it is a drolly affectionate panorama of university-town fauna. In form and function it is appealingly innovative and likable. Its richly detailed portrait gallery will seem oddly familiar to all who, while perhaps not knowing Austin, have done any time in similar university towns like Cambridge or Berkeley.

Linklater's next film, *Dazed and Confused,* is set on the last day of high school in Austin in June 1976. As in *Slacker,* Linklater tracks, through the course of a long day and night, a collective—here, teens coping, through rituals of cars and drink and dope and music, with the frustrations of their age. Although masquerading as a teen flick, *Dazed and Confused* is a sophisticated study of being lost in time and space.

Allison Anders, born in 1954, went to film school at UCLA and broke into film through a job on the movie *Paris, Texas* that she got after writing director Wim Wenders fan letters for over a year. *Paris, Texas* (1984) seems to have been, like *Pierrot le fou,* a seminal work for younger moviemakers.

Full of lonely highways, broken families, flat land-

scapes, and male anguish, *Paris, Texas* (great title) told of
a nomadic Dad coming back to try to rebond with his wife
and son. Recently, one of its writers, L. M. "Kit" Carson,
put down the contemporary generation of independent
filmmakers for lacking the "coherent vision" present in
the films of such 1970s upstarts as Martin Scorsese,
George Lucas, Dennis Hopper, and Bob Rafelson.

It could be said that Allison Anders's 1992 debut
movie, *Gas Food Lodging* is a feminist look at the *Paris,
Texas* universe. *Gas Food Lodging* was scripted by Anders
from a novel by Richard Peck and shot by Dean Lent.

Set in grimly horizontal Laramie, Texas, it centers on
a single mother, Nora (Brooke Adams), who works as a
waitress in a diner, and on her two teenaged daughters.
The older daughter, Trudi (Ione Skye), is by way of being
the school tramp; she is cruelly blown off by a rich jock
when she mistakes his nighttime lust for daytime friendship. But she reacts with spirit, putting up with no attitude.

Trudi's younger sister, Shade (Fairuza Balk), is also
having problems with men; she is attracted to punk-
rapper-cum-window-dresser Yves (Donovan Leitch), who
claims to live for risk and to like "the fuckin' edge."
Shade is the movie's observing consciousness and imagination, telling us that "women are lonely in the Nineties." She likes to go for mild walks on the wild side and
haunts a Spanish-language movie house on the wrong
side of the tracks that shows black-and-white Mexican
melodramas about passionate women and nuns, all starring the flamboyant "Elvia Ribero." Shade imagines her-

self in such a film. She craves passion and tarts herself up to give herself to a big-talking Yves: "Let's jump off cliffs, go to another planet." But Yves proves terrified of an actual woman.

Rejected, Shade finds herself in the Hispanic part of town in an outsize wig. There she is rescued by handsome Xavier, a Mexican-American youth who has been on the edges of life for a while: Trudi had gotten him fired from his job as a busboy in her mother's diner when he objected to Trudi's racist contempt, and he had then gotten a job as a projectionist in that Spanish-language cinema, where he had a fight with Shade when she tried to tell him how to do his job.

Romance begins to bloom all around. Trudi meets a gangly but quietly confident Sam Shepard type named Darius (David Lansbury) who turns out to be an English geologist hunting for rare rocks. He takes her to a cave lit with reflecting blue lights; she tells him cathartically of a gang rape that had gotten her started on the "bad girl" trail; they make love. Darius moves on, promising to return. Nora, after a disastrous dinner party for a persistent beau, starts talking very early one morning (his noise had woken her up) to a satellite-dish installer called Hamlet Humphrey. ("That's pitiful," she blurts out on first hearing his moniker.) She is surprised to find she likes him. She offers him coffee. He proves impotent, though, in their first sexual encounter.

*Gas Food Lodging* is very much a movie about three women inhabiting a very small space, a glorified trailer, and the tensions and abrasions that are bound to arise therefrom. Anders is superb at getting the feel of a place; we know exactly where we are in her interiors. The mother-daughter animosity that has been building between Nora and Trudi climaxes when Trudi announces she is pregnant by the vanished Darius and Nora insists she get an abortion or split. Trudi chooses to split and heads for the local metropolis, Dallas, to have the baby.

Shade's dad (James Brolin), a feckless, burnt-out sort, pops into her life to save her from some attackers. Shade makes the mistake of treating him as an adult and going to see him and his current woman in a nearby town to ask for fifty dollars. It is an uncomfortable visit, but she comes away with the money, which she wants in order to go looking for Darius, who she is sure has not deserted her sister. Shade is a natural romantic, and life, as it happens, endorses her romanticism. Xavier turns out to be a prince: he takes her to meet his mother in their simple, pleasing adobe ranch house. Xavier's mother is a beautiful old woman, deaf but able to dance soulfully by hearing the music through the ground. Xavier, then and there, pledges Shade eternal devotion in a scene excelling her most lurid Mexican-movie fantasies: as the camera closely circles the pair, he swears love "por todos los días, por todas las semanas, por todas las meses, por todos los años, por toda mi vida."

Trudi sends back home movies of her baby's birth from Dallas, while Shade goes off on a quixotic quest for the baby's father. She gets as far as New Mexico, staggering over cactus-studded mesas like someone in a Southwestern *Wuthering Heights*. At last, she spots exotic rocks being sold roadside by hippie Cecil, who explains that he got them from Darius and that Darius died in a cave accident. So Darius, as Shade knew, *had* been true; only death kept him from coming back to Trudi. It is, strangely, a happy ending. Fairuza Balk's questioning sweetness makes Shade a very appealing figure, while the bright Ione Skye does not shirk from rendering the princessy selfishness of Trudi.

*Gas Food Lodging* lacks the ironic, absurdist edge of much recent cinema. While it includes much quirky humor, it is at bottom a naturalistic study of the lives of three women. What is distinctive about it and gives it real artistic cachet is the go-for-broke romanticism of Shade in contrast to the beaten-down prosiness of her mother and her sister. Out of the myriad murk of losers and jerks in Laramie, Shade finds passion herself, *wills* her mother a nice man, and satisfies herself that her sister's love was, if tragic, at least true. *Gas Food Lodging* is finally closer to *Wuthering Heights* than to *Paris, Texas*. Anders believes in that movie-fed imagination of Shade's. If Xavier's mother can hear the music in the ground, so can we.

Anders's next film, *Mi Vida Loca*, deals with the girl gangs of East Los Angeles. Just as Leslie Harris brought the eye of a woman artist to the Brooklyn projects, so Anders can be counted on to give a place in the sun to the Angelenas of gangland.

*Gun Crazy* was a 1949 B-movie about a heartless femme fatale who lures a sweet gun nut into a life of sadistic crime. Directed by Joseph H. Lewis, it told the nastiest

and least sentimentally indulgent version of the Bonnie
and Clyde myth, which was filmed with varying amounts
of young-love romanticism by Fritz Lang in *You Only Live
Once*, by Nicholas Ray in *They Live by Night*, and by Arthur
Penn in *Bonnie and Clyde*. Lewis's low-rent flick was shot
with virtuoso skill. When critic Myron Meisel comments
on how its "famous single-take bank robbery reconciled
budget problems and dramatic impact with imaginative
flair," he might be talking about today's independent
cinema.

Almost a decade ago, writer Matthew Bright, who
scripted the campy *Forbidden Zone*, completed an update
of the noir classic. But the script was destined to wait
until 1992 to be filmed. It then came into the hands of
Tamra Davis, a native of Los Angeles who had appren-
ticed under Francis Ford Coppola at Zoetrope Studios in
1986 and gone on to become a star director of music
videos for such singers as Lou Reed and Bette Midler. By
the late 1980s, she had graduated from videos to documentary and fiction shorts. Enthusiastic about making
her debut feature with Bright's script, Davis sold the idea
to independent producers Zane W. Levitt and Diane Fire-
store. Davis was very leery of the way some music-video
makers focused exclusively on glitzy visuals in making
the transition to features. She said, "I really wanted to
concentrate on story. I intentionally focused on narrative
and character elements." She made her first movie in
twenty-three days for about a million bucks.

As in *Gas Food Lodging*, we are in trailer country, but
this time in "backwater" rural California and this time
not in a neat matriarchal space but in a grubby patriarchal

hell. Seventeen-year-old Anita (Drew Barrymore), a powder keg of the Id waiting to explode, lives in the trailer
with her mother's boyfriend, beefy, beery Rooney (Joe
Dallesandro, pioneer screen hustler in such Paul Morrissey flicks as *Flesh, Trash,* and *Heat*). The mother has
decamped to Fresno, and Rooney periodically rapes
Anita. She escapes his attentions only by sleeping outdoors in a blue bathrobe. Desperate for some recognition
by her peers, Anita has become the class slut, making
herself available to two fellow-student goons in a barrel
in the town dump.

It is, of all things, a class project that will match Anita
with her destiny. Assigned to find a pen pal, she starts
corresponding with twenty-four-year-old Howard (James
LeGros), who is doing three years in Chino on a man-
slaughter rap for beating to death a convenience-store
clerk and who had earlier served two years for pistol-
whipping his father. When Howard writes that ''I always
dreamed of a girl who liked guns,'' Anita determines to
measure up to his dream and starts shooting pumpkins
out behind the trailer. Rooney offers to help; he puts his
arms around her, advising, ''Squeeze it [the trigger] like
it was a zit.'' Classy guy.

Just as Anders showed Shade's fantasy images of herself as a passionate cinematic Latina, so Davis injects
images of Anita's visions of herself as a bespangled,
rootin', tootin', shootin' cowgirl. This imagery is actually
one of the few connections of this *Guncrazy* to the old *Gun
Crazy,* where the woman was a sort of Annie Oakley at a
traveling fair.

Anita concocts a cynical plan to spring Howard:

she'll get him a job at a local garage run by a rangy, snake-handling fundamentalist preacher (Billy Drago) if Howard will tell his parole board that he has accepted Jesus Christ as his personal savior. It works. The night before Howard is due to arrive, Rooney once again rapes Anita, who then showers and, wrapped in a bath towel, plugs him. She goes to meet Howard, who is shyly carrying a big painting of her, and takes him to Hank, the preacher, who imposes a strict regime of garage work, Bible-hollering, and snake-handling on Howard.

Hank, interestingly, is treated not as a hypocrite or a killjoy but as a tolerated, if bizarre, lawgiver; he is the film's only authority figure not viewed with disgust. It is just the opposite with Howard's stiff-necked and contemptuous parole officer (Michael Ironside), whose wild daughter, Joy (Ione Skye, a bad girl again), is, to her father's horror, Anita's best friend. "You're both trash. Stay away from my daughter," he warns. He is right, but perhaps unwise in saying so to their faces.

A bit of a puritan, Howard parries the sexual advances of the hot Anita until Hank insists the two get married at once. He performs the wedding himself in his dark, wooded chapel. That night, Howard is impotent. (Male impotence is rather a motif in recent films.) "I'm sorry I could not consummate our wedding night," he solemnly apologizes. But it does not really bother Anita, who instead shows her new husband a secret: Rooney's decomposing body in a dumpster.

Unfazed, Howard takes the body from the dumpster to the dump, where he shovels it into the furnace. Still a religious boy, he suggests that Anita "say a few words. I know he was a bastard, but it's the Christian thing to do." She, though, has passed beyond the petty hypocrisies and snarls, "Here lies a pig. May he rot in hell for all eternity." On the subject of sex, she reassures the anxious Howard: "I don't care if we never do have sex. I never understood why they call it making love." And speaking of sex, the two school goons show up and leeringly suggest a foursome with Anita. Howard demands they apologize. When they don't, he shoots them, counseling one groaning goon to "just think about Jesus." He douses their car and them with kerosene.

The lovers' body count is now three—three macho pigs, to be sure. The lovers shower together (overhead shot, a *Detour* echo) and cuddle each other to sleep. Things get out of control when the pair take Hank, bitten by a supposedly defanged rattler, to a hospital and are there told by the parole officer that Howard will have to go back to jail. They do not welcome this news. She shoots a cop. He pistol-whips the parole officer, only sparing his life at Anita's urging because he is Joy's father, and saying, "Trash, huh? So long as I got this gun, I'm smart and you're stupid."

*Guncrazy* now spirals down into lovers-on-the-lam tropes. Anita voices the requisite motto: "Our lives are over now. There's no place for us to go." But she does have a scheme of locating her mother in Fresno. This lightly sketched hunt for the mother, as if reestablishing a natal bond will somehow set right all that has gone wrong since the birth, is reminiscent, in a minor key, of

Mike's search for his mother in *My Own Private Idaho*. The two screw up a bar robbery when kind-hearted Anita cannot bring herself to take working guys' paychecks. Prissy Howard is still objecting to her use of the word *fuck*. After arriving in Fresno, they sit by a huge sculpture of a Mayan-like face for a bit and then go to Mom's address. It is a scrungy bordello, populated by run-down, stoned whores and a scummy pimp, whom Howard—can you guess?—pistol-whips. Anita's mom has decamped, perhaps to happier trails.

When the couple very properly return a stray dog to a lush, Tudoresque house, the owner (Jaid Barrymore, Drew's real-life mother) foolishly tells them she and her husband are going away. Next thing, husband and wife are enjoying a deferred consummation in a large, clean bed. "It's like you're part of my body," she coos. They dress up in the owners' duds. "We look like nice people," he marvels. "We *are* nice people," retorts Anita, as ever the stronger and surer of the two.

A climactic shoot-out in the borrowed house ends with Howard descending the staircase in slomo, six-guns blazing, into a hail of cop bullets. He kills a bunch before going down. He has persuaded Anita, possibly pregnant, to pretend to have been a hostage. Her last lying words, as she is solicitously led off, are, "He made me do it." The camera pans up to the sky.

*Guncrazy* is best at capturing the aroma of life in a trailer town where junk and pollution coat the surfaces of things and nobody puts down roots. As Joy remarks, the town sights are the dump and a drive-in movie theater that has been closed for ten years. As a study of the affectless youth spawned by these dumps, *Guncrazy* is much closer to *Heathers* than it is to any films noirs of the 1940s. But, despite its female protagonist (who is, be it noted, far less drastic than the heroine of Abel Ferrara's characteristically extreme *Ms. 45*), *Guncrazy* does not have the wit or anarchic energy of *Heathers* and often indulges its protagonists' self-pity. And the heavies are uninteresting, except for the shadings of gray that Dallesandro manages to bring to Rooney.

Instead, what gives *Guncrazy* a lift and offers the most promise for Tamra Davis's future work are the performances she elicits, often more complex and human than the script. Drew Barrymore, scion of America's premiere thespic family and adorable little sister in *E.T.*, has blossomed into a pint-sized blond Venus flytrap. This is her best work: biting that lower lip, smiling ambiguously, alive with hunger and humor and purpose, she has something of Jean Harlow about her, coarse and carnal but in amused control. Often compared to Lana Turner, Barrymore has a sassiness that recalls rather the earlier Metro sexpot. Drew Barrymore *is* what Madonna tries so painfully hard to be on screen. James LeGros is rivaling Steve Buscemi as a ubiquitous icon of independent cinema. First noticeable as the teenage cowboy terrorized in Kathryn Bigelow's *Near Dark* (1987) and really surfacing as Matt Dillon's imbecilic friend in *Drugstore Cowboy* (1989), LeGros excels at playing morons who seem to be *just* shy of reaching ironic self-awareness. A chunky and solid presence, LeGros is perfectly suited to these dawn-

ingly human types and is ideal here as the half nice boy,
half psychopath Howard. Ione Skye is fine in a sort of Eve
Arden, trampy-best-friend role, while Billy Drago impresses as an oddball but sincere Holy Roller—he looks
like John Sayles's evil twin.

Davis's next film, *CB4*, was written by Nelson George
and Chris Rock. Set in a world Davis knows—pop music
and video—it is a satirical farce about middle-class black
youths from ''Locash, California'' achieving musical
stardom by pretending to be prison-hardened street rap-
pers (*CB4* means Cell Block 4). But *CB4* comes nowhere
near the élan of its models, *This Is Spinal Tap* and *Wayne's
World*.

Davis's next project sounds more promising: a Western about women gunslingers in the 1860s, to be shot
near Sacramento, California, and to be called simply *Bad
Girls*. And Drew Barrymore is in it.

**W**omen and guns: once a shocking collocation, but now
the label for a nascent genre of female-avenger flicks on
the order of *Ms. 45*, Kathryn Bigelow's *Blue Steel*, Ridley
Scott's *Thelma and Louise*, and Tamra Davis's *Guncrazy*.
The special pleasure of Stacy Cochran's 1992 film, *My
New Gun*, is to inject into this heavy-breathing genre some
quiet lightness and revisionist delicacy of touch. Cochran, in her mid-thirties, with an M.F.A. in film from New
York's Columbia University, wrote and directed this, her
first film. She had actually written the script for a screenwriting class at Columbia. After graduation, she spent a
time shooting short films and with, as she says, surpris-

ing ease and "strange simplicity" saw the *My New Gun*
script accepted by IRS for production. The movie takes
place in, and is about, the eerily alienated universe of
suburbia; it was largely filmed in the very prim, very
proper, very socially anxious New York bedroom suburb
of Teaneck, New Jersey. The lunar oddness of Cochran's
northern New Jersey is very different from the boisterous
urban Jersey John Sayles films farther south.

*My New Gun* focuses on two neighboring houses and
evokes, for a while, a sort of slasher or occult movie. We
keep wondering: are these people vampires, serial killers,
what? It is Cochran's droll gift to rouse these apprehen-
sions and then ease them down into the actual—and in
some way not less strange—story she wants to tell.

Fastidious radiologist Gerald (Stephen Collins) and his
lovely wife, Debby (Diane Lane), have a "perfect" marriage in a neatly "perfect" house with a sliding-glass-
doored green backyard. If there's a fly in the ointment, it
is Crime: alarmed by a local mugging, Gerald buys Debby
a gun and forces her to shoot out back. Unlike Anita in
*Guncrazy,* Debby loathes the thing—she has to it about the
same attitude that Ann, in *Sex, Lies and Videotape,* has to
her husband's penis.

On her errands, Debby keeps bumping into an odd,
across-the-street neighbor—scruffy, laid-back, purringly
groovy Skippy (James LeGros). In a supermarket, he
stands up for her to a snippy clerk and gently brushes
back her hair. His face pops up at the kitchen window
asking to borrow the gun that she's let slip she has; she's
washing dishes (a woman's chore, clearly). She says no,

but he comes in anyway, ostensibly to borrow sugar. Patronizingly, Gerald quizzes Skippy about his life and his job until Skippy balks: "Excuse me. I'm not here to take your daughter to the prom. I'm here to borrow some sugar." But he isn't; he sneaks upstairs to glom the gun from her bedside drawer. Why?

Time-lapse shots of clouds moving over the street in Ed Lachman's somberly luminous cinematography do not solve the mystery, but perhaps hint that the solution is as much in the realm of poetry as of horror.

Debby covers for Skippy to Gerald, saying she lent him the gun. He freaks: "Are you back in the Valley of the Dolls, Deb? You loaned a loaded gun to a satan-worshipping junkie?" Storming over to Skippy's to repossess his gun, Gerald literally shoots himself in the foot. Skippy's place, quickly glimpsed, is bare, queer, with red linoleum floors in every room and a huge Ping-Pong table dominating the downstairs living room. We can, almost, agree with Gerald. Skippy claims to live with his mother, but that seems improbable.

Next day, rain. Gerald is in the hospital for his foot and blames Debby for the additional pain of the botulism he is sure he contracted from the egg-salad sandwich she brought him. Leaving the hospital, she drops in on The Red Chimney, the burger joint where Skippy works (this was actually shot in Hackensack, New Jersey) and promptly faints (a Hal Hartley moment). Skippy revives her with an iced Coke and onion rings but then suddenly dashes out into the rain in order, he says, to take a co-worker with appendicitis to the hospital. She does not believe him; she suspects drugs. But later she agrees to lend Skippy her car to drive a vague, dreamy woman in a white suit (Tess Harper), who he says is his mother, to the airport. When he returns the car, he comes inside, shows Debby the gun in his belt, and curls up on the floor by the door to sleep. She puts a blanket over him and then joins him, chastely.

Next day, to Skippy's annoyed surprise, "Mother" is back home. Echoing Skippy's earlier behavior in *her* house, Debby sneaks upstairs and finds a box of clippings that tells all about mother. She is indeed Skippy's mother, and also Kimmy Hayes, a famous country singer now retired after numerous breakdowns and married to a sinister cowboy type (a wedding portrait, posed in an outdoor setting, comes eerily to life as Debby looks at it—another visual reminiscence of *My Own Private Idaho*). Kimmy discovers Debby among her things and stabs her. Now it is Debby who is off to the hospital, where her husband's only reaction is: "Is there blood in the car? I knew we should have gotten mocha seats." He does, though, sheepishly admit that it was *another* egg-salad sandwich that gave him botulism.

We begin to see, along with Debby, that, against all bourgeois appearances, it is Gerald who has been wrong and Skippy who has been telling the truth. That night, a sort of musical houses is played, with Gerald still away in the hospital. A disoriented Kimmy is put to sleep in Debby's bed. Sitting at her kitchen table, Skippy at last kisses Debby as the camera slowly approaches. Then they, logically, go over to Skippy's to make love.

There is, and always was, some danger to Kimmy out there. Hence Skippy's taking the gun. An oily type asks Debby questions in her driveway and pursues her into her house. (It is Kimmy's husband.) There is an urgent need to flee. The now allied trio of Skippy, Kimmy, and Debby (sweet *e* sounds, as in Stacy) are seen, in long shot, heading into a Ramada Inn.

Gerald, back home, declares to Debby, "I want to try being apart from you. I cannot stand the unsurprising nature of the crap you get us into."

At the Ramada, Kimmy lolls in the Jacuzzi, oblivious of the nearness of the menace. The psycho husband is at that moment attacking a maid in her room. Sensing him near, Skippy soothingly ushers his mother out of the pool and out of the motel. At this point, the frightened trio go to the cops—another refreshingly realistic violation of the etiquette of genre movies. The police stake out the site of the film's tragic and madcap climax—a manicured country-club. At first, the jealous psycho husband thinks poor Gerald is coming on to his neurotic wife and punches him out. Guns are drawn, even by the terrified Debby. The wedded pair—psycho and neurotic—are slain. The movie ends with the lovers, Debby and Skippy, driving off. A newly emboldened, empowered Debby asks the shaken, desolated Skippy, "Can I drive?"

*My New Gun* takes a half-absurdist, half-despairing look at suburbia and at a bohemian-hippie-artistic alternative to that mode of being, with all its sexist, imprisoning, careerist antisepsis. In a way, Cochran's vision might come out of the beatnik 1950s, if, of course, women's voices were as audible then as they are now.

But *Gun* is definitely a movie of the 1990s, too. It has something in common thematically with *Sex, Lies and Videotape;* at moments, the later film might be called *Sex, Lies and Guns.* Plus, as noted above, it has a bit the look of *Idaho*'s melancholy Northwest transported to New Jersey. But none of this is to impugn the wonderful originality of Cochran's artistry, her voice and tone. To say that an artist is of a moment is not to deny her authenticity. Especially fresh here is the playful toying with genre: we think we are in a genre flick and then only gradually realize that it is only *Gerald's* movie that is a genre cheapie about satan-worshipping junkies. There *is* real evil about, though, and we need sharp antennae for it.

Sly, sexy rhythms of framing and speaking and, especially, playing are Cochran specialties. Diane Lane has never done finer work than her Debby; Lane does not, in a standard way, go from Stepford wife to Jane Fonda, from Mrs. M.D. to Ms. 45. She miraculously plays an alert and ironic woman from the start; the scenes of sexual and personal awakening come naturally and unforcedly. Diane Lane joins Jennifer Beals and Andie MacDowell among the brightest and loveliest women performing in the new cinema. And James LeGros, too, outdoes himself: he adds a dimension of goodness and authority to his gallery of dryly laconic losers. His Skippy is a wise protector of his mother (as far as fate allows) and a sexy lover of Debby. Finally, he will himself be in need of love and protection. The end of *My New Gun* is a true blank page, the beginning of an unimaginable road movie in which the strangely liberated lovers are not fugitives or robbers or addicts or assassins. Just lovers. Or loners.

Stacy Cochran's is a wonderfully subtle and humane talent whose evolution it will be a pleasure to watch. Her next project, she tells me, is a script called *Boys*—with an *s*, she laughs, not a *z*, since "women use an *s*, at least when talking about white boys."

James LeGros talked to me about his work in films, which has, in the course of some twenty-five features, ranged from independents to big-studio films. "I work better in the independent arena," he says, "in contrast to studio films, because, one, there is only one agenda there—to make the best possible film. In a studio, there are multiple agendas. Two, the filmmakers are not primarily interested in special effects; the restricted budget forces inventiveness. And three, mainstream movies seem shackled to a three-act-story structure. Every executive has read and taken to heart Syd Field's book on scenario construction. In general, the studios are going the way of the U.S. auto industry; they're not making an efficient or competitive product."

Born in Minnesota, LeGros started acting in high school in order to meet girls. He attended UC Irvine but did not study acting there. Afterward, on a lark, he took an apprenticeship in a theatrical company.

His big-studio experiences have run the gamut from one he labels "the slimiest operation, disillusioning though a good education" to another he recalls as "one of the most delightful experiences, largely because they were so wealthy they didn't bother to cheat us . . . my dresser was a millionaire."

Kathryn Bigelow, for whom he made *Near Dark* when he was quite young, he calls "a unique filmmaker who'll only get better." Of *My New Gun* and Stacy Cochran, Le-Gros comments, "I got very lucky. Everybody was really working on the same film. It was an incredibly tight script, and it was shot as it is on the page." *Guncrazy* he says he did not want to do at first because he did not believe in the character as written. But Tamra Davis proved very receptive to the actor's desire to make his character more rounded and sympathetic.

In contrast to his experience with Stacy Cochran, on Gus Van Sant's *Drugstore Cowboy* "there was a lot of improvisation. Between the script and the movie there was a lot of difference. I like to work loose. On *Drugstore Cowboy* there were so many different cuts and the movie ended up shaping itself. As storytelling *Drugstore Cowboy* is more coherent than *My Own Private Idaho,* but as pure vision it is not so good as *Idaho*. Gus was freer in *Idaho*."

LeGros's articulate and thoughtful intelligence should not surprise anyone who has perceived the cunning and economy with which he has played characters who may not themselves possess those attributes. His style may be minimalist, but style, as he says, "is not something you pick off a tree. That tree is within you."

*S*tyle can, of course, manifest itself as exterior flourish, as a twilit sheen. The work of Kathryn Bigelow is a case in point. After a visually stunning and verbally laconic debut with the 1983 biker flick *The Loveless,* set in the South and starring Willem Dafoe, Bigelow hit her stride in 1987 with the vampire film *Near Dark,* written by Bigelow and Eric Reid and filmed in Arizona and Oklahoma. The best bloodsucker saga since Lugosi (a claim unchallenged by Francis Ford Coppola's 1992 *Bram Stoker's Dracula),* *Near Dark* opens with young rancher Caleb (Adrian Pasdar) slapping a mosquito sucking his blood (an image that recurs in *Barton Fink).* It's a lazy summer night in a small Oklahoma *Last Picture Show*–ish town. Beautiful Mae (Jenny Wright) is licking a cone on the main street and Caleb goes up to her to ask, ''Can I have a bite?'' It is a request that will be answered beyond his dreams. They go for a ride in his pickup. ''Stop,'' she says. ''There's something I want to show you: the night. Listen. Do you hear it? It's deafening.'' Caleb drives to a corral to show her his white horse, which shies violently away from her, but Caleb, smitten, is deaf to premonitions and insists she kiss him. Though reluctant to invade him, she consents to bite his neck.

It is suddenly the next morning. Caleb is stumbling home across plowed land under a blazing, hostile sun— images of natural fertility that themselves now feel oppressive. A speeding, dark-windowed van scoops him up; inside it are Mae's ''family'': patriarch Jesse (Lance Henriksen) and his moll (Jenette Goldstein), a biker (Bill Paxton), and a boy of about thirteen, Homer (Joshua Miller). After a wild ride with the colorful hippies, Caleb politely pleads, ''I don't understand what's goin' on here. I like you, I really do, but I really gotta get home.'' They want to kill him, but at Mae's request and because she has already initiated him with a bite, they let him go in a place called Hope, Kansas. In the bleak bus station, he is three dollars shy of the money for a bus home and vomits up a candy bar he tries to eat. A kindly cop helps with the money, saying, "What are you on?" "You wouldn't believe me" is the answer. But he stumbles off the bus in the middle of nowhere, except that Mae is right there. She bites her wrist and says, "Drink this." He does and is relieved of his pain; he smiles; they kiss. "Look at the stars, so bright it'll blind you," she urges. Bigelow contrives in such scenes to evoke complication and fresh sensations about the vampire world: it becomes a place of poetry and wonder, of companionship and love, as well as of horror.

Back at the ranch, Caleb's father and little sister commence a worried search, but these forces of white-bread normality seem dull and overmatched.

The van family lives, though, not on love but on constant kills for blood. A montage of one night's activity show the family at work on the roads of the Southwest: Homer, pretending to have fallen off his bike, suckers a passerby; the biker picks up two women in a party mood; Jesse and his moll are attacked by two hoodlums. The group insists Caleb kill, too. He and Mae hitch a ride in a truck driven by a black man, but Caleb cannot bring himself to join in the man's murder. After Mae does the deed, Caleb sucks blood from her and smiles with repleted contentment.

Then occurs the movie's central and most defining episode: silhouetted against the nocturnal fog, the six descend on a redneck roadside bar and wipe it out. The biker reaches heights of sadistic and sarcastic glee in dispatching the hapless folk within. "Shit-kicker heaven," he calls the bar. "Finger-lickin' good," he pronounces after slicing and slurping from a waitress's throat; he draws his boot spur across the bartender's throat. A terrified young cowboy (James LeGros) is assigned to Caleb to kill; the cowboy leaps through a window, is chased by Caleb, and—under a billboard saying CLEAN HAY PAYS—let go. Caleb lies about the kid's fate. In a cackling Walpurgis Night, the group torch the place as Homer dances on the bar. It is clear now what the family is.

In a dazzling shoot-out riff, the cops, cued by the cowering teenage cowboy, surround the vampires in a motel. Their bullet holes poke diagonal shafts of wounding light into the dark room, burning the skin they hit. Caleb engineers a display of macho heroics by driving the van *into* and then out of the motel room. "You're one of us now," they all agree in complimenting the rookie.

At their next stop, the Godspeed Motel, Mae tells Caleb it's been four years since Homer "got" her. "You miss the sun," she pines, but Caleb now insists, "I can see better at night." At the soda machine, Homer picks up a little girl who turns out to be Caleb's sister, who is there on her brother's trail with her father. Dad shoots Jesse, who merely spits up the bullet. Given a moment of choice, Caleb opts to go with his prior "blood" family. He distracts the vampires by opening a door to daylight and drives off with his father, whom he convinces not to take him to a hospital, for he is suffering from no conventional ailment, as he proves by sticking his hand out the van into the searing sun and scorching his skin.

Back home, in images that evoke both Pietà and Resurrection (just as the earlier blood-sharing had parodied the Eucharist), the rancher father, an expert at inoculating cattle, undertakes to restore his beloved son. He lays Caleb out naked on a slab in the barn and transfuses all his old blood for new. He weeps over the body of his enfeebled son. But one dawn, the doors of the barn are opened, and the entering light no longer burns Caleb's flesh. He is whole again—in blood if not in heart—and family life resumes. But an ominous stillness hangs over the farm. Sure enough, one night, Mae is swinging on the squeaky swing; she is surprised at the warmth of Caleb's skin. Little sister is grabbed by Homer, who seems genuinely infatuated and not merely blood-hungry. Caleb must rescue his sister from the monsters (one of which he so nearly became himself). He contrives to blow up Jesse, the moll, and the biker and causes lovelorn little Homer to sizzle to death in the morning sun.

Mae is then transfused in the barn. When she emerges one fine morning, she says, "I'm afraid." "Don't be," Caleb reassures her. "It's just the sun." Love is the real transfusion.

*Near Dark* is a film of remarkable and subtle originality. It evokes the poetry and allure of the night, while finally siding with the day. Eros battles and vanquishes Thanatos. And setting the whole conflict on the dirty roads of the Southwest was a stroke of genius. It is the first vampire road film.

Bigelow has gone on to make two studio movies: *Blue Steel* (1990), about a New York cop (Jamie Lee Curtis) hunting and *dating* a serial-killing Wall Street broker (Ron Silver), and *Point Break* (1991), about an FBI agent (Keanu Reeves) turning surfer to nab a gang of masked bankrobbing surfers. The first is largely an exercise in the tight photography of sweat beads, but the second displays the kinetic Bigelow of hand-held, in-your-face bravura action. The trick for Bigelow is to find material worthy of her style.

Martha Coolidge's is a feminine and feminist sensibility that has brought warmth to genre films like *Valley Girl* (1983) only to get bogged down in genre quicksand in the like of *Joy of Sex* (1984) and *Real Genius* (1985). Born and bred in New Haven, Connecticut, Coolidge went to the Rhode Island School of Design and then moved to New York for graduate studies in film. After getting an M.F.A. at NYU, she began making documentaries (mostly about her family) in the early 1970s. In the late 1970s she was hired to make features by Coppola's Zoetrope Studios, the collapse of which enterprise more or less stranded her in genreland until *Rambling Rose* (1991).

This script, by Calder Willingham from his autobiographical novel, dealt with the intrusion of sex—in the form of Rose (Laura Dern), a near nymphomaniacal young woman servant—into the proper Hillyer family in the rural Georgia of 1935. That family consists principally of authoritarian father (Robert Duvall), flaky mother (Diane Ladd), and pubescent Buddy, thirteen (Lukas Haas).

Though it was all shot around Wilmington, North Carolina, the movie finds a real Deep South rhythm; it takes its time. Long, deep-breathing, two-character scenes let the characters get to know each other and let us get to know them: the father with the mother talking in bed at night, the mother and Rose on the lawn, Buddy and Rose strolling under the willows and talking about men and women. Two key scenes—the father in the kitchen with a smitten Rose, whom he commands to cover her nipple, and Buddy snuggling up to Rose in bed trying to get her to uncover it—are richly textured collisions of desire and conscience. The film wants us to understand, and shed our preconceived judgmentalism about, female sexuality; it achieves its purpose as art should—by making us know and love the individual person, Rose.

"I had," says Coolidge, "a deep understanding of the material. The South, with its traditions of education and class, was akin to how I grew up in New England." Ladd and daughter Laura Dern, who had earlier worked together in David Lynch's rather different *Wild at Heart,* ease into their roles perfectly. Duvall has never been better. He has Southern affinities—East Texas on his mother's side, Virginia on his father's—and relished both the quirky good-hearted character and working with Coolidge. "I'd rather work with Martha than most men I've worked with," he has said. "She's like a mother behind the camera, nurturing and comforting. She allows the atmosphere to be easy for you, which is right for an actor and certainly right for this film.'' But the film in a way belongs to its point-of-view character, young Buddy, beautifully played by Lukas Haas. It is Buddy who gets his sentimental education from Rose.

Coolidge next got the plum studio assignment of helming the movie of Neil Simon's *Lost in Yonkers,* again a costume coming-of-age-in-an-odd-family story. Perhaps she could become a modern Clarence Brown, that director of such romantic coming-of-age films as *Of Human Hearts, The Human Comedy,* and *Ah, Wilderness!*

*Lost in Yonkers,* unfortunately, is far less achieved than *Rambling Rose.* Coolidge's cinematic humanity is inaudible amid the theatrical artificialities of the script (Simon seems unsure whether he is telling the aunt's or the nephew's story) and the playing. Mercedes Ruehl as the simple aunt and Irene Worth as the granitic granny and Richard Dreyfuss as an uncle out of Damon Runyon all overdo it.

CHAPTER SIX

# *F*rom the Southland, with Detours

Among filmmakers of the Southwest, a new name has ridden into town. The legend of Robert Rodriguez has become at least as colorful as his first feature film, *El Mariachi*. Born in 1970, he is the third oldest of the ten children of Cecilio and Rebecca Rodriguez of San Antonio, Texas. Cecilio Rodriguez sells pots and pans from door to door and Rebecca is a nurse. They brought their boisterous, lively brood up to cherish education, thrift, hard work—and going to the movies.

Cecilio also bought one of the first VCRs, which came with a camera attached. Robert took to it at once. "I started filming short movies with my brothers and sisters, who were an endless supply of cast and crew." The plots dealt with time-honored family events like the revenge of a bullied sister. A filmmaker was born—and a cartoonist as well. After graduating from St. Anthony's High School in San Antonio, Robert went to the University of Texas at Austin in 1986. Despite all his home movies, his grades were not good enough to get into the film program, and so he invented a daily comic strip entitled "Los Hooligans" that featured characters based on his siblings, especially sister Maricarmen. It ran for three years in a local paper.

Rodriguez also entered his family tapes—now grandly entitled *Austin Stories*—in a local film contest. His entry won and got him, in the fall of 1990, into the film program at last. (He is still *in* that program.) There he made *Bedhead,* an award-winning 16mm short.

By the summer of 1991, he was ready to tackle his first feature. An old classmate from St. Anthony's, Carlos Gallardo, lived in the Mexican border town of Acuña, where Robert had often spent vacations making little Spanish-language action shorts for the Mexican video market. Rodriguez devised the character of El Mariachi, a sort of Mexican "Man with No Name" in tribute to the Clint Eastwood persona in Sergio Leone's Italian Westerns. El Mariachi is a nomadic guitarist and singer (a *mariachi*) who, through a bizarre chain of circumstances, becomes a free-lance avenger. The film *El Mariachi* is the story of his transformation into this avenger.

Where to get the necessary $9,000 for the bare-bones shoot? Robert and Carlos had a pit bull, a motorcycle, a school bus, a jail, a bar, and a ranch (Carlo's house) at their disposal. Carlos sold some land, and Robert checked himself into an Austin research lab, where he had to live for a month as a guinea pig for new drugs. Fee: $3,000. Incidental perks: he had leisure to finish the script (credited both to him and to Gallardo), and he recruited one of his key actors, Peter Marquardt.

**Richard Linklater.** *Richard E. Aaron.*

**Spike Lee.** *Copyright © 1989 Universal City Studios, Inc. All rights reserved.*

**Christopher Münch.**
*Wayne Shimabukuro.*

**David Angus and Ian Hart in** *The Hours and Times.*

Christian Slater in *Heathers. Copyright © 1988 New World Enter-tainment. All rights reserved.*

Winona Ryder and director Michael Lehmann discuss a scene from *Heathers. Copyright © 1988 New World Entertainment. All rights reserved.*

**Atom Egoyan.**
*Ego Film Arts.*

**Michael McManus in** *Speaking Parts. Ego Film Arts.*

Tony Chan (left) gives
direction to Jeff Lau in
*Combination Platter. Tony
Chan Productions, Inc.*

Jeff Lau in *Combination Platter. Tony Chan Productions, Inc.*

**Hal Hartley.**
*Susan Shacter.*

**Adrienne Shelly and Martin Donovan in** *Trust***.** *Chris Buck.*

**Matt Dillon and director Gus Van Sant on the set of** *Drugstore Cowboy. Copyright © 1989 Avenue Pictures.*

**River Phoenix and Keanu Reeves in** *My Own Private Idaho. Copyright © 1991 Fine Line Features. All rights reserved. Photo by Abigayle Tarsches.*

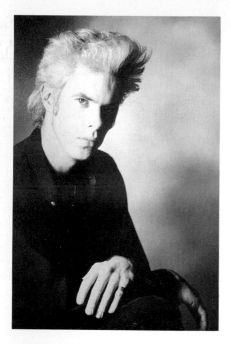

**Jim Jarmusch.** *Copyright*
*© 1989 Masayoshi Sukita.*
*All rights reserved.*

**Youki Kudoh and Masatoshi Nagase in** *Mystery Train.* *Copyright*
*© 1989 Mystery Train, Inc. All rights reserved.*

With a borrowed Arriflex, a tape recorder, and two aluminum modeling lamps, the project was a go, with Rodriguez doing the cinematography and sound (all post-recorded). The actors, who were mostly working for free, never saw a script, and were given their dialogue just before or even during (since it was essentially a silent film) the shot. The Anglo heavy (Marquardt) spoke his (Spanish) lines phonetically. Rodriguez did not want a rehearsed sound to his dialogue. Everybody ate at Gallardo's home. Filming took fourteen days. Final cost: $7,225. (Skeptics, be assured that the postproduction video transfer took a mere $2,824.) Good news: they came in $1,725 under budget. Bad news: the Mexican video industry in Acuña, destined customers for the film, were not interested in buying it. Then good news: Rodriguez drove to L.A. with the film, got a high-powered agent and a big-bucks production deal at a major studio—in fact, Columbia, which Rodriguez chose partly because John Singleton had made *Boyz N the Hood* there. It is possible that Rodriguez will be doing an English-language remake of *El Mariachi* with a six-million-dollar budget, but he may instead attempt something entirely new. He does in any case intend to make films in which Hispanics will be neither comic stereotypes nor gang members, but just "regular guys."

It is an amazing Cinderella story, an especially dramatic version of the story of many of today's independent filmmakers.

And the film itself? It is an exuberant triumph of high spirits and low style that is impossible not to like. The camera snakes around the dusty little Mexican town in and out of nooks and crannies—it was held either in Rodriguez's hands or in his lap as Gallardo (or somebody else, if star Gallardo was in the scene) pushed Robert around in a wheelchair. A good deal of time is spent in a local jail and at a luxury pool as the data of the story are put in place: Moco, a drug kingpin (Marquardt—a Christopher Walken look-alike), hires a pudgy hit man (Reinol Martinez) dressed in black and carrying his automatic in a guitar case to off some treacherous vassals. At the same time, a sweet but unsmiling wandering mariachi minstrel (Gallardo) hits town looking for gigs in bars. He, too, wears black pants, and he, too, carries a guitar case, containing a guitar. The mariachi is a fatalistic child of the road. Just as he calls today "un día sin amor, sin suerte, nada cambia [a loveless, luckless day, nothing changes]," his luck changes. A turtle waddles across the road; the minstrel is given a free coconut and gets a shoeshine. This new town will, obviously, bring "buena suerte [good luck]." He goes into a bar and softly orders a Fresca—a droll homage to the abstemious Shane. When the bartender explains they already have a resident mariachi, he splits. Then the hit man strides in with a similar case. The sarcastic bartender asks, "What is this, mariachi day?" Not exactly, for the hit man plugs three customers, pays for his beer, and splits.

The real mariachi has had more luck in the second bar he tries, a classy hotel bar run by Domino (Consuelo Gómez), a beautiful woman ("the most beautiful thing I've seen today, next to the turtle," he informs us in voice-over). He asks her for a job, saying, "Mi voz es mi vida [my voice is my life].'' She sends him upstairs to meet her pit bull and to take a bath in her bedroom. She is, alas, the kingpin's mistress and suspects the mariachi is the hit man—the whole movie is a tragicomedy of mistaken identity. Sneaking up behind him as he shampoos in the tub and holding a knife to his throat and then to his testicles, she demands he prove his identity as a musician. Squatting in the tub with his guitar in his watery hand, he improvises a hilarious tune about her northern eyes and his imminent castration. It is the movie's high point. Convinced, she laughs: ''It was only a letter opener.'' She gives him a job, and that night in the bar he sings a ballad about his nomadic life. In a smashingly tight red dress, she listens—with erotic intensity. That night, she and the mariachi and the harmless pit bull sleep innocently together. Domino wishes him sweet dreams—''Que tus sueños sean angelitos'' is the lovely Spanish phrase—but El Mariachi dreams, as he has earlier in the film, a disturbing dream about a child, a mask, and a cemetery.

But this note of romance is soon drowned in a cacophony of violence. El Mariachi keeps bumping into goons who mistake him for Azul, the hit man. ''If he's called Azul [blue], why doesn't he wear blue?'' plaintively queries El Mariachi. He winds up again and again, in his simplicity and dexterity, outfoxing and slaying these practiced killers.

Moco, who thinks he is in either a Sam Peckinpah or a Sergio Leone movie (he likes to strike matches on the faces of his goons, à la Lee Van Cleef in *For a Few Dollars*

*More)*, calls frequently for the head of El Mariachi. The guitar cases get switched and Azul heads for Moco's ranch carrying El Mariachi's guitar. El Mariachi, wanting his guitar back, follows on the motorcycle that was a present to his beloved Domino from the evil Moco.

It all ends in an orgy of slaughter as Moco shoots Domino and Azul and El Mariachi's guitar and El Mariachi's guitar hand. El Mariachi plugs Moco and strikes a match on the bastard's face. He mounts the bike, putting Domino's cherished letter opener between the handlebars and her pit bull on the backseat. Reflecting on the bloody rush of events, he comments that this town has brought not luck after all but a curse *(maledición)*. ''I have lost my guitar, my hand, and her.'' But it is the birth of a new persona, El Mariachi the Avenger. He rides off.

*El Mariachi* bears the marks of its intended destination on the action video shelves of Mexico. There are too many runnings down staircases and leaps into trucks and spreading bullet stains. There is too little time spent on character, and the end is too brutally curt. What we have seen of El Mariachi and of Domino was too seductive and amusing for such a send-off. But the movie has an impudence, energy, and salt that make Rodriguez a talent to watch. He brings a delightfully revisionist and specifically Hispanic spin to the clichés of the action genre that will be unlikely to desert him as he branches out into more demanding kinds of filmmaking.

*J*im Jarmusch is one of the key sensibilities in recent American cinema. He was born in Akron, Ohio, in 1953 and studied cinema under Nicholas Ray. He wrote and filmed three influential black-and-white films in the 1980s: *Permanent Vacation* (1980), *Stranger Than Paradise* (1984), and *Down by Law* (1986). Though living in New York City and thought of as a New York filmmaker, Jarmusch has in fact gone to the heartland in much of his work.

*Stranger Than Paradise* was a sort of road movie that looked at American oddities through the laconically unsurprised eyes of two dense guys and a young Hungarian woman; *Down by Law* put two dense Americans and a zany Italian guy in jail and on the lam together in backwater Louisiana. Again, it was foreign eyes taking in odd corners of the United States. But it was the form and tone of *Stranger Than Paradise* that really sounded a new and influential note. In each of its scenes, Tom DiCillo's camera would open with a shot of a space (interior or exterior) in which one, two, or three (rarely four) people would be statically situated or into which they would enter in the course of the shot. They would perform certain minimal behaviors and either leave the space or grow still in it so that at the end of the shot the space would reassert its integrity, its hegemony. During each shot, the camera might swivel but rarely would it move. Each of these setups ended with a fade to black.

The first third of the film takes place in New York, where Eva (Eszter Balint) drops in from Budapest on her American cousin Willie (John Lurie). Her arrival is lonely and pathetic: she stands glumly at the airport; she lugs a suitcase, a paper bag, and a cassette across dingy

streets in Manhattan's Lower East Side. She is installed
grudgingly in Willie's bare apartment, but her cousin has
no occupation save watching TV and doing a little petty
gambling at the races and at cards with his sadsack, look-
alike pal Eddie (Richard Edson, later to play in *Do the
Right Thing*). Eva hangs about posing unexcited questions
about TV dinners, the rules of football, vacuum cleaners,
solitaire. She puts Screamin' Jay Hawkins on her cassette, to Eddie's displeasure. On the eve of her departure
for Cleveland to stay with an aunt, Willie—who has
warmed to her a bit—buys her a dress, which she politely
puts on but later leaves on a garbage can, after changing
out of it into her usual uniform of jeans and sweater right
out on the cold street. At home, the guys drink beer out
of cans, listlessly and wordlessly.

In the second part, flush with six hundred dollars in
poker winnings, Willie and Eddie decide to drive to
Cleveland to see Eva. The camera spends a lot of time in
the backseat observing the snowy towns of Pennsylvania
and Ohio. DiCillo's gray-on-gray images rise to poetry in
the Cleveland streets, in shots like the one of the wet
street in front of the bus station and Nite Life Lounge. The
principal Cleveland interior is the living room of portly,
severe Aunt Lotte (Cecillia Stark in a genuinely comic
performance). Aunt Lotte fiercely grips her armchair
while watching TV, wins at cards, and compels the New
York visitors to chaperone Eva's dates with a coworker at
the hot dog stand where she is employed. This results in
an implausible and very-long-held joke shot of the four
watching a movie: Date—Eddie—Eva—Willie. Eva and
the guys go to see Cleveland's most famous sight, Lake

Erie, but a gusty, swirling blizzard is raging, and so they stand forlornly and forever at the lake railing—the shot is sad, funny, and pretty.

This inspires the two guys to head, in the film's third part, for warmth, for Paradise, for Florida. They set out by themselves, but, actually missing Eva, double back to pick her up, to Aunt Lotte's annoyance. Florida consists of a neon orange atop a motel sign, a motel exterior at sunset, and a motel bedroom where the trio sleep quite sexlessly—this is a rigidly unerotic film. Eva and Willie claim the two beds, at right angles to each other, and Eddie is forced to open up a fold-out bed in the space between them. Next morning, stewing that the guys have left her to go off to the dog races (they had not taken her to the track in New York, either), Eva mopes disconsolately at a stone table beside the winter sea. When they get back, having lost all but fifty dollars on Eddie's hunches, the guys quarrel and the trio go for a walk on the beach. The next day, with the guys again off without her (this time to the horses), Eva buys a big hat, is promptly mistaken by a hepcat for a drug dealer, and is given a huge wad of cash. Impassive as ever, she simply takes it. The guys, lucky at the ponies, get back to the motel room to find she has gone to the airport. There follows a laboratory demonstration of the randomness and whimsicality of fate. Through a series of mischances, regrets, and impulses, Willie winds up on a plane to Budapest, Eddie in a car on the way to New York, and Eva back in the motel sitting on the bed with her hat in her lap. And all have struck it rich.

*Stranger Than Paradise* is a film of beautifully wintry

images and a far-off, wintry wit, but it is hard not to want its three people to break out of their spatial and linguistic prisons of glum, monosyllabic affectlessness. A sort of February of the soul prevails in the film's symbolic segments of America: the big city, the heartland, the tropical South. It is a world where even wild strokes of good luck have no consequences. With its sad marginal screwballs and its hats, *Stranger Than Paradise* has something in common with Gus Van Sant's *Drugstore Cowboy*, but it is *Drugstore Cowboy* as if made by the James LeGros character.

In 1989, Jarmusch made *Mystery Train*, his first color film. The cinematographer was Robby Müller, who had filmed Jarmusch's *Down by Law* and had earlier shot *Paris, Texas* for Wenders. The film, Jarmusch's masterpiece, is an intense look at Memphis, Tennessee. It tells, in succession, three stories that occupy the same real time.

The first part, "Far from Yokohama," is about two Japanese tourists; the second, "A Ghost," is about an Italian widow bringing her husband's body home; the third, "Lost in Space," is about three local losers. All the characters wind up spending the night in adjoining rooms at the small and seedy Arcade Hotel.

In the first story, Jarmusch's penchant for looking at American civilization through alien eyes finds ideal expression. Two Japanese teenagers, Juni (Masatoshi Nagase) and Matsuko (Youki Kudoh), are sitting in a blue train on their way to Memphis to visit the founding shrines of rock. They come to Memphis (a perfect name, with its echoes of ancient Egypt) as representatives—in fact though never in attitude—of a richer and more developed country piously visiting the sacred places of an earlier civilization. It is exactly the spirit in which Henry James's American heiresses visited the Colosseum in the nineteenth century. It is a neat, and very understated, turn of the historical screw. As the train glides past car graveyards, Matsuko puts on white lipstick and opines that the train is slow; Juni says time is different in America. Time—its real differences within seeming simultaneities—is one of Jarmusch's constant themes. They detrain in Memphis, where she likes the train station because it is so quaintly antique, while he expresses a preference for Yokohama's modern terminal. In the station, he uses his ever-present lighter to light the cigar of an elderly black man (Rufus Thomas, a rhythm and blues legend), who offers a courtly thanks in Japanese. The young pair speak in subtitled Japanese throughout.

Leaving the station, the two tourists put a pole through the handle of their red suitcase, each carrying an end, and begin a long trudge through the pastel, run-down streets of Memphis. The journey starts on Chaucer Street, named fittingly after the poet of pilgrims. She is eager to get to Graceland, but for Juni Memphis is the city of Carl Perkins, Jerry Lee Lewis, and Roy Orbison more than of Elvis. By luck, they pass the Sun Records building and go in for the guided tour, given by a rapid-talking guide prattling about early Elvis recording sessions there. Back out in the sun, they admit they understood nothing.

They plod on past a barbershop, Shades Bar, and a parked Cadillac until, at nightfall, they spy the small

Arcade Hotel and decide to postpone Graceland. The hotel is run by a brilliantly comic duo of clerk (Screamin' Jay Hawkins, another rhythm and blues legend) and bell-boy (Cinque Lee, younger brother of Spike). These two spar throughout, as the wry, wise clerk teases the bellboy, vain about his little cap and impressed by a magazine article about how much Elvis would weigh on Jupiter (over six hundred pounds).

The Japanese pay the twenty-two dollars a room costs and tip the bellboy with a Japanese plum, which the clerk eats. Juni takes pictures of the hotel room, including the inevitable painting of Elvis on the wall. When Mitsuko asks him why he never takes pictures of the outdoors, Juni says he can remember what he sees outside but forgets interiors like hotel rooms and airports—a deft Jarmuschian reversal of the Japanese-shutterbug cliché. Elvis-addict Matsuko hauls out her scrapbook of Elvis avatars: an Assyrian king, the Buddha, the Statue of Liberty . . . Madonna. At this last, Juni sighs, ''Gimme a break.''

In an unusually beautiful, Hopperesque Müller shot, Juni stands at the window looking out at the blue night as a train goes by on an overpass across the street. ''It's cool,'' suddenly remarks this impassive and glum kid, ''to be eighteen and in Memphis . . . this is not Yokohama . . . this is America.'' It is a moment of rapture such as young Americans feel in, perhaps, Paris.

Matsuko, more playful and animated than he, smears her lipstick over his face in the course of a messy kiss. When he actually smiles, she asks, ''Why do you not smile and be happy?'' "I am happy," he answers. ''That's just the way my face is.'' They make love, have a mild quarrel, make up, and go to sleep intertwined. It is a passage, shot from above, of private tenderness. At 2:17 A.M. "Blue Moon" comes on the radio. (We will hear this very playing of that sad song twice more in other rooms.)

In the morning, she hears a loud report. "Was that a gun?" "Probably," he responds, "It's America.'' They shower, fight about what to pack, and leave the room.

In these young Japanese devotees of American pop music, Jarmusch has found the perfect vehicles for his take on our quirks. Their combination of deadpan detachment and passionate curiosity is exactly the filmmaker's. (By happy coincidence, *Mystery Train* is, according to Jarmusch, the very first American film entirely financed by Japanese capital.)

With the film's other aliens, the touch is less sure. For example, in the second story, ''A Ghost,'' the Italian widow walks similar streets from the station, is fleeced by local sharpies, and winds up in a room next to the Japanese couple's. She generously agrees to share it with a nervous, talkative woman. As one of the larcenous sharpies had prophesied, Elvis appears to her in the middle of the night—clad in silver lamé, fat, polite, transparent. Mildly funny as a sort of American equivalent of the religious iconography of her native Italy, the apparition really has no lasting effect on her or her story.

In the third segment, the barber from the barbershop in ''Far from Yokohama'' (Steve Buscemi, in one of his juiciest nerd roles), his hotheaded brother-in-law (musician Joe Strummer), and their black friend (Rick Aviles) manage to screw up their already marginal lives totally. The barber's sister (the motor mouth in "A Ghost") has left her husband, who, angry at the world, wantonly kills a liquor-store clerk in the course of a petty robbery and in the presence of the other two. The terrified trio take refuge in the Arcade, where a quarrel ensues and the barber gets accidentally but quite painfully shot in the knee. (This is that morning shot, which, amusingly, the seemingly otherworldly Italian woman had identified as coming from a .38.) The guys drink from a whiskey bottle and discuss such cultural topics as the old TV series *Lost in Space* and why there are no paintings of African-Americans like Otis Redding or Martin Luther King up there on the wall with Elvis. (The Elvis painting falls down, by the way, when the gun goes off.) Answer: the hotel is white-owned. It is unlikely to be a coincidence that a similar issue burns in Spike Lee's *Do the Right Thing*, made in the same year.

In *Mystery Train*'s last shots, threads cross. Juni and Matsuko are again forming the same composition in a moving blue train. They are on their way to New Orleans to see the house of Fats Domino. The barber's sister walks by and asks them if the train stops at Natchez. He understands *matches* and whips out his ever-ready lighter. Puzzled, she moves on and sits alone. Meanwhile, his pals have dumped the wounded and screaming barber in the back of a pickup to take him to a doctor-who'll-ask-no-questions they know in Arkansas. The pickup and train run parallel for a second right near the Arcade. Then the train curves off to the right.

*Mystery Train,* named after the haunting song sung by Elvis and others, is a thought-provoking meditation on time, on America, and on Memphis, that navel of the unceasingly bizarre Elvis cult. More than any of his other settings, Memphis works as a fertile metaphor for Jarmusch and for Robby Müller, who here at least equals his work in the similarly provocative *Paris, Texas.*

In 1991, Jarmusch wrote and directed *Night on Earth,* a five-parter about five simultaneous taxi driver-passenger encounters: in L.A. at twilight, in New York in early morning, in Paris after midnight, in Rome in the wee hours, in Helsinki at dawn. The five anecdotes range from the cute to the maudlin, with no Memphian resonance or illuminating depth about where they happen. But the camera of Frederick Elmes, a collaborator with John Cassavetes and David Lynch, as it glides along California freeways, mean Manhattan streets, and crooked little Parisian alleys, evokes so much sadness and loneliness we want to weep. What Jarmusch has to guard against is being satisfied with just such vague sentimentality.

In 1991, Tom DiCillo, who photographed Jarmusch's *Permanent Vacation* and *Stranger Than Paradise,* wrote and directed his feature debut, *Johnny Suede,* about a feckless Ricky Nelson wannabe (Brad Pitt) who sports a towering, lacquered pompadour and is forever falling for the wrong woman. Toneless and unfunny, *Johnny Suede* is enough to give a bad name to affectlessness.

Another director who has been said to be "poaching" on the works of Jim Jarmusch and on those of Hal Hartley, too, is Michael Almereyda, who was born under another name in Overland Park, Kansas, in 1960. Almereyda's biography says that he has written, over the past dozen years, various screenplays, mostly unproduced.

His first feature was *Twister* (1988), which he scripted from the novel *Oh!* by Mary Robison. Set around Wichita in Almereyda's native Kansas, *Twister* is a dysfunctional-family sitcom played in a manic key: patriarch Cleveland (Harry Dean Stanton) wants to breed miniature cows; his latest girlfriend Virginia (Lois Chiles) hosts a religious TV show for children; son Howdy (Crispin Glover) is a rocker fop; daughter Maureen (Suzy Amis) is a dreamy alcoholic. Maureen's ex-husband, earnest and straight Chris (Dylan McDermott), returns to reclaim his wife and daughter Violet (Lindsay Christman) and has a hard time of it. A twister strikes while the family watches TV. Brother Howdy and sister Maureen go off at one point in quest of their vanished mother. What they find is not Oz but William Burroughs taking target practice in a barn and droning on about a man who ate a clock. It all ends with a family tableau propped up in front of the TV: Howdy—Violet—Maureen—Chris. It is a sort of homage to the moviegoing scene in *Stranger Than Paradise*. *Twister* has a bad case of the literary cutes; it seems unaware that its targets (TV, families, mid-America) are old hat and its ammunition rusty.

Almereyda's second film, *Another Girl, Another Planet* (1992), is much more cinematic and original, although, paradoxically, it is also more primitive. The fifty-six-minute, black-and-white film was shot in Pixelvision; PXL Vision was a forty-five-dollar Fisher-Price plastic toy camera using audiotape cassettes and plugged into wall outlets. The toy is no longer on the market. The director wrote and shot the thing in New York in a week with unpaid actors in his and a friend's East Twelfth Street apartments. Total cost, including the blowup to 16mm, came to around $10,000. The low-definition images, called black-and-white but really gray, have a blurry, underwater, barely legible quality that has been compared to Seurat and might also be compared to the effect of strong eyedrops.

The episodic story counterpoints married Nic downstairs (Nic Ratner) with womanizing Bill upstairs (Barry Sherman). Bill's melancholy women recite to him tragic stories—tragic but funny, as when rocker Ramona (Mary Ward) tells of her dead artist husband being yelled at by a holy Tibetan lama—well, see the movie. What occurs is essentially the parable of the biter bit: Bill breaks hearts until his is broken by Romanian waitress Mia (Elina Löwensohn, who also played an elusive Romanian in Hal Hartley's *Simple Men*). Mia has, like Eva in *Stranger Than Paradise*, her own musical tastes, running to the group Psychic TV, and her own standards, saying, "I'm not into casual sex." She joins in childlike play about Nabu, an elephant she and Bill have seen in a movie. The couple find happiness "somehow exhausting." She recommends a culinary specialty of her Romanian grandmother: peanut butter inside two Ritz crackers covered with chocolate. (Too easy, Michael.) Then Mia springs Bill's comeuppance, saying, "I'm not in love. I have to go." Bill, smarting, realizes that "not to be in love is to be dying." He somehow finds himself sharing his tiny apartment with Nabu—a poetic answer to a prayer. Downstairs Nic contributes to the mood of magic realism with a fish called Nosferatu and with constant showings of a 1935 Max Fleischer cartoon called *Dancing on the Moon*, about animals escaping from a zoo to dance freely and happily with each other on the moon—a sort of utopian antithesis to the amorous mismatches upstairs. And Nic also tells a funny one-liner about the difference between a drunk and an alcoholic. Again, see the movie.

*Another Girl, Another Planet* may be derivative around the edges, but it has a wild poetry, a raucous humor, and a technological impudence that are very much Almereyda's own. It is far superior to *Twister*. The director is, according to a piece in *Premiere* magazine, planning another Pixelvision feature, a meditation on Edgar Allan Poe to be shot in Poe's old haunt of Richmond, Virginia, as it looks today. Almereyda is a visionary whose objects of vision are just starting to swim into focus.

Three independent films of recent years have played variations on that endlessly beckoning American trope—the road.

John McNaughton is a Chicago native who, on graduation from Columbia College in that city, caromed off a number of jobs, including carny, steelworker, silversmith, and boat builder until landing in an ad agency. From two brothers who packaged and distributed videos,

McNaughton, in 1986, got $100,000 to direct a thriller for the video market, which was to have been *El Mariachi*'s fate, too. From old *Chicago Tribune* files McNaughton and coscenarist Richard Fire wrote a screenplay loosely based on the career of serial killer Henry Lee Lucas. For one reason or another, the completed film, *Henry: Portrait of a Serial Killer,* languished for three years until it began to win acclaim at film festivals in 1989.

Filmed in the Chicago area by Charlie Lieberman, *Henry* opens with a montage of its protagonist's handiwork: a woman's neat corpse in a living room near a saucer and an ashtray, a bloodied woman slumped in a bathroom, a woman followed home but saved when her husband is there to welcome her, a woman's body wrapped in plastic in a stream in which a plastic carton drifts by. Then, economically, we see a hitchhiker get in a car whose driver says he is going to town. We fill in the rest.

Meanwhile, gaunt, scruffy Otis (Tom Towles) is picking up his blonde sister Becky (Tracy Arnold) at the airport. She is fleeing a no-good husband, having left her little daughter in the care of her own mother. Nomadic Henry (Michael Rooker) is staying with these people, for Otis is an old prison pal.

Henry gets a local job as an exterminator—always an ironic job description, as in *Blue Velvet* and *Naked Lunch.* He enters one house in his professional capacity, and, next thing, a cartoon is on the TV and the camera is slowly, slowly circling the corpse of a woman strangled with a wire on the sofa.

Otis is briefly glimpsed at his job—gas jockey in a

garage who also sells dope to adolescent male customers he comes on to sexually. Back home, Becky is gutting a fish and listening to her brother's story of how Henry, to whom she is instantly attracted, was in prison for killing his mother with a baseball bat. Later that night, Henry and Becky play cards and softly exchange horror stories from their respective childhoods: Henry's mother, one is not surprised to hear, was a "whore" who made him wear a dress while watching her perform with various men. Well, no wonder he turned out the way he did!

Becky, a nice but sad and rather dim young woman not unlike the barber's sister in *Mystery Train,* has gotten herself a job giving shampoos in a beauty salon; she buys an I LOVE CHICAGO T-shirt. When her brother starts kissing her suggestively after the fish dinner, Henry angrily separates them and takes Otis out to Cicero to pick up two hookers, but Henry's idea of a good time is to snap both their necks. Otis is upset for a moment, but quickly gets with the program. When the TV set in their ratty apartment dies, Henry and Otis go to buy a new one, but Henry's idea of making a purchase is to electrocute the salesman, who was, it is true, obese and nasty.

Things get still nastier soon. When a high-school kid rejects Otis's advances with a punch in the face, Otis steams and that night remarks to Henry, "I'd like to kill that kid." Henry, who is the intelligence to Otis's fool in this evil duo, explains that Otis has been seen with the kid. "Well, I'd like to kill *somebody,*" snarls Otis. "Repeat that," says Henry coolly—and in that brilliantly silhouetted instant we are made to understand the genetics of serial killing. Uncontrollable rage at life's slights, little and big, can become *this*. Henry takes Otis for a long, smooth, stalking drive along a Chicago highway and down under a viaduct. Henry has an eye for the best way to manage these things safely. Pretending to have car trouble, Otis shoots a motorist who stops to help. Always vary your modus operandi, explains the savvy Henry. Then comes a sequence difficult to watch—so unpleasant McNaughton mediates it through a videotape Henry and Otis made *in situ* and later run and rerun at home in slow motion: the torture and murder of a suburban family— mother, father, and son—in front of each other.

Henry is a still, stolid character, and Michael Rooker plays him without the slightest indulgence in any twitching neuroticism. Henry goes out one night for a long walk to get cigarettes: will he kill the guy in the store? No, he just answers a pleasant bit of small talk with, ''Fuck the [Chicago] Bears.'' Will he kill a woman out walking her dog? No, she gets just too far away. Two lucky, random escapes. But the evening is not a total loss for, when Henry gets home, he finds Otis raping Becky and intervenes. Otis gets poked in the eye with a comb by Becky, stabbed by Henry, and has his head sawn off in the bathtub (shades of *Ms. 45*)—also by Henry.

For a short while *Henry* becomes a lovers-on-the-road movie, as Henry and Becky take off at night, pausing briefly to dump a green plastic bag containing Otis off a bridge. Henry has shied away from sex with Becky, but he appears to consent in principle to her fantasies of a romantic future. She suggests returning to her mother's and bringing up her little girl together, while he mentions his sister's horse ranch in the San Fernando Valley in the California he has been vaguely headed for. To her "I love you" he answers, "I guess I love you, too. Want to listen to the radio?"

They stop at a motel. He brings out his guitar case, and she goes in the shower. Cut to the next morning, as he carefully shaves, in close-up, and quietly, calmly leaves the motel alone. Is he, perhaps out of shame at his clearly hinted impotence, sneaking out on her? Not exactly, for down the road a bit he stops the car and carefully deposits a big grayish-blue folding suitcase on the shoulder of the road. He drives off, but the camera lingers unbudgingly on the suitcase.

*Henry: Portrait of a Serial Killer*—a movie I resisted seeing for some time—is a work of great originality and insight, mixing ellipsis and reticence with an unfazable bluntness of presentation. Mostly, it avoids easy pop psychology (except for that overdetermining childhood) and lurid gore (except for that videotape). But in sticking to the *how* rather than the *why*, it manages to give a very full human picture of Henry. It puts Henry in a drolly evoked social context of marginal losers. And it is full of a lower-depths comedy, in the domestic scenes with the simian brother and the waiflike, trusting sister, both of whom rely for stability and common sense on a monster whose depths they cannot gauge. The movie does not bother with sympathy or condemnation; it is concerned with presenting. And just by presenting with such clarity, it offers a devastating analysis. Only intelligence, it seems to be saying, is of any use in this case. For *Henry* is not some *Friday the 13th* indulgence; it is a work of provoking coolness.

The largely smooth, unjumpy, cool images of Lieberman and the finely understated performances of Rooker, Arnold, and Towles match the director's intelligence. The whole thing is as if the dingy universe of John Waters were being gravely examined by the eye of an Errol Morris. Morris's poetic, intrusive, amused sensibility has recently revolutionized documentary filmmaking in *Vernon, Florida* (1981), *The Thin Blue Line* (1988), and *A Brief History of Time* (1992)—the last two with eerie scores by Philip Glass. *Henry* could be called an anti–*Thin Blue Line,* for that film set out to establish the existence of an innocent man among the screwballs that litter our bedraggled highways.

McNaughton then made *The Borrower* (1989), a sci-fi comedy heavy on special effects, and *Sex, Drugs, Rock & Roll* (1991), an Eric Bogosian concert movie put together from eight filmed performances. In 1993, he did *Mad Dog and Glory,* a darkish Chicago comedy about a shy police photographer (Robert De Niro), a small-time don who fancies himself a stand-up comic (the excellent Bill Murray), and a woman they, in a sense, share (Uma Thurman). David Caruso essentially reprises his *King of New York* role as De Niro's cop partner. Richard Price wrote it; Robby Müller photographed it, beautifully; Martin Scorsese produced it (it was, after *The Grifters,* the second movie not his own he produced). *Mad Dog and Glory* will look better with time; it was a film McNaughton managed to color with his own personality, but there were, perhaps, other agendas at work. He is planning to film a William Burroughs adaptation, as well as some scripts of his own. Good.

**M**ichael Steinberg was at UCLA from 1982 to 1988 getting an M.A. and an M.F.A. in film production. While there, he met fellow student and screenwriter Neal Jimenez, who actually wrote *River's Edge* (1987), a dark study of teen evil, while still a student.

Steinberg made his directorial debut in 1992 codirecting with Jimenez *The Waterdance,* a script Jimenez based on some personal experience. It dealt with the efforts of young Los Angeles novelist Joel Garcia (Eric Stoltz) to come to terms with incurable paralysis—the result of a climbing accident. *The Waterdance* broke some new ground in the rehab genre by its candor about sexual dysfunction and by its refusal of easy hope.

Steinberg's first solo directorial effort was *Bodies, Rest & Motion* (1993). Based by Roger Hedden on his own playscript that centered on four young people in their twenties, it is about roots, rootlessness, and lost homes. Hedden's play, produced at Lincoln Center in New York, was set in New England, but the film was made in Tuscon (renamed Enfield), Arizona, in the baking August heat of 1992. Hedden is candid in admitting that the first reason for the change of locale was that, closer to California, it was easier to attract financing and stars. Expediency brought artistic dividends, too: the piece's themes play better out amid the auto-dealership-infested desert towns where, except for retirees, everybody seems to be living by accident because they had to stop off on the way to someplace else. Another bonus was the region's Native American culture, which came to figure in the film. Such a combination of openness to what comes along with an overarching sense of goal is a hallmark of much (but not certainly all) independent filmmaking.

Nick (Tim Roth) is a rolling stone sick of *here* and itching to light out for anywhere else. He decides, for no particular reason, to head for Butte, Montana; his lover, Beth (Bridget Fonda), will go along obediently. Certainly, their jobs—appliance salesman and waitress—are nothing to keep them in Enfield. But Nick proves unable to wait even a day for Beth and drives off, after stealing her a TV from the store. Playing the car radio, swigging a beer, and smoking a cigarette, he drives happily into the dawn. He stops at a Navajo gift shop and buys a feathered headdress.

Later, he asks a Navajo gas jockey about the mystic meaning of the wind. "It's just the wind," says the man, refusing to be romantically ethnic on cue. "It'd be better if it meant something," replies Nick, unconsciously encapsulating his life.

He makes a detour to visit his own long-ignored family, but finds his parents' house occupied by an old deaf man and his little granddaughter. Then, in the middle of a storm, he tries to call Beth from a roadside phone booth (overhead shot) but encounters a nasty operator and screams, "Reconnect me . . . you heartless fucker." Again, symbolic words. The next morning, heading back, he drives by a huge statue of an Indian towering above a gas station.

Meanwhile, in Enfield, Beth is in a fix, for their apartment has been rented. She has one more day in it, and on that day painter Sid (Eric Stoltz) arrives to ready it for the new tenants. (Stoltz was also one of the film's producers. He remarked, "If I was going to do another independent movie, I wanted to find something new in the experience.") Sid is the antithesis of Nick in being contentedly rooted in Enfield, liking the place, liking his job, liking himself, happy in his skin. The heart of the story is Sid's gradual, gentle breaking down of Beth's cynical, tired, once-burnt resistance to trust. They coexist in the bare apartment and with the help of a few of his joints, she relaxes. They spend the night having sex. For her, it is a relaxing night; for him, love. "I'm twenty-eight; you're just the latest," she says the next morning. "I'm the last," he insists. But she heads out after a funny yard sale of everything left in the house.

Nick gets back and gets the picture about Sid and Beth at once. Bearing no grudge, he advises Sid that Beth is probably on Route 66 heading for her father's. In the film's last images, roadmaster Nick is nestling down with an ex (Phoebe Cates) while rootmaster Sid is off on the road, slowly circling through motel parking lots in search of his lost love's car.

Fonda and Stoltz manage to flesh out their characters more than Roth, whose clutch of complexes seems underwritten. But *Bodies, Rest & Motion* (the title is from Isaac Newton) certainly makes better sense as a film—and as an independent film—than as a closed piece of stagecraft. All of cinematographer Bernd Heinl's outdoor compositions show us what we are missing in that apartment.

*T*he Music of Chance comes not from a play but from a novel written by Paul Auster, an American writer, popular in France, whose philosophical fiction is sometimes compared to Beckett and Kafka. The story here is about what one might call the metaphysical hazards of the road: an ex-fireman from Boston (Mandy Patinkin) drives his red BMW on endless, pointless roads to escape the pain and meaninglessness of it all. He rescues a roadside mugging victim (James Spader) who turns out to be a professional card player. After losing a big card game, the two wind up as slaves constructing a meaningless wall with medieval Irish rocks across the remote Pennsylvania estate of two fastidiously unpleasant millionaires (Charles Durning and Joel Grey).

*The Music of Chance* is the feature debut of Philip Haas, a filmmaker who has over the last twelve years made some ten idiosyncratic and delightful documentary films with and about such artists as David Hockney. Scripted by Philip Haas and Belinda Haas, it was shot mainly in North Carolina for *American Playhouse*. The Auster book, apparently, dwells upon the mystiques of motion and of chance as determinants of fate. Good films, like, say, *Detour*, can embed such attitudes in image, narrative, and character, or they can, like *Slacker*, embody them in the very structure of a film. But here they are mainly talked about by the fireman, while what we get to watch is an elegantly photographed prison melodrama with an aroma of allegory. Try to imagine *Island of Lost Souls* remade by Merchant and Ivory.

The most startling thing in *The Music of Chance* is the usually cool James Spader in greasy black hair as a sleazy, fast-talking, streety gambler—the sort of role that might make a director say, "Get me Steve Buscemi." There are moments when Spader, like his character, almost breaks out of the prison of significance the movie has put him in.

*T*he cinematic laureate of Florida is native Victor Nuñez, whose ambition to become a "Southern writer on film" formed at Antioch College. His first two features—*Gal Young 'Un* (1979), a period romance about a widow and a conman from a Marjorie Kinnan Rawlings story and *A Flash of Green* (1984), a sweaty thriller about land, greed, and sex from a John D. MacDonald novel—were triumphantly set there. (*A Flash of Green* is the real *Blood Simple.*)

Nuñez's third film, the 1993 *Ruby in Paradise*, which he filmed on a shoestring budget with money from a legacy and with his own land as collateral, is an original script about a young woman on the run (Ashley Judd) who rolls to a stop in Panama City Beach, Florida, a town known as the "Redneck Riviera." There she finds a job she likes, a mode of self-expression (a journal: compare Justice's poems in *Poetic Justice*), and two differently imperfect men (Todd Field, Bentley Mitchum). But the real catalytic agent in the movie is Panama City Beach, whose mixture of sleazy, rootless kitsch, and found beauty Nuñez never patronizes but manages to find oddly redemptive.

# CHAPTER SEVEN

# *F*rom the Northwest and Canada

The evergreens and wide pale skies of the Pacific Northwest have, by virtue of their proximity to Southern California, served as backdrop to Hollywood films since the 1920s. In the summer of 1926, Buster Keaton used the small southwest Oregon town of Cottage Grove and its Row River environs as a convincing substitute for Civil War Georgia in his locomotive-chase masterpiece, *The General*. In 1930 Raoul Walsh filmed his majestic early 70mm Western *The Big Trail* in redwood country; the process used was called Grandeur, and the star was a very young John Wayne. And so it went: the Northwest was there, and it was used consistently over the years. But, as with so many American regions, the Northwest seems only recently to have been seriously contemplated—particularly with a questioning, quirky intensity by independent filmmakers eager to see into its very soul.

David Lynch was born in Missoula, Montana, in 1946, went to high school in Alexandria, Virginia, and wound up in the mid-Sixties as an art student at the Boston

Museum School, where he roomed with aspiring artist and later musician Peter Wolf in a small pad on Hemingway Street. Wolf and Lynch were both young artists in search of a form; Wolf was to go on to rock stardom. In those days, his tastes ran to progressive jazz, while Lynch was into pop. Wolf tells me, ''We'd take a one-ton truck to drive to New York to get drunk. I was being a debauched starving artist; David was just into being an artist. He was an optimist; I was an extremist. I drove him crazy.'' It is interesting to note that there were elements of detachment and control even in young hellion David. Later at Philadelphia's Art Institute, Lynch grew disillusioned with painting and turned to film.

His feature debut came in 1978 with *Eraserhead,* a black-and-white film Lynch produced, directed, wrote, and edited. Funded in part by a grant from the American Film Institute Center for Advanced Film Studies, it took two years to complete. *Eraserhead* is an imagistic collage that combines atomic neurosis about mutation, film-noir seediness, and a battery of surrealism: drawers full of water, giant wriggling spermatozoa, a character called The Lady in the Radiator. The title character wears his hair in a bolt-upright, finger-in-socket comic-book mode; his and his wife's mutant baby is both repulsive and affectionate. The film, very much an illogical and indulgent art movie, nevertheless contains in germ later Lynch obsessions, particularly his blend of terror at and fascination with sex and procreation.

Also in black and white was *The Elephant Man* (1980), which Lynch wrote. It was, as shot by Freddie Francis, an exquisite period exercise; it was, too, in John Hurt's title performance, an eloquent humanist statement. But Lynch's sensibility, except for those unsettling shots of thundering elephants, seems a bit smothered by all the high-mindedness.

In 1984, Lynch wrote and directed a $47 million Hollywood adaptation of the Frank Herbert futuristic sci-fi family drama *Dune*. It lasted 140 minutes and was a totally unintelligible mix of *Prince Valiant* and *Star Wars*. Such typical conceits as the Flying Fat Boy were wasted in fantasy. Lynchism works best when counterpointed to sober reality. But *Dune* did inaugurate Lynch's key collaboration with actor Kyle MacLachlan as the character Paul Atreides (the name pretentiously echoes Aeschylus's *Oresteia*).

It might have seemed, in 1984, as if David Lynch's career had already traversed the classic crash-and-burn trajectory of the unwary independent filmmaker. He had made his icky art flick *(Eraserhead)*; he had been hired to make a responsible movie of the week *(The Elephant Man)* for a big producer (Mel Brooks); he had undertaken a major-studio, megabudget, pop-genre blockbuster *(Dune)*, which proved a disaster. (Compare the Michael Lehmann trilogy of *Heathers, Meet the Applegates,* and *Hudson Hawk.*) But in truth Lynch was only now about to find his voice as an artist. And finding his voice went hand in hand with securing his terrain.

*Blue Velvet,* which Lynch wrote and filmed in 1986, was set in the Northwest, although filmed in North Carolina. The small town we're in is called Lumberton; logging trucks often lumber by; a cheery radio voice is heard advising, "It's a sunny warm day, so get those buzz saws out." *Blue Velvet* wants to probe into the life that lies hidden just beneath the surfaces of green, flowered Lumberton. As Jeffrey Beaumont's store-owner Dad is watering the front lawn, he is stung by a bee and collapses. The family dog unconcernedly drinks water from the dropped hose, while the camera noses through the grass and finds angry, scuttling bugs. While Pop is in the hospital, Jeffrey (Kyle MacLachlan) and his girlfriend (Laura Dern) grow intrigued by the mystery behind what the dog finds: a sliced-off ear being nibbled by ants in the grass. The insect life that pullulates beneath the pretty top layers is the master metaphor in *Blue Velvet*.

Jeff and his friend start out as a teen couple out of *It's a Wonderful Life:* he shows her his "chicken walk" stunt; they plot detective strategy in a Hardy Boys/Nancy Drew mode in Arlene's Diner. For Jeff feels drawn to investigate the secret of Dorothy Valens (Isabella Rossellini) in Apartment 710 of the Deep River Apartments building. He first gets in by pretending to be an exterminator ("It's only the bug man"). Dorothy's apartment, with its bare brown walls, long dark corridors, and freakishly solitary floor lamp casting aloft a fluorescent glare, is somehow like a nightmare version of sex organ; it contrasts vividly with Jeff's comfy family home.

That night he is in the Slow Club watching Dorothy, billed as the Blue Lady, torching "Blue Velvet" in a blue spot. We see him in close-up and then a wide shot of a stage. From left to right: neon, piano, blue spot on singer.

Then Dorothy in close-up. He is hooked; he is about to begin a descent into the vortex of the Id. His wearing of an earring in his left ear is perhaps a tiny sign of his readiness to take the trip, to transgress the Boy Scout persona.

For the second night, he returns to Dorothy's apartment. His girlfriend is disturbed at his growing obsessiveness, saying, "I don't know if you're a detective or a pervert." "That's for me to know and you to find out," he childishly answers. Once inside again, he urinates and the sound of the flushing toilet drowns out the four-honk warning that Dorothy is returning. He has to hide in a closet and gets to spy as Dorothy strips to her undies, removes her wig, and gets treated by a knife-brandishing Frank (Dennis Hopper) to a liturgy of sadistic rituals: "Get undressed . . . no lights . . . bourbon . . . it's dark . . . spread your legs, show it to me, don't you fuckin' look at me." A beat later, Frank is whimpering, "Mommy," but then he ties and gags her before climaxing and splitting.

Jeff, who has been eyeing all this half horrified and half excited from his peephole, emerges to confront Dorothy, who sits on the couch with him and pleads, "Do you like me? Do you like the way I feel?" He touches her breast, her nipple; their lips meet, upside down, in close-up. "Hit me," she begs. Jeff is caught. (While Dorothy is later in the bathroom, Jeff roots in her papers and finds a picture and a birth certificate of her son, who has been kidnapped by the bad guy. This whole murky plot about the kidnapped kid and drug deals and a corrupt cop is a kind of noise off; it is a mere MacGuffin.) The kidnapping that matters in *Blue Velvet* is the kidnapping of Jeff's white-bread soul by the powers of erotic darkness. Deep rivers indeed.

On the third day, Jeff tries ineptly to explain to his girlfriend what is happening to him: "I'm seeing something that was always hidden. I'm involved in a mystery. You're a mystery." She offers an optimistic perspective, telling of a dream she had of darkness that ended with "robins bringing a blinding light of love—there is trouble till the robins come." But Jeff is not ready yet for robins and returns again to Dorothy, who lures him into her sick scenarios: "Are you a bad boy? I want you to hurt me." He consents to hit her, and she grins ecstatically as they make love against that backdrop of brown walls: "You're my special friend. I still have you inside of me."

Dorothy's uninhibitedness, desperation, nakedness, and masochism are all somehow the same to Jeff. Rossellini's audacious, selfless, revealing performance is seductive and powerful enough to make us as complicit as Jeff. Not for nothing is the actress the daughter of the Ingrid Bergman who gave such insinuating representations of masochistically warped women in *Notorious* and *Dr. Jekyll and Mr. Hyde*.

On the fourth night at Dorothy's, Jeff is shanghaied by her sadistic masters to a queerly bare motel. Three obese whores pout. A lipsticked, berouged pal of Frank's (Dean Stockwell) lip-synchs, as lamplight falls on his powdered face: "A candy-colored clown they call the Sandman . . ." Frank is impressed: "Goddamn, you're one suave fucker." The room reeks of evil. In Lynch, the props of evil are drugs . . . makeup . . . cigarettes. Not for him the compassionate at-oneness with outcasts of a Van Sant or the satirical championship of them of a Cronenberg. Lynch looks with Jeff's eyes. Lynch is a torn choirboy holding his rosary in one hand and his hard-on in the other.

In a speeding car, Frank gets high, kisses Dorothy, and forces Jeff to kiss him. "I'll send you straight to hell," he leers in repellent close-up. On the ground, he makes Jeff feel his muscles and then beats him, leaving his bloody face in the mud of (the ironically labeled) Meadow Lane. What has happened to Jeff seems not just a pummeling but—in some way not visualized by Lynch—a sexual violation by the forces that have so brutalized Dorothy (a name that inevitably recalls *The Wizard of Oz,* whose imagery will pop up in *Wild at Heart).* And in flashback, Jeff is tormented by his own complicity in the brutalizing of Dorothy.

The next two nights Jeff spends mostly in wholesome surroundings: at home with his girlfriend, visiting his dad still hospitalized from the bee sting. By day, he waters the drying lawn. He and his girlfriend go to a normal teen party and slow-dance and kiss and pledge true love. Wholesomeness seems to be reasserting itself, but the feeling is illusory. A nude, battered Dorothy appears on Jeff's front lawn: the worlds of his Superego and of his Id have collided. The naked Dorothy moans to Jeff, "I love you," as she matter-of-factly explains to Jeff's girlfriend that "he put his thing in me." The girlfriend sobs, slaps Jeff, and retreats to her pink bedroom, crying, "Where is *my* dream?'' Things climax back in Apartment 710, now littered with the corpses of Dorothy's earless husband and of the corrupt cop, whose pocket police radio is still broadcasting warnings about Frank. Frank arrives in the apartment in a clumsy disguise determined to kill Jeff, who instead decoys Frank into a back bedroom. Jeff is hiding again in the closet—voyeur point of view again— but flings open the closet door to surprise and shoot Frank. Jeff's girlfriend and her cop dad show up to console a shaken Jeff: "It's all over." The lovers kiss in the corridor.

Next morning brings another horror: an extreme close-up of an ear, attached this time to a face, on a lawn. False alarm: it is just Jeff reclining in a lawn chair and watching a robin eating a bug. Even his girlfriend's greeting-card version of nature has, it appears, a nasty underside. But Lynch's camera is in these final moments in a mood more Hallmark than Hellish: shots of the robin, tulips, a passing red fire truck, roses, and we leave the happy lovers—happy but maybe a little warier about what lies at the bottom of life.

Dorothy leads her retrieved little son across a park and hugs him as the camera slowly pans up to a blue sky, which turns into a blue velvet stage curtain. Her voice singing, "I still can see blue velvet through my tears," rises on the soundtrack. There is a hint in this hauntingly ambiguous closure that Dorothy's need for artifice—velvet lounge drapes in the sky—might be a better prophylactic against the evil that is out there, surely, everywhere, than the young lovers' blissfully regained semi-innocence.

Kyle MacLachlan had starred in *Dune* for Lynch, but it was in *Blue Velvet* that he perfected his air of abused naiveté. Laura Dern brought more to her character than was written; she seemed more aware, alert, open to sex and danger than her Nancy Drew persona. It was only in Lynch's next film, *Wild at Heart,* and in *Rambling Rose,* Martha Coolidge's tender study of a flibbertigibbet teen-age sexpot in a Georgia town of the 1930s, that Dern got her chances. Dennis Hopper clearly relished doing Frank's in-your-face sleazy menace, but Dean Stockwell's cooler depravity left more impression.

In 1990 Lynch made *Wild at Heart,* which he adapted from a novel by Barry Gifford. Yet another screwed-up-young-lovers-on-the-highway-in-a-convertible epic, it stars Nicolas Cage as Sailor and Laura Dern as Lula. (*Sailor et Lula* was the film's title in France.) Never has psychology been further from Lynch's interest. *Wild at Heart* has a generic, almost allegorical feel, like a tale from Ariosto or Spenser. Sailor is an abstraction of "lover," with emblems and armor taken from the fertile Id of American pop culture. His governing metaphors are two: Elvis and *The Wizard of Oz.* He dresses throughout in a snakeskin jacket he refers to as a "symbol of my individuality and my belief in personal freedom." (It is a typically American paradox that individuality is expressed through slavish imitation.) Sailor engages in two renditions of Elvis songs: early on, he sings "Love Me" in a dance hall under pink and red spots, and at the end he sings "Love Me Tender" (a song he said he was saving for his wife) on the hood of a car. Nicolas Cage, in the performance of his career, sings these songs himself with abandon; by risking the ridiculous so fearlessly, he hits the sublime.

The witches and utopias of Oz are the imagistic decor of both Sailor and Lula: she sees her mother (Diane Ladd) flying about the sky as the Wicked Witch, and he is finally put straight by the celestial appearance of the Good Witch (Sheryl Lee).

The fairy tale-like narrative tells of the pursuit of the fleeing lovers by her operatically vicious, martini-slugging mother, determined to separate her daughter from the youth who knows her dark secret—that she had her husband torched. It opens in Cape Fear, North Carolina, as Sailor shoots one of Ma's violent henchmen at a dance where Glenn Miller's "In the Mood" is playing. After almost two years in the Pee Dee Correctional Institute, he finds Lula waiting for him with a convertible and they're on the road. To where? California? "I'd go with you to the ends of the world," she promises. "Rockin' good news," he responds.

Cigarettes and sex and cars pervade (even determine) the lovers' existence; unlike the lovers of courtly romance, Sailor and Lula are already enjoying carnal paradise. This is Lynch's most unshadowed celebration of sex, although he does give the exuberantly articulated raptures a comic edge. Lynch and cinematographer Frederick Elmes love to pose the two in bed. There is a delightful long shot of a bed with Sailor sitting off on the left in a blue shirt polishing his shoes and Lula off on the right in a black bra and pants polishing her toenails. They are getting ready to go dancing. Later, they lie in bed after

sex—feet to each other's knees, heads at different corners, the whole composition bathed in a mustard light—
talking of cigarettes (He: "I started smoking at four") and
sex (She: "You mark me the deepest"; He: "You're perfect for me, too").

They hit New Orleans, and in a motel the rapture esca-
lates. In bed Lula says, "You just about take me right over
that rainbow. You got the sweetest cock. It talks to me
inside. It's got this little voice." He is pleased at this:
"You really are dangerously cute. Let's go get a fried
banana sandwich." In a bar, as Sailor speaks about his
earlier sexual conquests, Lula says, "You get me hotter
than Georgia asphalt." Later we see, in quick succession,
the film's obsessions: a burning match, asphalt, and
Lula's fingers clenching and unclenching in orgasm.

Lynch's mock porn achieves a fragile mix of erotic heat
and deflating humor. Laura Dern's thorough enjoyment
of it all is infectious; she is a Kmart Dietrich *with* the erotic
wit but *without* the ironic superiority.

West of New Orleans, things get darker for the fleeing
pair; they descend, in fact, into hell. In Texas, the radio
reports necrophiliac horrors and then plays ugly heavy
metal (although they try to get in the mood, they are at
heart a romantic, Elvis pair); seeing clothes strewn on the
night road, they come on a bloody accident and a delirious victim who drools blood and dies. "Jesus, Mary, and
Joseph," mumbles the (Catholic?) Sailor. Next hot morning, they drive into the heart of hell: Big Tuna, Texas.
FUCK YOU is spray-painted over a burnt welcoming sign.
"It ain't exactly Emerald City—we're a long way off that

road to California," say the lovers, blending those two American Dream destinations.

The Big Tuna Motel is a familiar Lynch torture site: Lula vomits, obese grotesques cavort in the courtyard, the satanic, stub-toothed Bobby Peru (Willem Dafoe in excess) sexually terrorizes Lula and suckers Sailor into a heist. (The sadistic toying with Lula is a painfully long scene, marked with a reiterated obscenity that recalls the Bad Lieutenant, Harvey Keitel, and the two women in the car.) It is at this navel of evil that Lula realizes she is pregnant and ruefully decides she does not want the child. "Nothing personal . . . I love you," she assures Sailor, who replies, "I love you, too." We learn in flashback that Lula, raped by an uncle, had had an abortion, of which disturbingly vivid, fish-eye recollections are shown by Lynch. It was a trauma for Lula and has soured her on procreation. Lynch seems ambiguous about both procreation and abortion.

The air in Big Tuna unsexes the lovers. "This whole world's wild at heart and weird on top . . . I wish I was somewhere over the rainbow," Lula moans. She lies uneasy and weeping in bed in fishnets. The bed table contains a pack of Kools and a radio that doubles as the base of the statue of a bronze horse and is playing Richard Strauss's mournful "Im Abendrot." Sailor, meanwhile, motivated solely by a desire to get her some money, speeds to the robbery in a convertible with Bobby Peru and a bad dame (Isabella Rossellini). Lynch stages the robbery as a carnival of horrors: gloppy blown-off heads plop on the ground, a dog runs off with a severed hand,

Sailor clapped back in jail for nearly six years.

On his emergence, Lula is again waiting, but this time with a difference: she drives to the train depot wearing a polka-dot summer dress, sexy but grown-up, and she has a six-year-old son (she'd written Sailor about her decision to keep the child). The Wicked Witch, her mother, has gone up in smoke. Sailor has brought the boy a stuffed lion (more Oz imagery) and gets in the car. But something is wrong (this is a passage of unusual psychological insight for Lynch), and he gets out.

Trudging back to the depot, he provokes an assault from four street types. (''What do you faggots want?'' he snarls. ''A cigarette'' would have been the answer to a civil question.) As he lies beaten on the ground (this was filmed in El Paso), the Good Witch hovers above him, assuring him, ''Lula loves you and has forgiven you.'' ''But I'm wild at heart.'' ''If you're truly wild at heart, you'll fight for your dreams. Don't turn away from love, Sailor.'' Sailor listens. He apologizes to the toughs.

Leaping from hood to hood of cars stopped in a traffic jam, he reaches Lula's hood and sings the long-desired song as their son smiles and the camera slowly, caressingly circles the entwined couple. Not since the finale of Bertolucci's *Luna* has a nuclear family been reunited in such a baroque, ecstatic manner. It is a musical coda to what, at its best, has been a dark and dangerous love musical, the sort of thing Elvis *should* have made.

*Wild at Heart* won the Palme d'Or at the Cannes Film Festival the year after *Sex, Lies and Videotape* and the year before *Barton Fink*—a strange U.S. hat trick.

In the years 1989–1992 Lynch produced his *Godfather* saga—the *Twin Peaks* stories. Lynch and Mark Frost conceived and cowrote the TV series, and Lynch directed the 113-minute pilot, first telecast in 1989, as well as a few later episodes during its aborted two-season run and the dreary 1992 wrap-up feature prequel *Twin Peaks: Fire Walk with Me*. The hour-long programs were uneven and self-indulgent, and *Fire Walk with Me* was an anemic disaster, far sadder than *Godfather III*. But that *Twin Peaks* pilot contains some of David Lynch's best work. The medium of television, still under mainstream constraints, forced him to mediate his misanthropy through innuendo, menace, and salacious hint.

It all concerned, in theory, an endless investigation into the murder and dumping into the local lake of high-school cutie Laura Palmer (Lara Flynn Boyle), who turns out to have been a promiscuous coke slut. The first image was of her plastic-wrapped body dragged out of the deep lake, while at her home her mother worries. Her father is a businessman eager to lure new Norwegian businesses up into the "healthy air" of Twin Peaks. Her boyfriends include a brooding but sensitive biker (James Marshall). There is also a bad, sullen youth (Dana Ashbrook) lurking about.

Laura Palmer's death, like the deaths in *Heathers*, makes a stir in the school, and ripples from it spread out through the vulgar bourgeoisie and the colorful working-class of the town of Twin Peaks.

Lynch vividly imagined a menagerie of rustic eccentrics; before there was a *Northern Exposure*, there was a

*Twin Peaks.* Its oddballs, of whom the log lady and giggly coroner are perhaps only the most memorable, were not just coyly tolerant philosophers, but projected possibilities of nasty menace as well. But Lynch's creation of the fauna of the place would have meant little without the magnificently chilling Northwest photography of Ron Garcia, which achieved an intimacy with the region. The undulating hills carpeted in evergreens, the bleakly gleaming diner, the empty roadhouse bar, the wooden chalets, the logging mill, the redneck shacks—all dripped melancholy and madness, qualities enormously intensified by the plangent, lonely, baritone chords of Angelo Badalamenti's theme. The Northwest had found a cinematic poet, though perhaps not one it would have chosen.

Into this grim world comes a lawman, FBI agent Dale Cooper, played to earnest perfection by Yakima, Washington, native Kyle MacLachlan. With an anal fanaticism, he goes about turning over the community's stones and impassively watching what crawls out. Cooper dictates all the minutiae of his life on a pocket tape to an invisible secretary, Diane. He confides to the tiny machine his love for the haunted greens of this northerly outpost, its Douglas firs ("smell those Douglas firs"), its cherry pie and coffee and doughnuts, its snowshoe ("not cottontail") rabbits, its "reasonable" hotel. And he has a hawk's eye for clues: he finds the letter *r* under a fingernail on the corpse, and he spots a motorcycle reflected in the eyes of the murdered girl in a videotape. He has, in fact, a lot of the prissy, persnickety perfectionism of Basil

Rathbone's Sherlock Holmes—complete with a Watson in dim Sheriff Harry S. Truman (Michael Ontkean). This sheriff has a ditsy secretary, as if to give TV audiences something familiar to grab onto.

This colorful pilot, of course, just established a narrative atmosphere. The solution to the mystery involved an abusive, incestuous father, as was eventually revealed in *Fire Walk with Me*. This was not altogether surprising, for to Lynch family is at once ultimate security and ultimate danger. The endings of *Blue Velvet* and of *Wild at Heart* celebrate parental bondings that come after much turmoil. But it is largely the turmoil that remains most vividly in the eye from Lynch's work. Lynch is more comfortable, throughout, as a dissector than as a sewer-up of the human heart. He is a true Jacobean—the John Webster of American cinema.

Jennifer Lynch, David's daughter, made the most talked-about film of the 1993 Sundance Film Festival— her directorial debut. Called *Boxing Helena*, it tells of a surgeon (Julian Sands) who amputates the arms of a woman (Sherilyn Fenn, who was a star of *Twin Peaks*). The woman had already lost her legs in an accident and had rejected the doctor's affections. The quadruple amputee is then forced to watch him making love. At this rate, the Lynch family may become the first independent film dynasty—the Zanucks or Fondas of the cutting edge.

$G$us Van Sant was born in Louisville, Kentucky, in the early 1950s, but lived all over as a child—his father was then a traveling salesman—in such places as Colorado,

Illinois, California, and Connecticut, before settling in
Oregon. Drawn first to painting (like Lynch), he went to
the prestigious Rhode Island School of Design, but
switched there to cinema studies and wound up with a
B.F.A. in film. After college, he did time in Los Angeles,
where he began filming the first of his twenty or so shorts,
and in New York, where he worked briefly for his father
and did commercials for a Madison Avenue advertising
firm for two years. Then he moved back to Portland,
where he has been based ever since, turning out music
videos, commercials, and shorts such as *The Discipline of
D.E.*, an adaptation of a story by William S. Burroughs, a
Van Sant hero; the depressingly titled *Five Ways to Kill
Yourself;* and the possibly more upbeat *Five Naked Boys and
a Gun*. He also kept on painting—painting deserts, he
says, and farms and barns.

Van Sant made his first feature in 1985, *Mala Noche,*
which he scripted from an unpublished book, apparently
a sort of journal, by a friend, a Portland character called
Walt Curtis. The film, some seventy minutes long and
costing about $25,000, was shot in black-and-white by
John Campbell, a Portland-based cinematographer who
says he grew up in a revival house in Berkeley watching
Ingmar Bergman films. The images of *Mala Noche* are,
however, even more extremely and rigorously stylized
than those of Bergman and his cinematographer, Sven
Nykvist. *Mala Noche* is, to an amazing and beautiful degree, a movie shot in black, a black out of which will
emerge a face, a boot, a pumpkin, a coffee cup, an ashtray—little pieces of life fighting to be seen against an

enveloping darkness. This is a Portland of the lost and the losing.

*Mala Noche* is a story of *amour fou:* Walt (Tim Streeter), a bright but bedraggled guy of around thirty who works in a skid-row liquor store falls for a Mexican teenager named Johnny (Doug Cooeyate), who happens into the store after coming up to Oregon in a boxcar. (The movie's first image is of Northwest mountains as seen by the kid from a train.)

Walt is not just in love; he parades his besottedness; he wears it as openly and casually as his ubiquitous dirty raincoat. He boasts to a woman friend, "I'm in love with this boy . . . I want to show him I'm gay for him." He makes this obsession a definition of himself. But the "ignorant Mexican teenager" has eyes not for Walt ("Sorry, but I don't sleep with *putos*"), but for Walt's car; he achieves "pure ecstasy" driving it too fast in the night rain.

The movie is the litany of the humiliations and compromises of Walt, who, in fact, falls into a unsatisfyingly passive sexual relationship not with Johnny but with Johnny's buddy Roberto, a.k.a. Pepper (Ray Monge). This relationship starts in a virtuoso montage, evocative of Eisenstein at his most homoerotic: crosscuts between the sleeping Pepper and Walt standing in the kitchen and the water he's boiling; then a pan as the camera slowly traverses the inky room from Walt to Pepper, linking the two in spatial and carnal unity.

But the sex has a decidedly downside for Walt: Pepper takes ten dollars and, as Walt tells us in voice-over in a hilarious scene as he walks down a dingy commercial street the next morning, unshaved as ever and clad in his tattered, filthy raincoat: "He's probably laughing because he fucked the gringo *puto* . . . my ass is so sore . . . poor boys never win . . . mala noche . . . Every streetboy on Sixth Street will think he can stick it in me. Well, they can't, but they aren't too smart in the first place or they wouldn't be here." During this monologue, which is at once aggrieved, contemptuous, and compassionate, fleecy white clouds scurry across the gray sky in time-lapse quickness, as if to reach a dream world where things are better arranged—these images will become a Gus Van Sant–John Campbell signature.

On the tactical level, Walt has a plan, a zany one but a plan: "I go to his [Johnny's] room at midnight and lay down at his feet. How many gringos have responded that dramatically to him?" This scheme does not work out even in the *fantasy* version we see; the *real* version is even more humiliating, with Walt dangling from a fire escape as he is berated by a fat, angry concierge.

Gadgets, not Walt, are the love objects of Johnny and Pepper. They like video games about cars; they enjoy horseplay with a camera Walt picks up for ten dollars; they really get off abusing Walt's battered old car, seeing it as a toy to tease him with (they pretend to ditch him on a country road) and eventually to wreck. During one little rustic jaunt, wise Walt comments in voice-over: "I don't want to interfere with their lives. A gringo like me has an easy and privileged life. Just because I see somebody and they're attractive doesn't mean I should be able to buy him because he's hungry, on the streets, desperate, good-looking. That wasn't my intention exactly." On a final drive alone with Pepper, Walt ("I love the countryside here," he tells us) tries to teach the kid to take a curve, but Pepper cannot bend his rigid grip on the wheel and mulishly crashes the car. "You drive like you fuck," Walt angrily analyzes, showing his usual wry mixture of distance and involvement. The ultimate gadget that allures and destroys the youths is a gun—they are constantly prey to police and immigration and they foolishly see the gun as a magic talisman.

Johnny vanishes for a good bit of the movie, expelled to Mexico. When he gets back, Walt asks him, "Where were you, in Idaho?" If Portland is gritty reality in Van Sant, Idaho is the cloudy land of lost dreams, a utopia of the heart. While Johnny was gone, Walt has, almost accidentally, entered into a more substantial relationship with Pepper. He nurses Pepper through a case of pneumonia caught while hustling out in the cold rain. (The weather in *Mala Noche* is pretty thoroughly awful.) Cured, Pepper moves in and they seem to get along, despite some domestic abrasions. Walt, though, is never less than realistic, saying, "I don't think he likes me that much. I don't blame him . . . They don't have any imagination about sex or anything else. It's not their fault." But pigheaded Pepper insists on an armed showdown with some cops, and next thing Walt is weeping over Pepper's dead body in a pietà pose on a foggy night sidewalk. "They're people like we are," he says in voice-over, with lapidary dignity. When Johnny reappears, there is a moment of camaraderie as the two play at bull and torero, but, when Johnny hears about Pepper, he blames Walt and stalks out, pausing to carve PUTO on the door.

But Walt never gives up. He remains a man on a mission of Eros, on a crusade. He goes searching for his love object, in the ever-present car. The car is tool of search and also locus of meditation and longing. Walt sits in it smoking with head back; he lies flat in it, head out the door and photographed upside down. When, at the end, he spots Johnny loitering on a street corner, he leans out and uninsistingly offers, "Come down to the store and talk to me, all right?" (That store, by the way, like most else in *Mala Noche,* is a scruffy den of half-glimpsed scrunge.) There is a grainy shot of the car driving away from Johnny down the rain-slicked street.

*Mala Noche* is full of cars and rain and cigarette smoke. These cigarettes—tobacco and pot—symbolize Van Sant's overall attitude to pleasures, obsessions, addictions; to him they are simply inflections of character, modes of coping, ways of living. What interests the director more than the substance is the spirit: his heroes have an openness and a sometimes paradoxical innocence of spirit that, while leaving them defenseless before life's sucker punches, yet award them small decisions along the way.

A simple sad guitar and a Mexican-sounding song set a mood perfectly in *Mala Noche,* whose score is credited to Creighton Lindsay. The earnest, friendly, generous, common-sense, no-apologies demeanor of handsome, stubble-studded Tim Streeter establishes solidly this first incarnation of the Van Sant hero, a hero haunted but hip, driven but cool. The flavor of the Van Sant obsessive, deadly serious but alive to the humor and ridiculousness of his position, very much aware of the humbling possibilities of life, is born. It is also a tribute to Van Sant to have coaxed realistic and honest portrayals of the Mexican youths out of Doug Cooeyate and Ray Monge; they become not merely objects but feeling subjects.

The heroes of all three Van Sant movies, incidentally, wind up in vehicles: Walt sitting in his Johnny-searching heap, *Drugstore Cowboy*'s Bob supine in an ambulance, *My Own Private Idaho*'s Mike unconscious in the front seat of a car. Only Walt is active, a driver; Bob is dying, likely dead by the end; Mike is in a narcoleptic stupor. And all three end up deserted by their beloved.

*Drugstore Cowboy* was adapted by Van Sant in 1989 and Daniel Yost from a then unpublished autobiographical novel by longtime prison inmate James Fogle. The novel, since published, chronicles the Pacific Coast, pharmacy-robbing capers of Bob, "one of the ringiest and most notorious dope-fiend drugstore cowboys on the entire West Coast, including Alaska."

*Drugstore Cowboy* is the most pervasively playful of the Van Sant Portland-lower-depths trilogy. The episodic story, narrated by the wounded Bob, opens in Portland in 1971. Bob Hughes (Matt Dillon—the character is forty in the book, but Van Sant lowered the age when Dillon took the role) is a pill addict who runs a sullen little band—a family, as it were—of narcotics thieves. Bob devises dramatic little scenarios for his crew to distract the attention of druggists while he steals the pills. The ganglet consists of two parental ironists—Bob and his wife, Dianne (Kelly Lynch)—and two moronic children—Rick (James Le-Gros) and pretty Nadine (Heather Graham). Bob maintains running battles with a basically friendly, concerned cop (James Remar) who shares an addiction to golf and with a very unfriendly cop, whom Bob sets up to be peppered with buckshot by an angry father who suspects that the cop is a Peeping Tom. When cops wreck his house looking in vain for secreted drugs, Bob remarks, "Man, I love cops; they separate the good ones from the rest; if it weren't for them, there'd be so much competition there'd be nothing left to steal."

With the exception of Dianne, who proves more hardened and unregenerate than he, Bob is surrounded by what he sees as the straight and the stupid. When he visits his mother (Grace Zabriskie) to pick up some clothes, she berates him and Dianne as a "no-good bum dope addict and your nympho girlfriend." Rick is pretty much harmless and dim—"I always wanted to be a farmer, Bob"; "What's a transom, Bob?"—but his sweetheart, Nadine, is stupid in ways that spell trouble. She innocently asks for a dog, and she mischievously puts a hat on a bed. Such things spook Bob, whose daredevil breeziness is gloomily offset by a superstitious terror of such taboos as mentioning dogs (Bob was once betrayed to the cops by an unwitting dog) and putting hats on beds.

Nadine's bad luck falls hardest on herself: she ODs and has to be stashed by Dianne, at great damage to Dianne's nails, in a motel crawlspace. The three remaining desperadoes are forced to leave the motel because their room is reserved for a convention of sheriffs—the jinx in operation already. It is Bob who digs Nadine's grave out in the woods and crosses himself; a conservative, golf-playing guy in some ways, Bob had earlier put down Rick and Nadine as typically uncultured products of mass culture, "TV babies watching people killing and fucking each other on the boob tube for so long it's all they know." To this Dianne dutifully answers, "I know, hon." Bob likes to see himself as the paterfamilias of a slightly askew sitcom family: "Honey, I'm home," he announces once, striding in with his head bandaged from a botched hospital robbery. Dianne's take on the deficiencies of their life-style can be a little tarter. Says she to the nodding Bob, "I hate this. You won't fuck me, and I always have to drive."

Frightened by the hexed fate of Nadine, Bob promises "God, the Son, the Devil, whoever" to live "a virtuous life" if the burial goes all right. Dianne wants to stay with the life, and so Bob goes back to Portland (the gang had left there after the bad cop's humiliation). He enters a methadone program and gets a job in a machine shop drilling holes. But he reforms with the same cool, no-big-deal, fatalistic wit that he had earlier brought to crime and drugs. He had then said, "As soon as it entered my veins, I felt a warm itch, a gentle explosion that began in the back of my neck and rose rapidly . . . you could do no wrong as long as it lasted." "I'm a junkie, I like drugs, I like the whole life-style, but it just didn't work out," he frankly states to his methadone counselor (Beah Richards, Sidney Poitier's mother in *Guess Who's Coming to Dinner*).

Bob never, in a word, falls into self-righteousness. He rents a sunny little room in the St. Francis Hotel with a view of the station; he makes tea a lot (more Van Sant boiling water). He lends a patient ear to a raspy-voiced old junkie priest, Father Tom Murphy, "the most notorious dope fiend on the coast" (William Burroughs, who wrote his own lines), ranting about right-wing drug persecution. When Dianne visits, Bob shyly defends his present life, saying that "for all the boredom I'm a regular guy with a regular room and a regular job." He asks her to stay, but she embarrassedly (and implausibly) refuses on the grounds that "I'm Rick's old lady now." She leaves him some drugs, though, which he gives to a grateful Father Tom. Very soon an act of kindness—he had stopped a nasty drug dealer (Max Perlich) from beating up a kid—returns to fell Bob. The resentful dealer shoots him. Lying shot on the floor, Bob retains his dry, droll perspective, remarking in voice-over that "there's nothing more life-affirming than getting the shit kicked out of you. You can buck the system, but you can't buck the dark forces that lie beneath the surface, the ones that some people call superstitions, like howling banshees, black cats, hats on beds, dogs, the evil eye."

In the ambulance, he reassures Gentry, the nice cop, that it was not a rogue cop but "the hat" and the "TV baby" that got him. ("Good morning, I like your hat" were, by the way, Bob's first words in the movie, spoken to a lady walking her dog—an unheeded double warning from Fate.) Flat on his back, Bob does not lose his patronizing attitude toward the police: "The chicken-shit cops were giving me a police escort to the biggest pharmacy in town." There is something Nabokovian in the swank of *Drugstore Cowboy*'s wit.

Near death, Bob confides in us: "I was once a shameless, full-time dope fiend." Accent on *shameless*. Van Sant's people, the authentic ones, know no shame. They are directly, if sometimes painfully, themselves. Bob's last words, head on a blue pillow in the ambulance, are: "I was still alive; hope they could keep me alive." But no. The dark forces take this trick.

Matt Dillon's sad Irish eyes and somber gravity make Bob a decent as well as a smart man. Kelly Lynch is crystal-bright and needle-smart as Dianne. She projects an aggressive sexuality often comically frustrated by the limp dopers around her. James LeGros hones his *faux-naif* characterization, and Heather Graham contrives to add a sadness to the whining Nadine. Max Perlich, Grace Zabriskie, and James Remar bring colors to the palette, and one can spot *Mala Noche*'s Doug Cooeyate and Ray Monge in cameos.

The sound track, somewhat in the fashion of *Reservoir Dogs*, is festooned with Seventies hits, most memorably "Israelites," with its ironic allusion to Bonnie and Clyde—a demythification of whom this film is.

Stylistically, *Drugstore Cowboy* is more adventurous than *Mala Noche*, where the interruptions to the narrative are almost entirely flashbacks to the immigrant boys' earlier experiences. In *Drugstore Cowboy* the realms of fate and ecstasy invade the story's linear progress. In dope reveries and in simple visions, spoons or pills or leaves or hats tumble slowly through cloudy blue skies.

The poeticized geography of the Northwest, whose laureate—or rather whose inventor—Van Sant has become, was already visible in the dinky little rustic car jaunts and time-lapse clouds of *Mala Noche*. And *Drugstore*'s addicts also get to see some of the country in the poetic, blue-based images of Robert Yeoman. They go cross-roading—that is, they race in a car to catch up with their bus-borne stash. Bob takes a rainy and solitary bus trip back to Portland. The main outdoor sequence is Bob's transporting of the blue-wrapped Nadine to a grave deep in the autumnal woods. But nature is not user-friendly, and these cowboys and cowgirls tend to hug the indoors.

*My Own Private Idaho* (1991), Van Sant's third film, and an original script, was made for some $3.6 million. It could be called in a way Johnny's and Pepper's revenge, their side of the story. If *Mala Noche* was a john's-eye view of hustlers (hustler types, anyway), *Idaho* is a hustler's-eye view of johns, and they do not come off particularly well. The movie chronicles the progress of its hustlers—especially, its two central characters, Mike Waters (River Phoenix) and Scott Favor (Keanu Reeves)—through a parade of johns.

These johns are comic grotesques mainly, harmless maybe but definitely screwy: a fatty who tosses cash onto a spent crotch after a blowjob; a jingle-singing detergent freak (Mickey Cottrell, a well-known Hollywood publicist and producer) who has Mike scrub a sink and a table in Dutch Boy costume; a rich woman (Grace Zabriskie) who goes in for foursomes with three male hustlers; a German salesman named Hans who chants avant-garde lieder with a lamp shade at a fancy motel called the Family Tree Inn (Udo Keir, who played the title roles in *Andy Warhol's Frankenstein* and *Andy Warhol's Dracula,* both directed by Paul Morrissey, a director Van Sant admires); an Italian exquisite drooling about blue-eyed blonds, and so on. It's like a Brechtian musical comedy of sex and commerce. Two anonymous hustlers tell the camera, in mock documentary style, horror stories about bad "dates." It's a dog's life, this hustlering, exactly as Walt had sympathetically seen it to be in *Mala Noche.* But Van Sant laces his compassion for these kids with a clear-eyed sense of humor. In one hilarious, Busby-Berkeley-meets-Genet fantasy sequence, six muscle-magazine cover-boys come to life and discuss their profession. Scott, cover-boy on *Male Call,* announces his ass can be had only for cash and taunts *G-String* cover-boy Mike with giving it away and turning queer.

*My Own Private Idaho* is not, however, a film about prostitution. Hustlering is more background than theme; it is the heroes' job, not their story. The story concerns the intersecting lives of Scott and Mike. Van Sant had originally written two separate scenarios, one called *Modern Days,* which told Mike's tale, and a second that was an updating of Shakespeare's *Henry IV* plays and dealt with Scott. *Idaho* is an attempt to dovetail both stories. Van Sant has referred to it as a "cut-up" à la Burroughs, who likes to mix and match unconnected narrative fragments in his books. "One night I was watching Orson Welles's *Chimes at Midnight*," says Van Sant, "and I thought that the Henry IV plays were really a street story. I also knew this fat guy named Bob, who had always reminded me of Falstaff and who was crazy about hustler boys. It was then that I decided to combine the two stories."

Of the two stories, Scott's is the simpler. He is the son of the mayor of Portland, Oregon, Jack Favor, a wheelchair-bound incarnation of corrupt power whose heart has been broken by the "effeminate" slumming of his son. Scott has set out to trash his father's values by consorting with riffraff. He has substituted for his biological father a grizzled street character called Bob Pigeon (William Richert, himself an offbeat film director, who made *Winter Kills* in 1979 and, in 1988, *A Night in the Life of Jimmy Reardon*, with River Phoenix). This Pigeon, a down-market Falstaff/Fagin figure, arrives back in Portland from Boise, Idaho, reciting Joyce Kilmer on the subject of trees, and at once sets up shop in an abandoned building, snorting coke and masterminding a petty robbery. Says Scott, "I loved Bob more than my father. He taught me better than school did." Unshaven, bellowing Bob Pigeon is Walt from *Mala Noche* gone to seed; he is William Burroughs's junkie priest from *Drugstore Cowboy* without the steely glint of madness and with a more likable penchant for Falstaff beer; he is a fantasy antifather figure, all-permissive and all-corrupting, a promoter of pleasure and a wrecker of discipline and order.

Scott, like the Prince Hal he is modeled on, is planning to quit slumming and enlist in the paternal forces of law and order and oppression very soon. A week shy of twenty-one and aware his father has a bum ticker, Scott coldly calculates the timetable of his coming betrayal. Scott is the reforming Bob Hughes of *Drugstore Cowboy*, but curdled with self-righteousness and insincerity. The Scott/Hal, Bob/Falstaff aspect of *Idaho* is essentially confined to two longish sequences: the Gadshill robbery and Scott's subsequent discomfiting of Bob, and the cleaned-up Scott's repudiation of Bob in a yuppie restaurant, followed at once by Bob's death and raucous, disorderly funeral—right across the cemetery green from the decorous solemnity of the religious interment of Mayor Favor.

The notion of a revisionist, *street* take on *Henry IV* set in the Portland underworld was not in itself necessarily a bad one, but Van Sant's acoustic and aesthetic touch seems off in these sections. The problem may be that the contemporary version is not revisionist enough. The Shakespearean dialogue is half rewritten, with slang uncomfortably jostling Elizabethan locutions. When Bob/Falstaff asks, "What time is it?" (Shakespeare: "What time of day is it, lad?"), Scott answers, "What do you care? Why, you wouldn't even look at a clock unless hours were lines of coke, dials looked like the signs of gay bars, or time itself was a fair hustler in black leather" (Shakespeare: "What a devil hast thou to do with the time of the day? Unless hours were cups of sack, and minutes capons, and clocks the tongues of bawds, and dials the signs of leaping-houses, and the blessed sun himself a fair hot wench in flame-colored taffeta, I see no reason why thou shouldst be so superfluous to demand the time of the day").

What's wrong with Scott's language is not that it's not Shakespearean but that it is not street, either; who would say such things? And the actors' discomfort is visible. The Gadshill robbery is murky, the subsequent guying of Bob unfunny, and the antic capering at Bob's funeral embarrassingly stilted. It is telling, too, that Mike Waters seems at a loss and awkward in these Pigeon scenes. The whole thing should have been totally reimagined from the ground—or from the gutter—up.

That said, there are some felicities in this part of the movie: a certain rigidity and hauteur in the marmoreally handsome Reeves is right for Prince Hal, who here delivers his I-shall-reform speech outdoors leaning against a broken wall and in such a way as to be overheard by a deluded Bob. And many compositions echo *Chimes at Midnight*. This is not the first homage to Welles in Van Sant: Johnny's reappearance on a Portland street at night in *Mala Noche* is an elaborate and funny quotation of the nocturnal resurrection of Harry Lime (Orson Welles) in a Viennese doorway in Carol Reed's *The Third Man*. But Welles, largely perhaps because he had so much of the megalomaniac in him, wielded a worldly savoir and smiling complicity in depicting men of power or men of charisma. The quieter Van Sant turns his men of power into robotic caricatures, like the mayor here, and his men of charisma into bellowing bores, like Bob Pigeon.

But the heart and soul of *My Own Private Idaho* is elsewhere, in the story of Mike Waters. A trailer child, son of an evanescent waitress (and probable product of incest), Mike is a red-pantsed ragamuffin who sells his body but who—the killer catch—is a narcoleptic given to collapsing into twitching stupors under stress. His stress is especially likely to be triggered by anything that recalls his mother, his childhood in Idaho with her, or the trailer/ bungalow they lived in with Mike's older brother, Richard (James Russo, in a fine performance). Mike is throughout the film a nomadic seeker for both the literal Idaho of his early years and the utopian Idaho of rooted love. If Scott in his cold egotism kills the two fathers he possesses, Mike persists in a desperate search for a mother he never locates.

The movie's first image is of the word *narcolepsy* defined in a dictionary. This narcolepsy functions as an open sesame, a trigger into the dreaming and poetic unconscious of Mike: he images his mother cradling and comforting a grown Mike; he reruns in his mind home movies of his childhood; in his imagination, time-lapse clouds hurtle across wide Idaho skies; a brown barn keeps collapsing (barns are favorite subjects of Van Sant the painter). Van Sant has said that he and his cinematographers, Eric Alan Edwards and John Campbell, had amassed much of this "visionary" footage without knowing exactly what they were going to do with it. Remembering the use of memory images in Wim Wenders's *Paris, Texas* (a film, again, that has had deep influence on younger filmmakers' imaginings of America) helped Van Sant see what to do with these images: they became Mike's reveries. It was, somehow, the character of Mike that gave Van Sant the ideal objective correlative for his imagistic fragments.

What is miraculous in Mike is that he is at once pathetic flotsam, passive dreamer, and true visionary. He can be poet, sage, lover, mystic. We first (and last) see him on a maternally undulating and desolately beautiful ribbon of Idaho road talking to himself and to a rabbit. He is a bit of a rabbit himself, skittering off timorously whenever any authority figure (for example, a perfectly pleasant Native American cop) approaches. A child of the road, he is condemned to an eternal pilgrimage on it. His first words are, "I always know where I am by the way the road looks. . . . There's not another road anywhere that looks like this road, I mean *exactly* like this road. It's one kind of place, one of a kind, like someone's face, like a fucked-up face." The camera executes a playful iris in on a far configuration of facelike terrain. One thinks, with this iris, of Buster Keaton, whose simpleton-ness is kin to Mike's. Something about that "face," perhaps, has gotten to him, and he slithers down onto the asphalt in a trance, fingers twitching. This vagabond gives new meaning to "on the road."

Back on the same stretch in the final scene, Mike muses, "I'm a connoisseur of roads. I've been tasting roads all my life. This road will never end. It probably goes all around the world." And right then, naturally, something about this road brings on a seizure; images of clouds, a huge, snow-clad mountain, and his mother cradling him as he is today crowd into his brain.

In *My Own Private Idaho*, Van Sant has reanimated the tired tropes of the road movie by the power of these oneiric images: the road is an umbilical cord leading to a hallucinatory union with the author of one's being. Mike, looking back at Portland, could say, with the greatest of American road heroes, Huck Finn: "I been there before." Idaho is the territory he lights out for, both literally and psychically. It is, after all, a *private* Idaho. And all this is never pretentious, thanks in good part to Van Sant's, and Phoenix's, alertness for comic, deflating opportunities.

At one point, Mike calls Idaho "the potato state." And his very first narcolepsy segues into a scene of fellatio—obliquely presented and itself interrupted by witty images of a road, a plaster cowboy, salmon leaping upriver, a lake at twilight, and a barn crashing onto the middle of a road at the exact moment of Mike's orgasm. This fondness for humor is signaled in the music, too: "America the Beautiful" begins to sound when Mike looks out a suburban john's window and enviously murmurs "Backyard!" just before swooning (the john, a woman, does indeed look something like his mother). And that tune, played for irony but played for beauty, too, is last heard over the movie's final images.

In Phoenix's deft playing, Mike has a kind of wit so dry and so simple as to be indistinguishable from idiocy. He manifests, in the words of another American bard of the road, Walt Whitman, "behavior lawless as snowflake, words simple as grass, uncomb'd head, laughter, and naiveté." To a john babbling of numerology, he says, "You know your math." To Scott, asking what to do if a bomb drops on Portland, "Take shelter?" To the rich woman in her baronial home, "This is a nice home. Do you live here? . . . I don't blame you."

Reading a postcard from his lost mother that she has

mailed from the Family Tree Inn (perfect name) in Snake River, Idaho, Mike goes on to savor the card's printed descriptions of the motel's amenities and sighs, "It sounds so nice. I wouldn't mind living here." River Phoenix told me he inserted these lines here as a deliberate echo of Mike's earlier words to the rich woman. Any *nice* place seems homey to poor Mike. (In fact, he is soon being regaled with that motel's amenities, but he cannot really enjoy them since he has found out his mother has moved on—to Italy.)

The relationship of Mike and Scott is complex. "Some hustler, huh?" comments Scott while helping a third hustler lug Mike's body out onto the rich woman's lawn. Up to a point, Scott is a friend; he calls himself Mike's "best friend." He scrapes Mike up more than once; we see him cradling the inert Mike in a pietà pose at the foot of a Portland sculpture entitled *The Coming of the White Man.* This pose recalls not only Walt with Pepper in *Mala Noche* but Mike in the lap of his mother in his reveries. Both Scott and his mother falsely assure the unconscious Mike that "everything'll be all right."

Scott accompanies the mother-questing Mike to Idaho and to Italy. On the way to Idaho, the two buddies bed down by a roadside campfire and Mike opens his heart to Scott. In a passage of heartbreaking tenderness and vulnerability, shy Mike averts his eyes, grabs his ankles, and whispers his love into the night. Scott bristles and responds with cold capitalist and macho dogmas: "I only have sex with a guy for money. . . . Two guys can't love each other."

Mike thinks about this: "Yeah . . . well, I don't know
. . . I mean, I mean, for me, I could love someone even
if I, you know, wasn't paid for it. . . . I love you and you
don't pay me." This aching goodness of heart is enough
to flatten Scott's ideologies but not to soften Scott.

River Phoenix wrote this devastating scene himself—
Mike's part anyway—with the blessing of the director
and the collaboration of Reeves. To stress Phoenix's profound contribution to Mike is to take nothing away from
Van Sant. Quite the opposite. Again and again, this director's coworkers call him "open . . . totally nonjudgmen-
tal" (Reeves), "very collaborative" (Phoenix), "free,
loose, spontaneous" (Eric Alan Edwards, who adds, interestingly, that "improvisation can be as important in
camerawork as it is in acting"). Such qualities are,
clearly, not just operational strategies for Van Sant, but
moral imperatives in art and life. These virtues of relaxed
generosity, intelligence, and wit are visible in his
heroes—in Walt and in Bob Hughes and in Mike—and in
the performers who, creating these Van Sant figures, have
done the freshest and best male work on the recent American screen.

Mike and Scott are in Idaho to look up Mike's brother
Richard, a trailer-dwelling, boozy painter of kitschy por-
traits. Scott is coolly contemptuous of all this tackiness:
the awful pictures, the sandwiches, the cans of Alpo,
the smiley-face decals on a ceiling light—details tossed
off by Van Sant. Richard tries to fob Mike off with old
fictions about how Mom stir-fried vegetables with a .38
that she later plugged Mike's dad with at a drive-in. But

Mike isn't buying. He *knows* who his dad is. Richard is his dad, and he doesn't particularly care (nice touch, this). After a stormy fight and a tearful reconciliation with his-brother-and-his-father, he is off to the Family Tree Inn after what he really needs: his mother.

The road soon leads, as all roads are reputed to, to Rome—actually, to a farmhouse outside Rome. Mike stumbles into sunlit doorways, asking, "Mom?" but she, of course, has moved on. Mike sobs in Scott's arms, wondering, "My mom's house was blue . . . no . . . it was green, it was green. How could I forget that?" The conscious Mike does not have the instant-replay capacity of the dreaming Mike. Mike is ready to split, but Scott has fallen in love with beautiful Carmella (Chiara Caselli). Excluded Mike, who had told her to call him Michael on being introduced, tosses in his bed and sulks and pouts and blows smoke in his spaghetti—the same Mike who had earlier told a girl in a Portland diner à propos of smoking, "Not when I'm eating, and don't blow it in my face." Van Sant people smoke.

We get a sort of naked fashion shoot of Scott and Carmella being rigidly pretty at a window and on a bed, as if to rhyme with an earlier still-life montage of kinky sex à trois with the zany Teuton back at the Family Tree Inn. Scott's latent heterosexuality has been established from early on when he consoled a weeping girl in that Portland diner, while Mike sniffed, "She's only feeling sorry for herself." His walks on the wild side were only designer shocks aimed at his father. He and Carmella split for Portland, where she becomes his cool, yuppie consort. (She did, though, have an ephemeral moment of friendly contact with Mike, who told her, "I know how you feel.")

The whole Italian pastoral has been, besides a calvary for Mike, an evocation of a tamed and civilized landscape in harmony with a stone-solid, handsome human dwelling—all quite rooted and un-American. On leaving, Scott had slipped Mike a few bills, saying, "Maybe I'll run into you down the road." But this is perfunctory and insincere. Mike, berserk with hurt and rage, now induces attacks of his narcolepsy and goes into a suicidal tailspin that soon sees him crawling on broken glass on a Portland sidewalk.

But somehow—the luck of the innocent—Mike winds up for the third time on that rolling Idaho road. The full iconic repertoire of his subconscious—plus the salmon again—flashes by as Mike talks of the eternity of the road and slides slowly down onto the face of the hard macadam. In a long crane shot, a car stops. Cut to road level, as faceless guys take his shoes and duffel bag and frisk him for cash and drive off. The road as Darwinian hell. Back—and permanently now—in long shot as a second car stops. A driver gets out, shovels Mike into the front seat, and drives off. Richard? Scott? Just a john? It doesn't matter? A friendly pickup, maybe, one that will take Mike farther along his long road.

The very last image is of the brown barn, emblem of fertility and home, *uncollapsing*. A title card then repeats a message Mike had read into the road's "fucked-up face": HAVE A NICE DAY. Mere sarcasm? A nasty epitaph on

Mike's hopes? Or a note of promise for Mike Waters and all the salmon in our rivers?

Gus Van Sant likes to acknowledge the influence of William Burroughs, and it is there in such things as the refusal of bourgeois pieties about drugs and the embrace of various tribes of outcasts. There, also, in the cool homosexuality, although Van Sant is capable, too, of the thoroughly credible heterosexual ambiance of *Drugstore Cowboy*. But Burroughs's stony-hearted solipsism is much more limited than Van Sant's tender watchfulness for holiness in odd places, his unblinking and compassionate gaze at the awful absences of love, his unjudging observation of obsession—all of which remind me rather of the otherwise very different French filmmaker Robert Bresson. Van Sant loves his junkies, and hustlers, and lovers. David Lynch, shocked at discovering insects under, so to speak, Ozzie and Harriet's lawn, seems puerile when compared to Van Sant's Dostoevskian at-homeness in the hearts of his derelicts. When it came out, I called *My Own Private Idaho* the best American movie of the Nineties. Still is.

The collaborative work on *Idaho* is remarkable: Portland cinematographers Edwards and Campbell have created images luminous and numinous: the very clouds and sky and land seem to pulse with an inner sadness and longing. Keanu Reeves's stiffness, distance, arrogance are right for Scott. River Phoenix's creation of Mike is an act of powerful artistic daring. It is not that he plays a hustler—lots of actors would be up for such a ''stretch''—but that he immerses himself so deeply in the soul of sweet, doomed Mike. The role is largely his invention, and he swims dreamily in its depths. Sliding onto horizontal surfaces, coiling himself into agonized crouches, standing shivering on raw streetcorners, Phoenix takes the body language that was James Dean's great invention to richer and sadder depths.

Phoenix was, in fact, born in Madras, Oregon, not far from Portland, in 1970, and spent some of his childhood traveling the Northwest with his parents, then working as itinerant fruit pickers. River and his siblings sometimes entertained in public places to get the family money to afford good schools. They were, he says, "humbling" experiences. The family later went to South America to work with a religious group, but returned to America after a disillusioning experience. From this eccentric but nourishing familial matrix River emerged a brave and original artist. After *Idaho* he made an independent movie, Sam Shepard's *Silent Tongue,* and two commercial films, *Sneakers* and *The Thing Called Love* ("you can work on different levels just as you live on different levels," he suggested); he died suddenly and shockingly in Los Angeles on October 31, 1993. Death, as often, had taken the best.

He never studied acting, he told me, but rather evolved a method: "I create space in my mind. I section off and organize the parts of my brain that I need to inhabit." When it works, "I feel completely overwhelmed to the degree of unconsciousness, but I'm completely awake and waiting for the spontaneous pop that makes it real for the first time." His own private method not only works for Phoenix, but seems a valid analysis of how he got to the point of imagining a Mike Waters. Art can have a spiritual dimension. It seemed completely unphony when Phoenix remarked that "I won the [National Society of Film Critics Best Actor] award, but Mike didn't win the award. It would have made him happy."

Van Sant's next film is *Even Cowgirls Get the Blues*, which he scripted from the Tom Robbins cult novel and which stars Uma Thurman as Sissy Hankshaw, a legendary hitchhiker whose roads lead from New York City to the Rubber Rose Ranch in the Dakota plains, where she encounters militant lesbians, migratory whooping cranes, the FBI, and the meaning of life. Costarring with Thurman are John Hurt as the Countess, Keanu Reeves as a Mohawk, and River's sister Rain Phoenix as Bonanza Jellybean. Heather Graham pops in. It sounds like a giddy satyr play after the somber Portland Trilogy.

*A* film that might be said to be in the fledgling Van Sant mold is 1992's *Where the Day Takes You,* directed by Marc Rocco and written by him with Kurt Voss. Rocco, born in 1964, is a graduate of the USC Film School and the son of actor Alex Rocco. The movie is about Los Angeles street waifs and stars Dermot Mulroney, Lara Flynn Boyle, and the ever-popular James LeGros. Unfortunately, it made self-pitying and humorless victims and martyrs out of its characters. A key lesson to be learned from Van Sant is that sinners are more interesting and more human than plaster saints.

A more solid stab at a street movie is *American Heart* (1993) by Martin Bell. In 1984, Bell made *Streetwise,* a sad and despairing documentary about Seattle street kids. *American Heart* constructs a fictional story in the milieu and spirit of *Streetwise*. Jack (Jeff Bridges), a cynical, long-maned, tattooed loser, gets out of jail and slowly, grudgingly bonds with his teen son, Nick (Edward Furlong), whose only alternative to street existence he represents. Father and son together come to dream of an escape from the urban hell of Seattle to the purity of Alaska. But the film is finally too busy, too scatter-brained: the father-son scenes inside their ratty rooming house never gibe with the glimpsed street scenes or with the various criminal enterprises the two get involved in. A falsely tragic climax on a ferry lets down the film. Furlong, of *Terminator 2* fame, is a tight-lipped and judgmental kid; it is Jeff Bridges who saves the film with a bold, grim exploration of a lost soul struggling for the last light. With none of the perverse glamour that can enshroud Van Sant's young losers, Bridges leaves an afterimage of adult waste and sorrow that lingers in the mind's eye when the shaky sentimentalities of *American Heart* are gone.

Another William Burroughs fan is David Cronenberg, the distinctive Canadian filmmaker. Born in Toronto in 1943, he attended the University of Toronto, switching while there from science to literature to film. He has been making features since 1975. After *Shivers/They Came from Within/The Parasite Murders* in that year, he went on to *Rabid* in 1977, *The Brood* in 1979, *Scanners* in 1981, *Videodrome* in 1983, and *The Dead Zone* in 1983.

By that time Cronenberg had concocted a visual vocabulary of glop, splatter, and ooze—a vocabulary that was really making points about the malignant deformations and terrible stresses that technology can beget. He hit his stride with *The Fly,* a 1986 remake of the 1958 mutant flick; it had an empathetic, sad-sack performance by Jeff Goldblum. One critic wrote, in words that must have been uttered someplace about *every* Cronenberg movie, that *The Fly* "goes over the line to be gross and disgusting."

Of his next film, *Dead Ringers,* a 1988 study of mad twin dope-addict gynecologists (both played by Jeremy Irons) given to wielding sadistically misshapen gynecological instruments, *another* writer unsurprisingly opined that the film "sinks into a depressing spiral of depravity and gratuitous gore." *Sinks* is good!

Cronenberg cowrote *The Fly* and *Dead Ringers* and was to take solo script credit on his next venture, a 1991 adaptation of *Naked Lunch,* a 1959 novel by Burroughs. Cronenberg had fancied himself a novelist back in the early 1960s, and his two favorite writers were Burroughs and Vladimir Nabokov. Burroughs proved the more lasting and congenial influence over the years. By 1990, Cronenberg had met Burroughs and secured his assent to the Canadian's strategy for a filmic adaptation.

The celebrated novel itself was radically experimental in form and in content. Jumbled together according to an aleatory, cut-up principle, it featured scenes of disemboweling, anality, and drug pathology. Excess was all. *Unfilmable* is too mild a word for *Naked Lunch.* As Cronenberg admitted, "a literal translation . . . would cost $400 million and would be banned in every country in the world." So Cronenberg fused *Naked Lunch* with other Burroughsiana like *Exterminator!* and *Junkie* and with biography and gossip to construct a sort of animated psychofantasy about the birth of a writer and about a writer's relation to technology—above all, given the period, to typewriters.

Things start in New York in 1953 with Bill Lee (Peter Weller as the Burroughs figure) working as an exterminator ("Exterminator!" is the film's first word—compare Jeff's disguise in *Blue Velvet*.) He is, though, about to lose his job because his wife, Joan (Judy Davis), is swiping his roach powder to shoot up with it (in the breast). She recommends it to Lee, saying, "It's a very literary high. It's a Kafka high. You feel like a bug. Try it." "My God, Joan, you're acting like a full-fledged junkie," sniffs the censorious Lee.

Lee has two writer pals, Hank (Nicholas Campbell as the Jack Kerouac figure) and Martin (Michael Zelniker, who was Red Rodney in *Bird*, Clint Eastwood's Charlie Parker biopic, as the Allen Ginsberg figure). Kerouac and Ginsberg and Burroughs were, in the Fifties, the stars of the beat movement; in fact, it was Kerouac, author of *On the Road*, who gave Burroughs the title *Naked Lunch*. (It would be fanciful, and only remotely accurate, to compare that trio with, respectively, Lynch, Van Sant, and Cronenberg today.) These two pals debate, in a greasy spoon (*Naked Lunch* is very much an indoors, Toronto studio movie), some ethics of writing; Catholic Hank declares that to rewrite or to rethink is a sin, whereas Jewish Martin insists on the joys of feeling guilt and rewriting everything a hundred times. Lee insists he gave up writing when he was ten and proclaims as his aesthetic: "Exterminate all rational thought!" He very soon becomes a passive medium, oddly called an "agent," for the CIA—or is it the Id? It is hard to identify his controlling powers exactly, for they are all huge talking insects.

The usual Cronenberg tics kick in with a vengeance: bugs, injections, paranoia, conspiracy, double agents, doppelgängers, plain doubles. His slurping control bug inducts Lee into the rites and technology of spying and writing and drug-ingestion—which are all the same thing here. He is told his wife is a dangerous agent of Interzone and ought to be eliminated because, besides being a spy, she isn't human really, she is actually an insect in human disguise. Oh, well then. When Lee catches Joan in a half-assed orgy with Hank and Martin, he shoots her "accidentally" while playing their well-known glass-on-the-head "William Tell routine."

The uxoricide flees to Interzone, his own private Tangiers. (Happily, Cronenberg was prevented by the outbreak of the Gulf War from shooting in the real Tangiers and had to come up with a better one in Toronto, à la Von Sternberg's Hollywood Morocco. Interzone is less a place than a hallucination, anyway.) The first thing Lee is asked in Interzone is, "You a faggot?" "Not by nature" is his answer, but that soon changes, although one never loses a sense that Cronenberg is rather squirmy at the seeping homosexuality.

Lee's first order of business is to buy a typewriter to type a report to his control bug about Joan Lee's death.

The one he gets quickly metamorphoses into a gloppy and sarcastic bug, who tells a nodding Lee, "This is no time to doze off like a freckle-faced boy on a fishing raft." Hardly a Huck Finn, Lee sits up and listens with relief when the type-bug assures him he is not responsible for killing his wife and advises him that "homosexuality is the best cover an agent ever had." Having said that, the type-bug squirts orgasmically.

Lee then meets the literary lights of Interzone, novelists Tom and Joan Frost (Ian Holm and, again, Judy Davis as the Paul and Jane Bowles figures). In a funny scene, Tom's Id chatters to Lee of his murderous hatred of his wife, while his lips are talking of typewriter makes. The care and feeding of typewriters is, indeed, the governing obsession of the writers in the film, and the scribblers' keyboards have a habit of turning into viscous, gluey, and verbally demanding blobs from the Id. Their shapes are visual riffs on vaginas and penises. But if Lee's typewriter is a martinet, in return it writes Lee's "reports" all by itself. It is these reports that become the text of *Naked Lunch,* not a word of which Lee is conscious of having written.

When Hank and Martin, on a visit to Interzone, praise Lee's novel, he is mystified at its existence and says he suspects "some colossal con, a well-orchestrated cabal." Martin, seeing publishing glory ahead for Lee, counsels, "For God's sake, play ball with the conspiracy." Martin and Hank try to woo Lee back to America, but he refuses, saying, "America is not a young place, it's old, it's dirty, it's evil"—a characteristic Burroughsian sentiment.

Lee's control bug pressures him to seduce Joan Frost, who is a threat because she writes in longhand (like Jane Austen, one presumes) and thus escapes the dominion of the machine. At need, Joan Frost, who is attracted to Lee, can do some typing for him on an Arabic keyboard, but that turns into a messy orifice. And another difficulty with Joan Frost is that she is in thrall to her housekeeper, who is a lesbian dominatrix witch—not to mention drug queenpin, not to mention monstrous centipede.

Metamorphosis is everywhere in the movie, but it is never a happy change. It is always ugly, negating, befouling, belittling. Lee's local minion, for instance, is buggified while being buggered in a cage by Swiss decadent Yves Cloquet (Julian Sands), himself a big bug. Lee watches with only mild interest.

Lee's typewriter now produces not only his writing and his writing fluid but his narcotic fluids as well. He is enslaved to the prolific insect, which has become his supplier of everything, dispensing "two kinds of intoxicating fluids." His dependence becomes total; he gets hooked on "mugwump jissom," a combination bug excretion/ink/drug. It is an ironic fate for a former exterminator.

At the end, he takes off with Joan Frost, the only non-bug left in Interzone, in a van on the road to Annexia (read U.S.S.R.). Forced by Annexian customs to "write something," he plugs Joan, who, like Joan Lee before her, had trustingly put a glass on her head, in the forehead. He is at once let in to Annexia. Again, murdering a woman is somehow a validating act for a male writer—a concept *Barton Fink* toyed with, too. And, dis-quietingly, the victim in both films is played by the pow-erfully intelligent, radiantly ironic, candidly sensual Judy Davis.

Peter Weller's gaunt face and insinuatingly nasal drone work well in the Burroughs role; they suggest, without impersonating. Ian Holm is enjoyable in the Paul Bowles role. (*Naked Lunch*, by the way, is the real *The Sheltering Sky,* for it puts into a context of wit and humor the inertly oddball Bowles couple who were the affectless subjects of that Bertolucci movie.)

Cronenberg's dazzling iconic repertoire here is as inge-nious as the invention of a new language. It fleshes out (or at least rubbers out) the monsters of the Burroughsian Id, Ego, and Superego. And it finds a witty theme inside its visual games: the potential enslavement of an artist to the demonic side of technology or the soul.

In Cronenberg's film *about,* rather than *of, Naked Lunch* one can sense the differences between the two men: in Cronenberg there is an Apollonian attraction to control and order that is at war with the gloppy and disintegrat-ing forces of Dionysus, to which alone Burroughs is drawn. And, in photographer Peter Suschitzky's gloomy colors, the sadism and misogyny come out looking cold-bloodedly awful.

But Cronenberg's achievement in making cinematic such a vacant vision is astounding. *Naked Lunch* is an inexhaustibly original act of independent cinema. It makes Uli Edel's film version of Hubert Selby, Jr.'s novel *Last Exit to Brooklyn*—another so-called daring adaptation of an unfilmable book—look like the conventional tear-jerker that it is. And it makes Soderbergh's *Kafka* look even more trivial.

Cronenberg's next project is *M. Butterfly,* from the play about a French diplomat (Jeremy Irons) in Peking who had an affair for twenty years with an opera singer who he thought was a woman but who was in fact a man. Compared to *Naked Lunch,* it sounds like a walk in the park.

Another brilliant Canadian independent filmmaker is Atom Egoyan. Born in Cairo in 1960 of Armenian descent, Egoyan was raised in British Columbia and moved at eighteen to Toronto, where he studied international relations and classical guitar at the University of Toronto. As a student, though, he turned his attention to film and began writing and directing shorts and programs for the Canadian Broadcasting Corporation. He made his first feature, *Next of Kin,* in 1984. It dealt with two persisting and interlocking Egoyan concerns: video technology and familial dysfunction. A spoiled son in "video therapy" with his rich parents grows obsessed with another family video depicting the anguish of a poor Armenian family giving a little son up for adoption.

In *Family Viewing,* which Egoyan wrote and directed in Toronto in 1987, we are again in the bosom of an unhappy rich white family, where Van (Aidan Tierney), a glum teenaged son, compulsively watches videotapes of his vanished mother, but his cold father Stan (David Hemblen), a VCR dealer, erases these priceless records to tape sex with his mistress, Sandra (Gabrielle Rose). To compound his heartlessness, Stan is unwilling to bring home his aged mother-in-law from a nursing home. Van dotes on the old lady and grows close to a young woman, Aline (Arsinée Khanjian, Egoyan's wife), who is often in the same room visiting her own old mother. When Aline's mother commits suicide, Van concocts an idea: switch the old ladies, bury Aline's mother as his grand-mother, and stash Granny in an unused wing of a big hotel, where they can both get jobs to keep an eye on her. Why not?

Aline's day job is giving phone sex. Sure enough, one day Stan calls. He talks to Aline and videotapes Sandra at the same time. The beast. He also grows obsessed with the real Aline, the nonphone Aline, for he has seen her visiting what he thinks is the grave of his mother-in-law with flowers. He hires a detective to have her followed. The film ends with an angry and unhinged Stan running through hotel corridors in a vain search for the nurturing community where Van and Aline have hidden Granny. All is intercut with videos.

*Family Viewing*, which could serve as the all-purpose Egoyan title, seems to believe that there was once an Edenic time of technological innocence when close, lov-ing families made home movies of the kids. Then came a fall, with technology becoming a tool of sexual exploi-tation and authoritarian intrusiveness.

*Speaking Parts* (1989), too, deals with the corruption of a home movie by cold commerce. A professor, Clara (Ga-brielle Rose, whose warm, laughing sensuality was the best thing in *Family Viewing*), cherishes home movies (we get to see a lot of them) of her brother, who died giving her a lung transplant. Clara haunts his cinerarium. She has written a TV script about his heroic sacrifice and has unwisely put it in the hands of a vulgar, ratings-hungry producer (David Hemblen, as the heavy again).

Preproduction meetings are being held in a big hotel that employs Lisa (Arsinée Khanjian), a towel folder, and Lance (Michael McManus), a housekeeper. Lance has a crowded schedule: besides being pimped to guests by an icily chic head housekeeper, he plays silent cameos in local films and asks Clara if he can audition for her TV film. Attracted in the course of the audition, they make love first in the hotel and then, after she has returned home, by means of a remote video hookup through which both masturbate to a screen image of the masturbating other.

Poor loser Lisa, hopelessly addicted to Lance, puts roses in his laundry and rents his movies again and again to watch alone in her bare room (one Lance cameo: Saint Sebastian wearing a Star of David). Eventually, she befriends a guy in the After Dark Video store in order to become, like him, a video filmmaker. But her insane questions so unnerve the bride at a wedding where she is working as the guy's assistant that this career comes to a quick halt.

Vain Lance, meanwhile, is having his conscience awakened by two developments: smitten by Lance, one of his sexual customers in the hotel (male, apparently) has killed himself, while Clara begs Lance, now playing her brother, to protest the absurd distortions the producer is inflicting upon her intimate story. Lance redeems himself by crying out, in midfilming, against the rape of the story and by befriending and kissing the besotted Lisa. In both cases he opts for tenderness and kindness over commerce. His first spoken word in his first speaking part was "No," precisely a refusal of corrupt discourse.

To describe the self-reflexive ingenuities of an Egoyan plot is to exhaust a good deal of the pleasure of an Egoyan movie. The actual visuals tend to be busy, functional illustrations of the theses, and the performances somewhat stiff. But in *Speaking Parts* there are two richly cinematic performances: Gabrielle Rose manages once again to bring a ripe sexuality to a monotonously written character, and pony-tailed Michael McManus injects a perfect note of laconically smug narcissism into Lance. And their sex by video remote, in Paul Sarossy's mobile photography, is erotic and genuinely witty. It is so startling and ripe a scene, in fact, as to unbalance the dynamics and thematics of the film, which remains, however, Egoyan's best.

*The Adjuster* (1991), also written by Egoyan and filmed in a surprisingly sinister-looking Toronto by Sarossy, broadens the canvas. Noah Render (Elias Koteas), an insurance adjuster specializing in arson cases, dwells with his family in an abandoned (but for their house) development, where he practices archery from his bedroom, shooting at a large billboard advertising the unbuilt "model homes." The reality of his job is taking pictures, both of fire's ravages and of his clients and their possessions. With these snapshots as stimulus, he sexually seduces his clients: a vampirish woman in black leather, a man in leather, among, no doubt, others.

Noah's wife, Hera (Arsinée Khanjian), is a film censor who surreptitiously tapes the porn she is judging for the private delection of her sister. (Her fellow censors turn out to be similarly corrupt.)

Actually, *The Adjuster* opens not with the Render family but with a pair of amateur pornographers/performance artists: obese Bubba (Maury Chaykin) and depraved Mimi (Gabrielle Rose), who are given to staging lubricious playlets in public settings like subways and football fields. (Bubba is an ex-jock). They rent the Render house to make some kiddie porn, while the obliging Renders move into the very motel where Noah has been servicing his burnt-out and horny clients. Finally, the evil Bubba burns down the Render home, and Noah has himself become the client of another adjuster.

Again, Egoyan queries the role of images—still or moving—in mediating, inflaming, and poisoning desire and in destabilizing the family unit. Bubba and Mimi are more destructive and nihilistic than similar exploitative types like the father in *Family Viewing* and the producer in *Speaking Parts*. Again, the character Khanjian plays seems trapped in a private nightmare. Noah seems an elaboration of polymorphous Lance—both clearly derive from the Terence Stamp character (pansexual servicer of a whole family) in what Egoyan has called "my favorite film," Pasolini's *Teorema*.

Egoyan's 1993 film *Calendar*, set in Canada and in

Armenia, offers a kaleidoscopic interplay among art, adultery, technology, and family.

One feels in Egoyan different personae at play and in conflict: a semiotic theoretician of images, a moral critic of technology, a warm chronicler of Armenian family values, a puritanical censor, a sweaty sensualist. In his art, these Atoms collide, often explosively and wittily, sometimes dully and predictably.

# CHAPTER EIGHT

# *P*oets of Dialect

*S*ome films have so unusual a texture and sound they may be said to employ a dialect of their own. A film of which this is literally true is Julie Dash's *Daughters of the Dust*. Dash is a native New Yorker, born in the early Fifties, who first discovered film when, at seventeen, she accompanied a friend to a cinematography workshop at the Studio Museum in Harlem. By nineteen, she was making her first short films. After graduating from the City College of New York and trying without success to get into the film program at UCLA, she spent some ten years writing and rewriting and trying to make her dream project; part of that time she was at the Center for Advanced Film Studies at the American Film Institute. By the time she came to make *Daughters of the Dust*, her eleventh film but first feature, in the summer of 1989, she had a budget of $800,000 from *American Playhouse*.

*Daughters of the Dust* is a film of memory, of place, of language, of religion. Filmed on the beautiful sandy islands off the coasts of the Carolinas and Georgia that served as the black Ellis Island, where chained African people were brought and processed, it tells of the Gullah, a West African people brought thither in the days of slavery. Spoken in an artful mixture of the Gullah dialect and more standard English, the story is told in voice-over by the Unborn Child of the two lovers in the film.

The present tense of the film is August of 1902, when many Gullah people are leaving the islands to go up north to make a living in the boom metropolises. A small boat approaches, bringing bossy, statuesque mainlander Viola and a photographer, Snead, who is to snap commemorative poses of the community on the eve of its breakup. On the boat also are haughty beauty Yellow Mary (Barbara O, the standout performance in a film that for the most part pointedly emphasizes the communal groupings of life), who ran away years ago after a rape to give birth to daughter Eula, also aboard, out of wedlock. What will Yellow Mary and the proud Gullah make of each other?

Snead is a learned, fastidious man who discourses on the kaleidoscope, explaining the etymology of the word and calling it an example of "beauty, simplicity, and science all rolled into one tube." His attitude to the people of the islands (most of the filming was done on Hunting Island) has the shadow of a similar patronizing condescension.

*Daughters of the Dust*, however, brings before us modes of memory more ancient and strong than the snapshot. Wise old Nana anguishes lest the upcoming move will eradicate the texture of Gullah history; she impresses on the travelers that ancestors are watching and that memories of Africa are—in the arresting Gullah dialect—"inside of we." It is the matriarchal religion of West Africa that has above all kept the folk memories alive as a vital tradition passed from mother to daughter; it must not be lost in the imminent passage north. (Dash inserts some Mother Goddess passages from the Gnostic Gospels to establish the universal validity of these cosmic aspects of woman.)

African words are taught to the boys, too; a dance is taught on a beach to seven girls robed in white. A whole culture is transplanted and passed on before our wondering eyes in the solemn, long-held images of cinematographer Arthur Jafa.

At first, Mary and daughter Eula are standoffish. Mary calls the island "the most backwater place on earth." Bringing a sophisticated city eye to the rapturously beautiful views, she merely squirms at its infestation of gnats. It is only by the time of the great feast that she is relaxing and feeling at home: this cornucopia of shrimp, yellow rice, corn bread, and other riches is lovingly and ritually prepared. As okra is chopped for the gumbo, okra stumps are places on the foreheads of the children. Dash has meticulously traced all these culinary and cultural details to the practices of her own Gullah ancestors. (Not everything, it should be mentioned, is explained; this is not an anthropological documentary. Dash *visualizes* and lets the images work their explanatory way into our eyes and brains and hearts.)

A key image in the film is a stark, sprawling, bare-branched tree in whose picturesque crooks and angles Mary and Eula take and hold long poses in their cinched gowns and parasols. Slowly, the majestic beauty of these women becomes at one with the majestic beauty of the place. (Dash has written, amusingly, that she had debated until the last minute putting old Nana up in the tree's crook but was afraid the elderly actress might fall out.) At issue throughout the film is a proposal of marriage made to young Eula (scheduled to depart north) by handsome young Cherokee St. Julian Last Child. Eula and the Cherokee are also posed in the tree as tableaux of true love fighting the community opposition to the young woman's remaining behind.

As the photographer busily arranges group photographs on the sandy beaches and dunes where so much of *Daughters of the Dust* transpires and ducks his head behind his camera's black cloth, aged matriarch Nana recites the tragic fate of the earliest Gullah arrivals on these haunted shores: legend may have it that the Ibos left their slave ships and walked away from their captors in chains upon the surface of the swampy water (to commemorate this legend we have seen a floating wooden statue that looks like a ship's figurehead), but the old woman avers that those arriving Ibos strode toward the water only to drown in it.

What a powerful recuperation of a human history Dash achieves in this movie and with what simple means. Julie Dash is a perfect illustration of how American independent film is giving artistic voice to the untold stories of America. Later, Gullah labor over indigo dye vats is vividly pictured, too.

Nana insists memories like these must never fade: she has everyone kiss some African soil kept in a treasured box. Dash has said that each character in the film represents in her mind a specific African deity like Ogun. And after the African religion, with its matriarchal flavor, the film clearly respects Islam, as practiced on the beach with an old Koran by Bilal Muhammed as he remembers it from his native Sudan. The Christianity seen in the film is an arrogant and artificial property of unsympathetic Viola.

As the departing Gullah pull away in the boats, Nana, reassured at last, gives her blessing to the venture. But Mary, vowing, "I'm Yellow Mary Peasant, I'm a proud woman, I want to stay," has found a home. And at the last minute, the handsome young Cherokee gallops up on a dappled horse; his young lover Eula breaks away from the boats to join him in a romantic finale and the two gallop off together—it is, also, a symbolic union of America's two oppressed races. It is their Unborn Child who has been narrating the film. Over images of the paddling boats, she says that "we remained behind growing older, wiser, and stronger" in "this quiet place [where] simple folk live and catch a glimpse of eternity."

*Daughters of the Dust* ends with an image of the generations of women turning to dust but leaving behind to daughters and granddaughters a living, breathing culture with memories of glory and of suffering. Dash has a little fun with the male photographer and his technical swagger, but she and her amazing cinematographer Jafa have created a visual cornucopia of unhurried and lingering images of garments and veils and trees and sand and wind and sunrise and sunset—and always those lived-in women's faces that are the *imagination* of a people's history. At one point, the Gullah watch moving slides of jerky, busy, crowded urban streets like those they will soon be walking. One is fearful of that northern future that in fact awaits them. But those slides are also, on the positive side, going to lead in the fullness of time to the commemorating, reanimating art of Julie Dash.

Whit Stillman grew up in the Fifties and Sixties in Manhattan and in posh upstate Cornwall on the Hudson. After graduating from Harvard in 1973 he did time as a writer of fiction and nonfiction and as an editor in New York. In 1980, in Barcelona, he married a Spanish woman; in New York, he then represented Spanish filmmakers and indeed played the comic American in some Spanish films that had scenes in New York. It took him four years to write his first feature, *Metropolitan,* which he envisaged as, and which indeed became, a small-scale film in the spirit of the first comedies of John Sayles, Spike Lee, and Jim Jarmusch.

*Metropolitan* (1990), which Stillman wrote, directed, and produced, brings the eye of an anthropologist and the ear of a comic novelist like Trollope to bear upon a vanishing tribe of Manhattanites: debutantes and preppies on a round of fancy-dress dances during Christmas break "not so long ago." After a girl complains to her mother about her bust size, we see signs of Christmas in New York: a fluorescent cross in the windows above Grand Central, snowflakes falling outside the Plaza. A dance is letting out, and a relative outsider, redheaded Tom Town-send (Edward Clements), is shanghaied back to the East Side apartment of Sally Fowler and becomes an instant member of the Sally Fowler Rat Pack. *Metropolitan* is essentially about his accommodation to them and theirs to him. He is only *somewhat* an outsider: he has been at the dance and is at a proper school. He calls himself a Fourier socialist, which delights the girls and amuses the group's conservative boys; he is, though, as the group learns only when they see him later from their taxi waiting for a bus, a resident of the middle-class West Side, where he lives with his divorced and frugal mother. He boasts of his closeness to a father who, it is clear, ignores him.

At Sally's he does not join in the communal cha-cha but spends time in the kitchen talking to serious Audrey (Carolyn Farina) about his maybe-finished-maybe-not relationship with icy beauty Serena Slocum. Stillman's character names are drolly perfect.

Though he does not quite realize it, Tom, with his chatty earnestness, has been a hit with the Pack, who invite him the very next night—an invitation he is able to accept only because he is too late returning his rented tux. Outfitting himself for running with the Pack is Tom's next challenge. His mentor Nick (Christopher Eigeman) persuades Tom that the round of balls, with its "hot nutritious meals," is a good investment, in fact "the only economical social life." He also assures Tom that "these girls *like* you." Tom agrees to meet Nick at Brooks Brothers, "where the pajamas intersect with the expensive shirts." Nick is a sartorial extremist and opines that the loss of the detachable collar "makes our generation the worst since the Protestant Reformation." The sequence is a gentle parody of the outfitting of the needy Perceval in the Chrétien de Troyes romance.

Tom wavers in matters of the heart. He has talks with Audrey about Jane Austen. He ignorantly rejects Austen on political grounds: "I don't read novels; you don't have to have read a book to have opinions." She firmly demurs, asking, "Has it ever occurred to you that, looked at from her perspective, today would look even worse?" But these conversations bring the two youths together, and Tom unbends to join Audrey in a conga line at the St. Regis. But he remains erotically obsessed with the glamorous Serena, who is now apparently involved with the heartless seducer Rick von Slonicker (Will Kempe—is it descent or accident that gives this actor the name of the famous clown in Shakespeare's theatrical company?).

Serena turns up at the Plaza, draws Tom out onto a balcony for a kiss, and makes him see her home. Audrey, noting Tom's disappearance, fears he has locked himself out and frets; when he apologetically returns, Audrey is devastated. Tom is attacked as "a bastard and an egoist" by gloomy Charlie (Taylor Nichols), himself a secret admirer of Audrey's. But Audrey seems to forgive Tom, remarking as they leave the St. Regis that "there's something about winter in the city with everyone dressed up that reminds me of *War and Peace*. Do you know what I mean?" Says Tom, "I think so, although I haven't read it."

On Christmas Eve, Audrey buys a Fourier book in Doubleday's on Fifth Avenue, looks at the Oxford Jane Austen in Scribner's, also on Fifth Avenue, bumps into the heartbreaker Serena at Rockefeller Center, and goes with her mother to a midnight service at fashionable Saint Thomas Church, where she cries while everyone sings, "O come, all ye faithful."

After a quick ellipse for Christmas Day, Orgy Week begins on the twenty-sixth. Tom tells Audrey that his dad has suddenly moved to Santa Fe and that he is reading *Persuasion:* "I like it. I was quite surprised." The Pack plays strip poker one night at Sally's (most memorable line, in reference to silly Cynthia: "Playing strip poker with an exhibitionist somehow takes the challenge away").

The next night, they play a trickier game, the Truth Game. Audrey, like Fanny Price, the *Mansfield Park* heroine she admires, is wary of "dangerous" games and "the harm that excessive candor can do." Her knight Charlie defends her reluctance to play and opens his heart to Audrey, after hers has been broken by Tom's confession of continued devotion to Serena.

When Rick von Slonicker himself shows up at Sally's the next night after attending the tacky International Ball, Nick, who, like Charlie, is a chivalrous sort and who has confected chilling stories about Rick's driving young women to suicide, punches him out. When Serena remonstrates, he angrily remarks, "It's incredible the eagerness of girls like you to justify the worst bastards imaginable. . . . *He's* the scoundrel. I should have thrashed him. He's one of the worst guys of modern times." Stillman captures the dialect of this tribe with just a bit of artistic exaggeration, with a heightened formalism that blends parody and affection. One thinks of Tarantino's hoods or Harris's Brooklyn women.

The out-of-synch rhythms of the human heart are such that, no sooner is Tom beginning to feel "a warm glow at the prospect of seeing Audrey" than he hears she has gone with the silly Cynthia to Rick von Slonicker's house party at his Southampton house. Alarmed, Tom confides in his rival Charlie, whose reaction is "No, she's not [there]. She's a big admirer of Jane Austen."

They determine to rescue the endangered maiden from the seducer who has "ruined girls." But it proves hard to find a steed: Hertz and Avis insist on a driver's license, so they take a taxi from Manhattan to the end of Long Island. It is a long ride to the wintry summer resort, and in the course of it Tom announces he has modified his Fourierism. Once there the driver balks at the agreed fee, demanding, "What's this shit?" Charlie's pompous response is "A gratuity *is* included." It is a clash of dialects.

Finding panties on the lawn outside, the two knights barge nobly into the lair of the dashing Von Slonicker. They find a shirtless Rick, a topless Cynthia, and a fully clothed Audrey, who is reading a society novel, *The Rector of Justin* by Louis Auchincloss—all basking under a sunlamp. The macho Rick smites Tom, despite Charlie's saying, "I warn you, he's a Fourierist." Tom brandishes a magic sword in the form of a harmless gun, and in a flash the good trio are on the beach.

Audrey did not really need rescue, but she clearly

relishes the gesture. Charlie, accepting his "defeat" by Tom, goes to make a phone call while Tom—now openly admiring of the Audrey he had earlier treated merely as a confidante—talks of a possible meeting in France (she's off to continue her studies there) and of how she shouldn't worry about the size of her bust (an echo of the film's opening scene).

As the shivering trio walk along a cold Southampton street and vainly try to hitch a ride, they sheepishly admit that the recent melodrama was "not something Jane Austen would have done."

Stillman's achievement in this small masterpiece is to have risked that audaciously formal, balanced, archaic diction and to have worked it into the rondo of Jane Austen–like dances, courtings, and misunderstandings. There is a delicate contrast between the youngsters' sophisticated utterances and their fumbling feelings, between their metropolitan heads and their provincial hearts.

The glib pomposity of the young men is further counterpointed by the more honest vulnerability of the young women. And, as in Austen, fineness of heart finally tells. The visual style of the film, shot by John Thomas, embraces all the extravagant decor with a joyous, never belittling irony. And the actors bring a fragile sincerity. It is stressed that these are, in the main, children of broken families (most pathetically, Tom finds his childhood toys in the garbage outside the building from which his father has, without telling him, moved).

*Metropolitan* is a movie about the children of a culture

trying to cope with that culture's altering shapes. Although differing in class and in dialect from the films Stillman mentioned as his models, *Metropolitan* has human similarities to them.

Stillman's next film is *Barcelona*, a story of two American cousins in Barcelona in the late 1970s and their involvements in romance and politics in that dangerously beautiful place.

*A*nother amazingly original film that creates a language, an idiom, to fit its themes is Christopher Münch's *The Hours and Times* (1991).

Münch was born in Pasadena, California, in 1962. His father was then an astronomer at Cal Tech; Christopher chose to grow up with his mother, a writer who lived in La Jolla, near San Diego. His education was, he says, unstructured, free-form; a key educational site was the Unicorn Book Store and Cinema in La Jolla, which also served as publisher of Green Tiger books. He frequented it while his peers surfed. Münch started making shorts as a kid; by the time he was fifteen he was making documentaries about the animals at the San Diego Zoo, one of which won a PBS prize offered to young filmmakers. He later crewed for the local PBS station and learned equipment.

His first two features are unreleased. Indeed, the first one, *Goldenoise*, remains uncompleted. Made in 1985 in 16mm color, it is a story, set in Los Angeles at the end of the 1970s, about greed, ambition, and romance in the music business. The second, *In Laura's Garden*, made in

1987 in 35mm color, is a wry romance about a young man of twenty-five meeting the woman he had had a distant crush on in high school. These films do at least seem to indicate that the music business and erotic obsession were of interest to Münch before *The Hours and Times.*

*The Hours and Times* covers a weekend vacation that Beatle manager Brian Epstein and John Lennon took, alone together, in Barcelona in April 1963, on the very eve of the group's global superstardom. The friendship of the two men had long fascinated Münch. After researching it thoroughly and talking to people who had known both of them, especially to those who had known Epstein, he wrote the script very fast. "The script just came to me," he says. "I was compelled to do it." With no financing to speak of, merely a sense that it was a cheap project "I could see the end of," Münch went to London to cast it (the Lennon role proved the hardest to fill) and to Barcelona to film it in four days in black-and-white.

The sixty-minute movie opens with a grainy montage of Barcelona: waterfront, ships, cranes, Gaudi buildings (the Casa Milá, the unfinished Sagrada Familia cathedral, the Park Güell), a final overhead shot of the waterfront and the Ramblas. There is an impression conveyed of Barcelona as a mannerist, visually distorted place outside time.

Then the first of Münch's signature two-shots: on the plane coming in, a close-up of Brian (David Angus) looking solicitously at a sleeping John (Ian Hart), half out of the frame. John awakens to say, "I had a dream I was a circus clown, but the circus was underwater, somewhere in Japan I think, everything was blue, I think me costume was red." Brian compares John's dream to Matisse's *La Danse*, whose patterns of interlocking dancers, with a solitary unlinked dancer, he describes to a quickly comprehending John. The dynamics of the relationship are before us, with a Japanese minimalism: adoring teacher; bright, teasing pupil.

A stewardess, Marianne (Stephanie Pack), suggests drinks and flirts with John, who orders Brian to give her their hotel phone number. Brian complies, with a moue of annoyance—not so much perhaps that she is a woman as that she is a potential interruption into a private weekend. "She's just a bird," soothes John, in the spirit and language of the time. "Birds are harmless." "Someone should put music in these planes" is his next, bored remark, to which Brian answers, "Not a bad idea."

Münch's wit, audacity, and assurance are already impressive. In writing, shooting, and casting he is walking boldly along a tightrope between the mere impersonation of his two celebrities and dissolving their identities in some Münchian fantasy (in the manner, say, of tactlessly appropriating artists like Ken Russell or Peter Greenaway). But David Angus's masochistic epigrammatism and Ian Hart's street cheek evoke the originals and then let us forget them. The minimalist bravado of the thing is very deft.

At first, in the taxi to their hotel, John is unimpressed by Barcelona (or "Bar*the*lona," as he sneeringly and pedantically referred to it on the plane), saying, "I only came here to get away with you, we could've gone to the fuckin' North Pole for all I care." That night, they dine in John's room in the Avenida Palace hotel, where much of the film was shot. Münch carefully composes the two in a succession of lengthy shots: in a mirror, at a table, one standing behind the other. Conversation at dinner and at cards after dinner centers on John's fascination with Brian's promiscuous homosexual sex life: "Is it [being buggered] painful?" "It's a question of relaxation." But John is eager to delineate the boundary of his interest: "I like hearing about your conquests—this lorry driver, that docker. I find you an engaging and remarkable man, Brian. I've never met a man like you, but I don't really want to have it off with you." The words are said with a measure of kindness, but they visibly inflict pain. After Brian goes to his room, John receives a call from his wife, Cynthia, and speaks to her admiringly of Barcelona ("This man Gaudi was an original in his day . . . his work stands outside of time"). One sees the wary, undereducated impressionability of Lennon.

Brian cuts out of the paper an advertisement for Ingmar Bergman's new film, *The Silence,* and takes John to it the next day. Their visit to the little cinema is represented by a single, lengthy shot of the two men seated in the dark gazing intently at a flickering light. The camera moves close in on John raptly chewing gum. We have heard Bach's *Goldberg Variations* before in *Hours,* and it sounds again in *The Silence,* where it was indeed played. After the movie, Brian explains to John that Bach wrote the variations to relieve his patron's "pain and insomnia"—the (perhaps blasphemous) parallels are left unspoken.

*The Silence*, too, takes place largely in a hotel and deals with sexual frustration, masturbation, and (heterosexual) buggery. (Sven Nykvist's difficult images, at once puritanical and sensual, count among the inspirations not only for Münch here but also for John Campbell in *Mala Noche*. Münch cites as among his admirations Antonioni, Bergman, Ray, and "in a lesser way" Ford, Kubrick, Wenders, Van Sant, and Malick.) *The Silence* sets John to thinking about women: "Sometimes I want a woman to push me like a strong wind; sometimes I want a woman to eat my shit." An easy prophecy of Yoko Ono, one may think at first, but second thoughts endorse its insight into Lennon's turbid psyche.

After an edgy conversation in a gay club with an aristocratic Spanish stockbroker and an ineffectual flirtation with a hotel bellboy, Brian takes a call from his mother in his room—a rhyme to John's call from his wife.

Strolling through a park, John photographs Brian holding a flower, but not without a dose of mockery ("Dandies love to pose") that causes Brian to ask, "How can you do this to me?" John's immediate response is "What choice have you but to let me?" This brutal exchange reminds us that Münch's title comes from love poetry that has been called masochistic:

> *Being your slave, what should I do but tend*
> *Upon the hours and times of your desire?*
> *I have no precious time at all to spend*
> *Nor services to do till you require.*

It is Shakespeare's Sonnet 57.

Back in the hotel, the whimsical John attempts a kindness. While Brian sleeps in a chair, John strips to enter a tub, sips a Scotch, and tootles on a harmonica by way of waking Brian and summoning him to "scrub me back." A lengthy, coolly unflinching shot of the tub shows an ungainly and misbegotten sexual fumble that, just as Brian heats up, John aborts by rising and leaving. Cut to close-up of John in a chair, sitting and smoking; Brian enters the frame, rear right, out of focus. With sphinxlike impassivity, John stares forward (as at *The Silence*). Brian: "Are you angry?" John: "No . . . don't pretend to know what I think." Brian: "And with that what never was is ended." The opaque beloved stays in tight focus; the anguished lover is blurred.

At this point occurs a welcome interruption, a visit from Marianne, the stewardess. As played by Pre-Raphaelite beauty Stephanie Pack, she turns out to be much more than a bird; she may be got up like a Sixties dolly, but she has the mind of a Nineties feminist. And the anachronism works well in the movie, giving John just what he needs.

As Marianne comes in, Brian pauses to kiss her on his way out, and she sees his ravaged face. When he leaves, she asks John: "You torment him, don't you?" "He torments himself. Maybe we torment each other," says John. She promptly assures the cocky rocker that "you don't torment *me*, but then again no one does. . . . I'd just as soon skip the whole ordeal [of marriage] and remain imbalanced and free." John suggests, in his patentedly provocative way, cunnilingus; Marianne counters by pulling out the latest Little Richard single, which John has not heard.

What follows is a minicatharsis for Lennon. The sexy music seems to dissolve what was bitter and brittle in him, to free him from demons. First, it makes him praise Brian, telling Marianne that, when the Beatles were opening for Little Richard, only "Brian understood Richard, Brian understands everybody besides himself." We get to see, as Lennon gets into the record, how he is irradiated by the music; it is Münch's inspired way of revealing the artist within the punk. He begins to move to the music, in rapt, jerky, lost movements that playfully allude to the twist, the monkey, and other stylized crazes of the hour. He urges her to join; she refuses; he reaches again; she consents. As they dance, they have a smooth, amused carnal harmony—the very opposite of that angular awkwardness in the tub.

And yet this easy passage with a woman does not work against John's closeness to Brian. After Marianne leaves, we see John trying to tie a Windsor knot in a mirror and engaging in an imaginary conversation with Brian about social graces ("I don't need to learn, you can tie it for me," he characteristically but now self-mockingly says to his imaginary Brian). In the lobby, he cheekily assures Brian he is looking forward to the bullfights with "all that pageantry and grace with pressure and so forth." What a brilliant writer Münch is!

On a bench, Brian makes John promise to meet him in ten years' time, "or at least remember it [the weekend]." As all reviewers pointed out, by 1973 Brian was dead and the Beatles over; this particular irony is perhaps a bit too obvious.

The scene fades to white—a punctuation mark used throughout the movie—and reveals Brian lying awake next to a sleeping John. As the two have separate rooms, we can draw our own conclusions. We hear bullfight noises and a classical seventeenth-century guitar piece that has been heard more than once before. Brian smiles, strokes John's arm, and walks out onto the hotel roof. This triggers a flashback to a rooftop in Liverpool early in Brian's friendship with John. On the roof of his parents' department store, Brian plies the youth with a lover's pleas: "You're not bored, are you? I never want to bore you. . . . These times we have together are very special to me, you know that? . . . You'll never leave me, will you?" John, tolerant and respectful, yet eludes the nets of Brianic entanglement and declares he's hungry.

Back in Barcelona, the two friends sit at an outdoor table before going to the bullfight. "We can always leave," suggests Brian. "And have a cigarette?" ambiguously answers John, in the film's last words.

"I had a dream I was a clown" was how John began the film, and we have observed the growth, precisely in the dream town to which Brian has introduced him, of a humility and compassion in him that may, it is implied, have had a sexual expression. Brian, intuitive, cultured, Jewish Brian, opens the city of Gaudi and Picasso (though it is only Matisse who is, in 1963, mentioned) to John, a brilliant pupil but a slippery customer—not to mention a genius. Poor sad Brian seems sentenced to tragedy. As fulfilled as he may be by this ecstatic moment out of time with John, he is unlikely to be able to come down from it when they return to the waking prose world of England. Heartbreak seems in store from John even at his kindest.

As it traces with extraordinary insight the boundaries of an intense friendship, *The Hours and Times* manages to be at once a case study of two exceptional individuals and a parable of more general suffering. In this sense alone, Münch earns his references to Bach, Bergman, and Shakespeare.

His next project, called *Color of a Brisk and Leaping Day* from an Octavio Paz poem, is about a young man, one-quarter Chinese and grandson of immigrant railroad workers, who buys a little railroad up near Yosemite to keep it from going out of business in the years after World War II. It is an original story that reflects Münch's lifelong interest in railroads. Although he has called it a combination of *Fitzcarraldo* with *Days of Heaven*, it seems more likely to be marked by Münch signatures: complete originality and the invigorating unpredictability of a fresh breeze at sea.

**J**ohn O'Brien's *Vermont Is for Lovers* (1992) places three fictional characters among real people playing themselves. O'Brien hails from the film's setting, Tunbridge, Vermont, where he was born and still helps to run his family's sheep farm. While a political science major at Harvard, he took a film course and began working with a friend on short documentaries about, for example, classmates. His first feature, codirected and cowritten with Harvard friend Gordon Eriksen, was *The Big Dis* (1989), about a soldier on a three-day leave looking to get laid but getting only dissed instead.

But O'Brien's real inventiveness surfaces in *Vermont Is for Lovers*. Although he loves the great silent comedians like Keaton and Chaplin and Lloyd, he has found their kind of life lacking in the Hollywood of the last generation. He knew, he told me, that his Vermont neighbors, people he has known all his life, were more interesting characters than what he was seeing at the multiplex. How to put them on screen, though, in an entertaining, non-documentary way—and in what had to be a small-budget film financed by family and neighbors? What he came up with was a fresh and funny mix of fiction and fact.

New York architect George (played by architect George Thrush, in reality an old boyfriend of O'Brien's sister) and his fiancée Marya (played by Marya Cohn, a Harvard fellow student and filmmaker) come to Vermont to get married at the sheep farm of Marya's aunt (played by Ann O'Brien, O'Brien's very own mother). On the eve of the big day, the lovers grow testy and quarrelsome. She has little patience with his absorption in covered bridges; he grows restless as her aunt prattles on about sheep. While distorted versions of "Old Macdonald Had a Farm" and "The Wedding March" play on the soundtrack, he has a tantrum about being unable to find a touch-tone phone to call his answering service in New York.

The film's relaxed structure then separates the lovers so

they can wander about the landscape talking to real local types about, above all, the pitfalls of marriage. George, in a self-deprecating and openhearted way, manages to loosen up, more or less, one Vermont interlocutor after another; a way of life begins to emerge. (The sense of the slow discovery of a culture recalls, of all things, *Daughters of the Dust*.)

The men George meets—they are all men and they are mostly either old themselves or associated with aged fathers—speak quietly and unemotionally of lifelong marriages lasting thirty or forty or fifty years or at least until the death of the spouse. These men, farmers mainly, grow more garrulous on the subject of the decline of the small farm and the snapping up of local land by vacationing city folk. One man in his nineties tells of courting in a sleigh before World War I; another lectures George on ''pre-Indian'' rock incisions lying about.

Marya, likewise, tries to gather wisdom from the locals: told by her aunt that one of the dogs on the farm is not only blind and retarded but psychic, Marya asks the dog about the prospects for her upcoming marriage. She, too, quizzes a spirited nonagenarian—a woman, this time—about the ups and downs of marriage. Her aunt brings out a pretty but intimidating family album of wedding snapshots.

George rises on the foggy dawn of his wedding day to watch the milking and the sheep shearing on the farm and to arrange a symbolic show of apology and reconciliation for his bride. After a secular exchange of vows on the lawn, various locals parade by with their animals:

oxen, ponies, rabbits, whatnot. It works; she is softened and gladly agrees to his compromise suggestion of Paris as a honeymoon site.

He actually blames their quarrel on Vermont: "The rural scene has brought out the worst in us; there wasn't enough noise here so we made our own noise; we need crime around us; up here the purity just magnifies our troubles." So Vermont is not for these lovers. George's verbal aria is a pleasing variation on what we had been suspecting was going to be clichéd schmaltz about rustic harmonies reconciling urban cacophonies. O'Brien's heart is probably more with his toughly unsentimental Vermonters than with the glibly self-justifying George, but a little superficial glibness has not come amiss.

O'Brien worked from a three-page story. All the dialogue was improvised, which was no problem for all those superbly weathered and rooted locals but was a challenge for the three actors—a challenge met well, be it said, and especially well by George Thrush.

*Vermont* is a deceptively intelligent and complex film in its balance of local and alien virtues and vices. O'Brien's is a very Vermont voice, with granite lurking beneath the green. His next film, *Man with a Plan*, filmed in 1992, takes one of the real locals from *Vermont Is for Lovers* and has him run an imaginary campaign for Congress around Tunbridge. There is indeed something of a Harold Lloyd and a gentler Preston Sturges lurking in John O'Brien.

# Conclusion

*T*he undercover cop in *Reservoir Dogs* tells a lying flash-back and then steps out of his lie within the flashback. The tribal voices of a Brooklyn street in *Do the Right Thing* pour forth paroxysms of stylized hate that somehow have a cathartic effect. Six talking porn magazine covers in *My Own Private Idaho* clarify the nexus between cash and sex. Parasoled women recline up a smooth tree in *Daughters of the Dust*. People meet in bookstores in the films of Hal Hartley and Richard Linklater.

These flashes of formalist brio that stud a few recent films are an index of ease with the medium. It is an ease at once playful and serious, self-referential but not self-indulgent. And behind technique is attitude. A compli-cated and adroit and ironic and passionate attitude to life so often emerges in the tones of these images and words.

There are recurring themes, too—like a centripetal nos-talgia for family counterpointed to a centrifugal itch for the road, like an anger at the failed American promise of education, like an insistence on cultural memory.

Many cameras are being turned on American life for the first time, or with a fresh urgency: those in the hands of women, African-American women, African-American men, Hispanics, Asians, openly gay and lesbian filmmakers.

But it would be absurd and insulting to attempt to make such a diversity of voices into a choir. What *is* common in new American filmmaking is an assumption that movies are any artist's prerogative to make. No longer need one submit to the mandarin cultural and craft rituals of the industry. Except as a cash machine, that industry is creatively as dead as the Manchus. Hollywood is as hollow as the Forbidden City (although chic winds of Cultural Revolution may blow from time to time through its empty temples).

There has been an irrevocable change in the weather of American movies. Local forecasts matter most now— those clouds above the backyard, the landscape of the dream, the heat of the street.

# Winners of the Independent Spirit Awards

The Independent Feature Project/West is a nonprofit membership organization dedicated to the support of the independent filmmaker and the spirit of independent films.

Founded in 1981 by a small number of independent filmmakers, its membership now numbers in the thousands. Among its activities are the Independent Film Market, held in New York in the fall and the publication of the excellent quarterly journal *Filmmaker*. The most visible of its projects is the Independent Spirit Awards awarded in March of each year, just before the Oscars, to celebrate the outstanding independent work of the preceding year. These awards have been given since the spring of 1986, when the awards celebrated the work of 1985.

## 1985

Best Feature: *After Hours*
Best Director (tie): Joel Coen, *Blood Simple;* Martin Scorsese, *After Hours*
Best Screenplay: Horton Foote, *The Trip to Bountiful*

Best Cinematographer: Toyomichi Kurita, *Trouble in Mind*
Best Actor: M. Emmet Walsh, *Blood Simple*
Best Actress: Geraldine Page, *The Trip to Bountiful*
Special Distinction (Foreign Film): *Kiss of the Spider Woman* (director, Hector Babenco)

## 1986

Best Feature: *Platoon*
Best First Feature: *She's Gotta Have It* (director, Spike Lee)
Best Director: Oliver Stone, *Platoon*
Best Screenplay: Oliver Stone, *Platoon*
Best Cinematographer: Bob Richardson, *Platoon*
Best Actor: James Woods, *Salvador*
Best Actress: Isabella Rossellini, *Blue Velvet*
Special Distinction (Foreign Film): *A Room with a View* (director, James Ivory)

## 1987

Best Feature: *River's Edge*
Best First Feature: *Dirty Dancing* (director, Emile Ardolino)
Best Director: John Huston, *The Dead*
Best Screenplay: Neal Jimenez, *River's Edge*
Best Cinematographer: Haskell Wexler, *Matewan*
Best Actor: Dennis Quaid, *The Big Easy*
Best Actress: Sally Kirkland, *Anna*
Best Supporting Actor: Morgan Freeman, *Street Smart*
Best Supporting Actress: Anjelica Huston, *The Dead*
Best Foreign Film: *My Life as a Dog* (director, Lasse Hallstrom)

## 1988

Best Feature: *Stand and Deliver*
Best First Feature: *Mystic Pizza* (director, Donald Petrie)

Best Director: Ramon Menendez, *Stand and Deliver*
Best Screenplay: Ramon Menendez and Tom Musca, *Stand and Deliver*
Best Cinematographer: Sven Nykvist, *The Unbearable Lightness of Being*
Best Actor: Edward James Olmos, *Stand and Deliver*
Best Actress: Jodie Foster, *Five Corners*
Best Supporting Actor: Lou Diamond Phillips, *Stand and Deliver*
Best Supporting Actress: Rosana De Soto, *Stand and Deliver*
Best Foreign Film: *Wings of Desire* (director, Wim Wenders)

**1989**
Best Feature: *Sex, Lies and Videotape*
Best First Feature: *Heathers* (director, Michael Lehmann)
Best Director: Steven Soderbergh, *Sex, Lies and Videotape*
Best Screenplay: Gus Van Sant and Daniel Yost, *Drugstore Cowboy*
Best Cinematographer: Robert Yeoman, *Drugstore Cowboy*
Best Actor: Matt Dillon, *Drugstore Cowboy*
Best Actress: Andie McDowell, *Sex, Lies and Videotape*
Best Supporting Actor: Max Perlich, *Drugstore Cowboy*
Best Supporting Actress: Laura San Giacomo, *Sex, Lies and Videotape*
Best Foreign Film: *My Left Foot* (director, Jim Sheridan)

**1990**
Best Feature: *The Grifters*
Best First Feature: *Metropolitan* (director, Whit Stillman)
Best Director: Charles Burnett, *To Sleep with Anger*
Best Screenplay: Charles Burnett, *To Sleep with Anger*
Best Cinematographer: Frederick Elmes, *Wild at Heart*
Best Actor: Danny Glover, *To Sleep with Anger*

Best Actress: Anjelica Huston, *The Grifters*
Best Supporting Actor: Bruce Davison, *Longtime Companion*
Best Supporting Actress: Sheryl Lee Ralph, *To Sleep with Anger*
Best Foreign Film: *Sweetie* (director, Jane Campion)

## 1991

Best Feature: *Rambling Rose*
Best First Feature: *Straight Out of Brooklyn* (director, Matty Rich)
Best Director: Martha Coolidge, *Rambling Rose*
Best Screenplay: Gus Van Sant, *My Own Private Idaho*
Best Cinematographer: Walt Lloyd, *Kafka*
Best Actor: River Phoenix, *My Own Private Idaho*
Best Actress: Judy Davis, *Impromptu*
Best Supporting Actor: David Strathairn, *City of Hope*
Best Supporting Actress: Diane Ladd, *Rambling Rose*
Best Film Music: *My Own Private Idaho*
Best Foreign Film: *An Angel at My Table* (director, Jane Campion)

## 1992

Best Feature: *The Player*
Best First Feature: *The Waterdance* (directors, Neal Jimenez and Michael Steinberg)
Best Director: Carl Franklin, *One False Move*
Best Screenplay: Neal Jimenez, *The Waterdance*
Best Cinematographer: Frederick Elmes, *Night on Earth*
Best Actor: Harvey Keitel, *Bad Lieutenant*
Best Actress: Fairuza Balk, *Gas Food Lodging*
Best Supporting Actor: Steve Buscemi, *Reservoir Dogs*
Best Supporting Actress: Alfre Woodard, *Passion Fish*
Best Original Score: Angelo Badalamenti, *Twin Peaks: Fire Walk with Me*
Best Foreign Film: *The Crying Game* (director, Neil Jordan)

# *F*ilmography of Directors

These filmographies cover the fictional feature-length works of directors discussed in the text. Many of these films are now available on video, and more are becoming so every day. Both large national video outlets and smaller, more specialized stores are increasingly responding to the growing audience for independent films. This availability is equally apparent in catalogues and guides for purchases of independent cinema on video.

## MICHAEL ALMEREYDA

**Twister** (1988)
Screenplay: Michael Almereyda, based on the novel *Oh!* by Mary Robison. Director of photography: Renato Berta.
CAST: Harry Dean Stanton, Suzy Amis, Crispin Glover, Dylan McDermott, Jenny Wright, Lois Chiles, Charlaine Woodard, William S. Burroughs, Lindsay Christman, Tim Robbins.

## Another Girl, Another Planet (1992)

Screenplay: Michael Almereyda; "Most of Nic's Dialogue": Nic Ratner. Director of photography: Jim Denault.

CAST: Nic Ratner, Barry Sherman, Mary Ward, Lisa Perisot, Maggie Rush, Paula Malcomson, Thomas Roma, Elina Löwensohn, Bob Gosse, Daisy.

## ALLISON ANDERS

## Gas Food Lodging (1992)

Screenplay: Allison Anders, based on a novel by Richard Peck. Director of photography: Dean Lent.

CAST: Brooke Adams, Ione Skye, Fairuza Balk, Donovan Leitch, James Brolin, Robert Knepper, David Lansbury, Jacob Vargas.

## GREGG ARAKI

## Three Bewildered People in the Night (1987)

Screenplay: Gregg Araki. Director of photography: Gregg Araki.

CAST: Darcy Marta, Mark Howell, John Lacques.

## The Long Weekend (o' Despair) (1989)

Screenplay: Gregg Araki. Director of photography: Gregg Araki.

CAST: Bretton Vail, Maureen Dondanville, Andrea Beane, Nicole Dillenberg, Marcus D'Amico, Lance Woods.

## The Living End (1992)

Screenplay: Gregg Araki. Director of photography: Gregg Araki.

CAST: Mike Dytri, Craig Gilmore, Mark Finch, Mary Woronov, Johanna Went, Darcy Marta, Scot Goetz.

## MARTIN BELL

**American Heart** (1993)
Screenplay: Peter Silverman, based on a story by Silverman and Martin Bell and Mary Ellen Mark. Director of photography: James R. Bagdonas.
CAST: Jeff Bridges, Edward Furlong, Lucinda Jenney, Tracy Kapisky, Don Harvey.

## KATHRYN BIGELOW

**The Loveless** (1983)
Codirected with Monty Montgomery. Screenplay: Kathryn Bigelow and Monty Montgomery. Director of photography: Doyle Smith.
CAST: Willem Dafoe, Robert Gordon, Marin Kanter, J. Don Ferguson, Tina L'Hotsky, Liz Gans.

**Near Dark** (1987)
Screenplay: Eric Reid and Kathryn Bigelow. Director of photography: Adam Greenberg.
CAST: Adrian Pasdar, Jenny Wright, Lance Henriksen, Bill Paxton, Joshua Miller, James LeGros, Jenette Goldstein, Tim Thomerson.

**Blue Steel** (1990)
Screenplay: Eric Reid and Kathryn Bigelow. Director of photography: Amir Mokri.
CAST: Jamie Lee Curtis, Ron Silver, Clancy Brown, Elizabeth Peña, Louise Fletcher, Philip Bosco.

**Point Break** (1991)
Screenplay: W. Peter Iliff; story: Rick King & W. Peter Iliff. Director of photography: Donald Peterman.

CAST: Patrick Swayze, Keanu Reeves, Gary Busey, Lori Petty, John McGinley, James LeGros, John Philbin, Bojesse Christopher, Julian Reyes, Sydney Walsh, Vincent Klin.

## CHARLES BURNETT

**Killer of Sheep** (1981)
Screenplay: Charles Burnett. Director of photography: Charles Burnett.
CAST: Henry Sanders, Kaycee Moore, Charles Bracy, Angela Barnett.

**My Brother's Wedding** (1984)
Screenplay: Charles Burnett. Director of photography: Charles Burnett.
CAST: Everett Silas, Jessie Holmes, Gaye Shannon-Burnett, Dennis Kemper, Ronnie Bell.

**To Sleep with Anger** (1990)
Screenplay: Charles Burnett. Director of photography: Walt Lloyd.
CAST: Danny Glover, Paul Butler, Mary Alice, Carl Lumbly, Vonetta McGee, Richard Brooks, Sheryl Lee Ralph, Ethel Ayler, Julius W. Harris, Sy Richardson, Davis Roberts, DeForest Coven, Jimmy Witherspoon.

## TONY CHAN

**Combination Platter** (1993)
Screenplay: Edwin Baker and Tony Chan. Director of photography: Yoshifumi Hosoya.
CAST: Jeff Lau, Colleen O'Brien, Lester "Chit-Man" Chan, Colin Mitchell, Kenneth Lu, Thomas K. Hsiung.

## STACY COCHRAN

### My New Gun (1992)
Screenplay: Stacy Cochran. Director of photography: Ed Lachman.
CAST: Diane Lane, James LeGros, Stephen Collins, Tess Harper, Bill Raymond.

## JOEL COEN

### Blood Simple (1984)
Screenplay: Ethan Coen and Joel Coen. Director of photography: Barry Sonnenfeld.
CAST: M. Emmet Walsh, John Getz, Frances McDormand, Dan Hedaya, Samm-Art Williams.

### Raising Arizona (1987)
Screenplay: Ethan Coen and Joel Coen. Director of photography: Barry Sonnenfeld.
CAST: Nicolas Cage, Holly Hunter, Trey Wilson, John Goodman, William Forsythe, Sam McMurray, Frances McDormand, Randall (Tex) Cobb, M. Emmet Walsh.

### Miller's Crossing (1990)
Screenplay: Ethan Coen and Joel Coen. Director of photography: Barry Sonnenfeld.
CAST: Gabriel Byrne, Albert Finney, Marcia Gay Harden, John Turturro, Jon Polito, J. E. Freeman, Mike Starr, Al Mancini, Michael Jeter.

### Barton Fink (1991)
Screenplay: Ethan Coen and Joel Coen. Director of photography: Roger Deakins.
CAST: John Turturro, John Goodman, Judy Davis, Michael

Lerner, John Mahoney, Tony Shalhoub, Jon Polito, Steve Buscemi, David Warrilow, Richard Portnow, Christopher Murney, Megan Faye, Isabelle Townsend.

## MARTHA COOLIDGE

### Valley Girl (1983)
Screenplay: Wayne Crawford and Andrew Lane. Director of photography: Frederick Elmes.
CAST: Nicolas Cage, Deborah Foreman, Colleen Camp, Frederic Forrest, Elizabeth Daily, Lee Purcell.

### The City Girl (1984)
Screenplay: Judith Thompson and Leonard-John Gates; story: John McDonald and Martha Coolidge. Director of photography: Daniel Hainey.
CAST: Laura Harrington, Joe Mastroianni, Carole McGill, Peter Riegert, Jim Carrington, Geraldine Baron, Colleen Camp.

### Joy of Sex (1984)
Screenplay: Kathleen Rowell and J. J. Salter, based on the book by Alex Comfort. Director of photography: Charles Correll.
CAST: Michelle Meyrink, Cameron Dye, Lisa Langlois, Charles Van Eman, Christopher Lloyd, Colleen Camp, Ernie Hudson.

### Real Genius (1985)
Screenplay: Neal Israel, Pat Proft, Peter Torokvei, based on a story by Neal Israel and Pat Proft. Director of photography: Vilmos Zsigmond.
CAST: Val Kilmer, Gabe Jarret, Michelle Meyrink, William Atherton, Jonathan Gries, Patti D'Arbanville.

**Plain Clothes** (1988)
Screenplay: A. Scott Frank, based on a story by A. Scott Frank and Dan Vining. Director of photography: Daniel Hainey.
CAST: Arliss Howard, Suzy Amis, George Wendt, Seymour Cassel, Abe Vigoda, Robert Stack, Harry Shearer.

**Rambling Rose** (1991)
Screenplay: Calder Willingham, based on his book. Director of photography: Johnny E. Jensen.
CAST: Laura Dern, Robert Duvall, Diane Ladd, Lukas Haas, John Heard, Kevin Conway, Robert Burke, Lisa Jakub, Evan Lockwood, Matt Sutherland.

**Lost in Yonkers** (1993)
Screenplay: Neil Simon, based on his play. Director of photography: Johnny E. Jensen.
CAST: Richard Dreyfuss, Mercedes Ruehl, Irene Worth, Brad Stoll, Mike Damus, Jack Laufer, David Strathairn, Susan Merson, Robert Miranda.

## DAVID CRONENBERG

**They Came from Within** (1976)
Screenplay: David Cronenberg. Director of photography: Robert Saad.
CAST: Paul Hampton, Joe Silver, Lynn Lowry, Allen Magicovsky, Barbara Steele, Susan Petrie.

**Rabid** (1977)
Screenplay: David Cronenberg. Director of photography: René Verzier.
CAST: Marilyn Chambers, Frank Moore, Joe Silver, Patricia Cage, Susan Roman.

**The Brood** (1979)

Screenplay: David Cronenberg. Director of photography: Mark Irwin.

CAST: Oliver Reed, Samantha Eggar, Art Hindle, Cindy Hinds.

**Scanners** (1981)

Screenplay: David Cronenberg. Director of photography: Mark Irwin.

CAST: Jennifer O'Neill, Stephen Lack, Patrick McGoohan, Lawrence Dane, Charles Shamata.

**Videodrome** (1983)

Screenplay: David Cronenberg. Director of photography: Mark Irwin.

CAST: James Woods, Sonja Smits, Deborah Harry, Peter Dvorsky, Les Carlson, Jack Creley, Lynne Gorman.

**The Dead Zone** (1983)

Screenplay: Jeffrey Boam, based on the novel by Stephen King. Director of photography: Mark Irwin.

CAST: Christopher Walken, Brooke Adams, Tom Skerritt, Herbert Lom, Anthony Zerbe, Colleen Dewhurst, Martin Sheen, Nicholas Campbell, Jackie Burroughs.

**The Fly** (1986)

Screenplay: David Cronenberg and Charles Edward Pogue, based on a story by George Langelaan. Director of photography: Mark Irwin.

CAST: Jeff Goldblum, Geena Davis, John Getz, Joy Boushel, Les Carlson.

**Dead Ringers** (1988)

Screenplay: David Cronenberg and Norman Snider, based on the book *Twins* by Bari Wood and Jack Geasland. Director of photography: Peter Suschitzky.

CAST: Jeremy Irons, Genevieve Bujold, Heidi von Palleske, Barbara Gordon, Shirley Douglas, Stephen Lack.

**Naked Lunch** (1991)
Screenplay: David Cronenberg, based on the book by William S. Burroughs. Director of photography: Peter Suschitzky.
CAST: Peter Weller, Judy Davis, Ian Holm, Julian Sands, Monique Mercure, Nicholas Campbell, Michael Zelniker, Joseph Scorsiani, Robert A. Silverman, Roy Scheider.

## JULIE DASH

**Daughters of the Dust** (1991)
Screenplay: Julie Dash. Director of photography: Arthur Jafa.
CAST: Cora Lee Day, Alva Rodgers, Adisa Anderson, Kaycee Moore, Barbara O, Eartha D. Robinson, Bahni Turpin, Cheryl Lee Bruce.

## TAMRA DAVIS

**Guncrazy** (1992)
Screenplay: Matthew Bright. Director of photography: Lisa Rinzler.
CAST: Drew Barrymore, James LeGros, Joe Dallesandro, Billy Drago, Robert Greenberg, Michael Ironside, Ione Skye, Rodney Harvey, Jeremy Davies, Dan Eisenstein, Jaid Barrymore.

**CB4** (1993)
Story: Chris Rock and Nelson George. Screenplay: Chris Rock, Nelson George, and Robert LoCash. Director of photography: Karl Walter Lindenlaub.
CAST: Chris Rock, Allen Payne, Deezer D., Chris Elliott, Phil Hartman, Charlie Murphy, Khandi Alexánder.

## TOM DICILLO

**Johnny Suede** (1991)
Screenplay: Tom DiCillo. Director of photography: Joe De Salvo.
CAST: Brad Pitt, Catherine Keener, Calvin Levels, Alison Moir, Nick Cave, Tina Louise.

## ERNEST R. DICKERSON

**Juice** (1992)
Screenplay: Gerard Brown and Ernest R. Dickerson; story: Ernest R. Dickerson. Director of photography: Larry Banks.
CAST: Omar Epps, Tupac Shakur, Jermaine Hopkins, Khalil Kain, Cindy Harren, Vincent Laresca, Samuel L. Jackson.

## ATOM EGOYAN

**Next of Kin** (1984)
Screenplay: Atom Egoyan. Director of photography: Peter Mettler.
CAST: Patrick Tierney, Berge Fazlian, Arsinée Khanjian, Sirvant Fazlian.

**Family Viewing** (1986)
Screenplay: Atom Egoyan. Director of photography: Robert MacDonald.
CAST: Aidan Tierney, David Hemblen, Garbrielle Rose, Arsinée Khanjian, Rose Sarkisyan, Jeanne Sabourin.

**Speaking Parts** (1989)
Screenplay: Atom Egoyan. Director of photography: Paul Sarossy.

cast: Michael McManus, Arsinée Khanjian, Gabrielle Rose, David Hemblen, Patricia Collins, Frank Tata.

## The Adjuster (1991)

Screenplay: Atom Egoyan. Director of photography: Paul Sarossy.

cast: Elias Koteas, Arsinée Khanjian, Maury Chaykin, Gabrielle Rose, Jennifer Dale, David Hemblen, Rose Sarkisyan, Armen Kokorian, Jacqueline Samuda, Gerard Parkes, Patricia Collins, Don McKellar, John Gilbert, Stephen Ouimette, Raoul Trujillo, Tony Nardi.

## ABEL FERRARA

## The Driller Killer (1979)

Screenplay: Abel Ferrara. Director of photography: Ken Kelsch.

cast: Carolyn Marz, Jimmy Laine, Baybi Day, Bob DeFrank, Peter Yellen.

## Ms. 45 (1981)

Screenplay: Nicholas St. John. Director of photography: James Momel.

cast: Zoe Tamerlis, Steve Singer, Jack Thibeau, Peter Yellen, Darlene Stuto, Editta Sherman, Albert Sinkys, Jimmy Laine.

## Fear City (1984)

Screenplay: Nicholas St. John. Director of photography: James Lemmo.

cast: Tom Berenger, Billy Dee Williams, Jack Scalia, Melanie Griffith, Rossano Brazzi, Rae Dawn Chong, Joe Santos, Michael V. Gazzo, Jan Murray, Ola Ray, Maria Conchita Alonso.

**China Girl** (1987)

Screenplay: Nicholas St. John. Director of photography: Bojan Bazelli.

CAST: James Russo, Richard Panebianco, Sari Chang, David Caruso, Russell Wong, Joey Chin, James Hong.

**Cat Chaser** (1989)

Screenplay: James Borrelli and Elmore Leonard, from the novel by Elmore Leonard. Director of photography: Anthony Richmond.

CAST: Peter Weller, Kelly McGillis, Charles Durning, Frederic Forrest, Thomas Milian, Juan Fernandez.

**King of New York** (1990)

Screenplay: Nicholas St. John. Director of photography: Bojan Bazelli.

CAST: Christopher Walken, David Caruso, Larry Fishburne, Wesley Snipes, Victor Argo, Janet Julian, Joey Chin, Steve Buscemi, Giancarlo Esposito.

**Bad Lieutenant** (1992)

Screenplay: Zoe Lund and Abel Ferrara. Director of photography: Ken Kelsch.

CAST: Harvey Keitel, Victor Argo, Frankie Thorn, Zoe Tamerlaine Lund, Paul Calderone, Leonard Thomas, Robin Burrows, Victoria Bastel, Paul Hipp, Eddie Daniels, Bianca Bakija.

**Body Snatchers** (1993)

Screenplay: Stuart Gordon, Dennis Paoli, Nicholas St. John; story: Raymond Cistheri and Larry Cohen, based on the novel by Jack Finney. Director of photography: Bojan Bazelli.

CAST: Gabrielle Anwar, Terry Kinney, Billy Wirth, Meg Tilly, Forest Whitaker, Christine Elise, R. Lee Ermey, Reilly Murphy, G. Elvis Phillips, Kathleen Doyle.

## JAMES FOLEY

**Reckless** (1984)
Screenplay: Chris Columbus. Director of photography: Michael Ballhaus.
CAST: Aidan Quinn, Darryl Hannah, Kenneth McMillan, Cliff De Young, Lois Smith, Adam Baldwin, Dan Hedaya, Jennifer Grey.

**At Close Range** (1986)
Screenplay: Nicholas Kazan, based on a story by Elliot Lewitt and Nicholas Kazan. Director of photography: Juan Ruiz Anchia.
CAST: Sean Penn, Christopher Walken, Christopher Penn, Mary Stuart Masterson, Millie Perkins, Eileen Ryan, Candy Clark, David Strathairn, Crispin Glover, Kiefer Sutherland.

**Who's That Girl?** (1987)
Screenplay: Andrew Smith and Ken Finkleman, based on a story by Andrew Smith. Director of photography: Jan De Bont.
CAST: Madonna, Griffin Dunne, Haviland Morris, John McMartin, Robert Swan, Drew Pillsbury, John Mills.

**After Dark, My Sweet** (1990)
Screenplay: James Foley and Robert Redlin, based on the novel by Jim Thompson. Director of photography: Mark Plummer.
CAST: Jason Patric, Rachel Ward, Bruce Dern, George Dickerson, James Cotton, Rocky Giordani, Corey Carrier.

**Glengarry Glen Ross** (1992)
Screenplay: David Mamet, based on his play. Director of photography: Juan Ruiz Anchia.
CAST: Al Pacino, Jack Lemmon, Alec Baldwin, Ed Harris, Alan Arkin, Kevin Spacey, Jonathan Pryce.

## CARL FRANKLIN

### Eye of the Eagle II: Inside the Enemy (1988)
Screenplay: Carl Franklin and Dan Gagliasso, from a story by Carl Franklin. Director of photography: Christopher Jones Lobo.
CAST: William (Todd) Field, Andy Wood, Ken Jacobson, Ronald William Lawrence, Shirley Tesoro.

### Nowhere to Run (1989)
Screenplay: Jack Canson and Nancy Barr, based on a story by Jack Canson. Director of photography: Phedon Papamichael.
CAST: David Carradine, Jason Priestley, Jillian McWhirter, Kieran Mulroney, Henry Jones.

### Full Fathom Five (1991)
Screenplay: Bart Davis, based on the novel by Brad Davis.
CAST: Michael Moriarty, Maria Rangel, Daniel Faraldo, John LaFayette, Michael Cavanaugh, Todd Field, Orlando Sacha.

### One False Move (1992)
Screenplay: Billy Bob Thornton and Tom Epperson. Director of photography: James L. Carter.
CAST: Bill Paxton, Cynda Williams, Billy Bob Thornton, Michael Beach, Jim Metzler, Earl Billings, Natalie Canerday, Robert Ginnaven, Robert Anthony Bell, Kevin Hunter, Phyllis Kirklin, Meredith "Jeta" Donovan, James D. Bridges, Phyllis Sutton, Derrick Williams, June Jones, Loren Tyler.

## NICK GOMEZ

### Laws of Gravity (1992)
Screenplay: Nick Gomez. Director of photography: Jean de Segonzac.

CAST: Peter Greene, Adam Trese, Edie Falco, Arabelle Field, Paul Schulze, Saul Stein, Tony Fernandez, Larry Maistrich.

## PHILIP HAAS

**The Music of Chance** (1993)
Screenplay: Philip Haas and Belinda Haas, based on the novel by Paul Auster. Director of photography: Bernard Zitzermann.
CAST: James Spader, Mandy Patinkin, M. Emmet Walsh, Charles Durning, Joel Grey, Samantha Mathis, Christopher Penn.

## LESLIE HARRIS

**Just Another Girl on the I.R.T.** (1993)
Screenplay: Leslie Harris. Director of photography: Richard Connors.
CAST: Ariyan Johnson, Kevin Thigpen, Ebony Jerido, Chequita Jackson, William Badget, Jerard Washington, Karen Robinson, Tony Wilkes.

## HAL HARTLEY

**The Unbelievable Truth** (1989)
Screenplay: Hal Hartley. Director of photography: Michael Spiller.
CAST: Adrienne Shelly, Robert Burke, Christopher Cooke, Julia McNeal, Mark Chandler Bailey, Gary Sauer, Katherine Mayfield, David Healy, Matt Malloy, Edie Falco, William Sage, Jeff Howard.

**Trust** (1991)

Screenplay: Hal Hartley. Director of photography: Michael Spiller.

CAST: Adrienne Shelly, Martin Donovan, Rebecca Nelson, John MacKay, Edie Falco, Marko Hunt, Gary Sauer, Matt Malloy, Karen Sillas, Mark Chandler Bailey, Thom Thon, Susanne Costollos, Jeff Howard, Patricia Sullivan, William Sage, Julie Sukman, Christopher Cooke, John St. James, Robbie Anderson, Bea Delizio, Kathryn Mederos.

**Surviving Desire** (1991)

Screenplay: Hal Hartley. Director of photography: Michael Spiller.

CAST: Martin Donovan, Matt Malloy, Rebecca Nelson, Julie Sukman, Mary Ward.

**Simple Men** (1992)

Screenplay: Hal Hartley. Director of photography: Michael Spiller.

CAST: Robert Burke, William Sage, Karen Sillas, Elina Löwensohn, Martin Donovan, Mark Chandler Bailey, Christopher Cooke, Jeffrey Howard, Holly Marie Combs, Joe Stevens, Damian Young, Marietta Marich, John Alexander MacKay, Bethany Wright, Matt Malloy.

## TODD HAYNES

**Poison** (1991)

Screenplay: Todd Haynes. Director of photography: Maryse Alberti.

"HERO" CAST: Edith Meeks, Millie White, Buck Smith, Anne Giotta, Lydia LaFleur, Ian Nemser, Rob LaBelle, Evan Dunsky, Marina Lutz.

"HORROR" CAST: Larry Maxwell, Susan Norman, Al Quagliata, Michelle Sullivan, Parlan McGaw, Frank O'Donnell.

"HOMO" CAST: Scott Renderer, James Lyons, John R. Lombardi.

## ALLEN & ALBERT HUGHES

### Menace II Society (1993)

Screenplay: Tyger Williams, from a story by Allan and Albert Hughes and Tyger Williams. Director of photography: Lisa Rinzler.

CAST: Tyrin Turner, Jada Pinkett, Bill Duke, Charles S. Dutton, Samuel L. Jackson, Larenz Tate, Glenn Plummer, Vonte Sweet, Ryan Williams.

## JIM JARMUSCH

### Permanent Vacation (1980)

Screenplay: Jim Jarmusch. Director of photography: James A. Lebovitz and Tom DiCillo.

CAST: Chris Parker, Leila Gastil, Maria Duval, Ruth Bolton, Richard Boes, John Lurie, Frankie Fason, Sara Driver, Jane Fire.

### Stranger Than Paradise (1984)

Screenplay: Jim Jarmusch. Director of photography: Tom DiCillo.

CAST: John Lurie, Eszter Balint, Richard Edson, Cecillia Stark, Danny Rosen, Tom DiCillo.

### Down by Law (1986)

Screenplay: Jim Jarmusch. Director of photography: Robby Müller.

CAST: Tom Waits, John Lurie, Roberto Benigni, Ellen Barkin,

Billie Neal, Rockets Redglare, Vernel Bagneris, Nicoletta Braschi.

**Mystery Train** (1989)
Screenplay: Jim Jarmusch. Director of photography: Robby Muller.
"FAR FROM YOKOHAMA" CAST: Masatoshi Nagase, Youki Kudoh, Screamin' Jay Hawkins, Cinque Lee, Rufus Thomas.
"A GHOST" CAST: Nicoletta Braschi, Elizabeth Bracco.
"LOST IN SPACE" CAST: Rick Aviles, Joe Strummer, Steve Buscemi.

**Night on Earth** (1991)
Screenplay: Jim Jarmusch. Director of photography: Frederick Elmes.
"LOS ANGELES" CAST: Winona Ryder, Gena Rowlands.
"NEW YORK" CAST: Giancarlo Esposito, Armin Muller-Stahl, Rosie Perez.
"PARIS" CAST: Isaach De Bankole, Beatrice Dalle.
"ROME" CAST: Roberto Benigni, Paolo Bonacelli.
"HELSINKI" CAST: Matti Pellonpaa, Kari Vaananen, Saku Kuosmanen, Tomi Salmela.

## NEAL JIMENEZ

**The Waterdance** (1992)
Codirected with Michael Steinberg. Screenplay: Neal Jimenez. Director of photography: Mark Plummer.
CAST: Eric Stoltz, Wesley Snipes, William Forsythe, Helen Hunt, Elizabeth Peña.

## TOM KALIN

**Swoon** (1992)
Screenplay: Tom Kalin. Director of photography: Ellen Kuras.
CAST: Daniel Schlachet, Craig Chester, Ron Vawter, Michael Kirby, Michael Stumm, Robert Read, Paul Schmidt.

## SPIKE LEE

**She's Gotta Have It** (1986)
Screenplay: Spike Lee. Director of photography: Ernest R. Dickerson.
CAST: Tracy Camilla Johns, Tommy Redmond Hicks, John Canada Terrell, Spike Lee, Raye Dowell, Bill Lee, Joie Lee.

**School Daze** (1988)
Screenplay: Spike Lee. Director of photography: Ernest R. Dickerson.
CAST: Larry Fishburne, Giancarlo Esposito, Spike Lee, Tisha Campbell, Joie Lee, Bill Nunn, Ossie Davis, Kyme, Joe Seneca, Samuel L. Jackson, Art Evans, Ellen Holly, Branford Marsalis, Kadeem Hardison, Darryl M. Bell, Jasmine Guy, Angela Ail.

**Do the Right Thing** (1989)
Screenplay: Spike Lee. Director of photography: Ernest R. Dickerson.
CAST: Spike Lee, Danny Aiello, Ossie Davis, Ruby Dee, John Turturro, Richard Edson, Giancarlo Esposito, Bill Nunn, Paul Benjamin, John Savage, Rosie Perez, Joie Lee.

**Mo' Better Blues** (1990)
Screenplay: Spike Lee. Director of photography: Ernest R. Dickerson.
CAST: Denzel Washington, Spike Lee, Wesley Snipes, Giancarlo

Esposito, Robin Harris, Joie Lee, Bill Nunn, John Turturro, Dick Anthony Williams, Cynda Williams, Nicholas Turturro, Ruben Blades, Abbey Lincoln.

**Jungle Fever** (1991)
Screenplay: Spike Lee. Director of photography: Ernest R. Dickerson.
CAST: Wesley Snipes, Annabella Sciorra, Spike Lee, Ossie Davis, Ruby Dee, Samuel L. Jackson, Lonette McKee, John Turturro, Frank Vincent, Anthony Quinn, Halle Berry, Tyra Ferrell, Veronica Webb, Tim Robbins, Brad Dourif.

**Malcolm X** (1992)
Screenplay: Arnold Perl and Spike Lee, based on the book *The Autobiography of Malcolm X* as told to Alex Haley. Director of photography: Ernest R. Dickerson.
CAST: Denzel Washington, Angela Bassett, Spike Lee, Al Freeman, Jr., Delroy Lindo, Carl Lumbly, Albert Hall, Theresa Randle, Kate Vernon, Lonette McKee, Tommy Hollis, James McDaniel, Ernest Thompson, Jean Lamarre, Bobby Seale, Al Sharpton, Christopher Plummer, Karen Allen, Peter Boyles, William Kunstler, John Sayles, Nelson Mandela.

### MICHAEL LEHMANN

**Heathers** (1989)
Screenplay: Daniel Waters. Director of photography: Francis Kenney.
CAST: Winona Ryder, Christian Slater, Shannen Doherty, Lisanne Falk, Kim Walker, Penelope Milford, Glenn Shaddix, Lance Fenton.

### Meet the Applegates (1991)

Screenplay: Michael Lehmann and Redbeard Simmons. Director of photography: Mitchell Dubin.
CAST: Ed Begley, Jr., Stockard Channing, Dabney Coleman, Cami Cooper, Bobby Jacoby, Glenn Shaddix.

### Hudson Hawk (1991)

Screenplay: Steven E. DeSouza and Daniel Waters, from a story by Robert Kraft and Bruce Willis. Director of photography: Dante Spinotti.
CAST: Bruce Willis, Danny Aiello, Andie MacDowell, James Coburn, Richard E. Grant, Sandra Bernhard, David Caruso.

## RICHARD LINKLATER

### Slacker (1991)

Screenplay: Richard Linklater. Director of photography: Lee Daniel.
CAST: 97 local residents.

### Dazed and Confused (1993)

Screenplay: Richard Linklater. Director of photography: Lee Daniel.
CAST: Jason London, Michelle Burke, Wiley Wiggins, Anthony Rapp, Adam Goldberg, Marissa Ribisi, Milla Jovovich, Cole Hauser, Christin Hinojosa, Matthew McConaughey.

## DAVID LYNCH

### Eraserhead (1978)

Screenplay: David Lynch. Directors of photography: Frederick Elmes and Herbert Cardwell.
CAST: Jack Nance, Charlotte Stewart, Allen Joseph, Jeanne Bates, Judith Anna Roberts, Laurel Near, V. Phipps-Wilson.

**The Elephant Man** (1980)

Screenplay: Christopher DeVore, Eric Bergren, and David Lynch, based on *The Elephant Man: A Study in Human Dignity* by Ashley Montagu and *The Elephant Man and Other Reminiscences* by Sir Frederick Treves. Director of photography: Freddie Francis.

CAST: Anthony Hopkins, John Hurt, Anne Bancroft, John Gielgud, Wendy Hiller, Freddie Jones.

**Dune** (1984)

Screenplay: David Lynch, Eric Bergren, and Christopher DeVore, based on the novel by Frank Herbert. Director of photography: Freddie Francis.

CAST: Kyle MacLachlan, Francesca Annis, Brad Dourif, José Ferrer, Linda Hunt, Freddie Jones, Richard Jordan, Virginia Madsen, Silvana Mangano, Kenneth McMillan, Jack Nance, Sian Phillips, Sting, Dean Stockwell, Max Von Sydow, Patrick Stewart, Sean Young.

**Blue Velvet** (1986)

Screenplay: David Lynch. Director of photography: Frederick Elmes.

CAST: Kyle MacLachlan, Laura Dern, Isabella Rossellini, Dennis Hopper, Hope Lange, Dean Stockwell, Jack Nance, Brad Dourif.

**Twin Peaks** (1989)

Screenplay: David Lynch and Mark Frost. Director of photography: Ron Garcia.

CAST: Kyle MacLachlan, Michael Ontkean, Joan Chen, Richard Beymer, Peggy Lipton, Jack Nance, Piper Laurie, Russ Tamblyn, Sheryl Lee, Sherilyn Fenn, Lara Flynn Boyle, James Marshall, Dana Ashbrook.

**Wild at Heart** (1990)
Screenplay: David Lynch, based on the novel by Barry Gifford.
Director of photography: Frederick Elmes.
CAST: Nicolas Cage, Laura Dern, Diane Ladd, Willem Dafoe, Isabella Rossellini, Harry Dean Stanton, Crispin Glover, Grace Zabriskie, J. E. Freeman, Calvin Lockhart, Freddie Jones, John Lurie, Jack Nance, Sherilyn Fenn, Sheryl Lee.

**Twin Peaks: Fire Walk with Me** (1992)
Screenplay: David Lynch and Robert Engels. Director of photography: Ron Garcia.
CAST: Kyle MacLachlan, Sheryl Lee, Moira Kelly, David Bowie, Chris Isaak, Harry Dean Stanton, Ray Wise, Kiefer Sutherland, Peggy Lipton.

### JOHN MCNAUGHTON

**Henry: Portrait of a Serial Killer** (1990, filmed in 1986)
Screenplay: Richard Fire and John McNaughton. Director of photography: Charlie Lieberman.
CAST: Michael Rooker, Tracy Arnold, Tom Towles.

**The Borrower** (1991)
Screenplay: Mason Nage and Richard Fire, from a story by Mason Nage. Directors of photography: Julio Macat, Robert New.
CAST: Rae Dawn Chong, Don Gordon, Antonio Fargas, Tom Towles, Neil Giuntoli, Pam Gordon, Madchen Amick, Tony Amendola, Robert Dryer, Richard Wharton, Bentley Mitchum.

**Sex, Drugs, Rock & Roll** (1991)
Screenplay: Eric Bogosian. Director of photography: Ernest R. Dickerson.
CAST: Eric Bogosian.

## Mad Dog and Glory (1993)
Screenplay: Richard Price. Director of photography: Robby Müller.

CAST: Robert De Niro, Bill Murray, Uma Thurman, Kathy Baker, David Caruso, Mike Starr, Tom Towles.

### PAUL MORRISSEY

## Civilization and Its Discontents (1962)
Screenplay: Paul Morrissey. Director of photography: Paul Morrissey.

CAST: Jared Martin, Pierre Blanchard, Larry McGinn, Jennifer Salt.

## Chelsea Girls (1967)
Screenplay: Paul Morrissey. Director of photography: Paul Morrissey.

CAST: Nico, Ondine, Gerard Malanga, Bridget Berlin, Eric Emerson, Mary Woronov, International Velvet, Ed Hood, Patrick Fleming.

## I A Man (1967)
Screenplay: Paul Morrissey. Director of photography: Paul Morrissey.

CAST: Tom Baker, Nico.

## Bike Boy (1967)
Screenplay: Paul Morrissey. Director of photography: Paul Morrissey.

CAST: Joe Spencer, Viva, Vera Cruz, Bridget Berlin, Ed Hood.

## Lonesome Cowboys (1968)
Screenplay: Paul Morrisey. Director of photography: Paul Morrissey.

CAST: Tom Hompertz, Viva, Taylor Mead, Eric Emerson, Joe Dallesandro, Francis Francine, Julian Burroughs.

**San Diego Surf** (1968, unreleased)
Screenplay: Paul Morrissey. Director of photography: Paul Morrissey.
CAST: Tom Hompertz, Viva, Joe Dallesandro, Taylor Mead.

**Flesh** (1968)
Screenplay: Paul Morrissey. Director of photography: Paul Morrissey.
CAST: Joe Dallesandro, Geraldine Smith, Patti D'Arbanville, Candy Darling, Jackie Curtis, Geri Miller, Maurice Braddell, Jennifer Roberts.

**Trash** (1970)
Screenplay: Paul Morrissey. Director of photography: Paul Morrissey.
CAST: Joe Dallesandro, Holly Woodlawn, Jane Forth, Geri Miller, Andrea Feldman, Michael Sklar, Bruce Pecheur.

**Heat** (1972)
Screenplay: Paul Morrissey. Director of photography: Paul Morrissey.
CAST: Sylvia Miles, Joe Dallesandro, Andrea Feldman, Pat Ast, Ray Vestal, Lester Persky.

**L'Amour** (1972)
Screenplay: Paul Morrissey. Director of photography: Paul Morrissey.
CAST: Jane Forth, Michael Sklar, Donna Jordan, Max Delys, Patti D'Arbanville, Karl Lagerfeld.

### Women in Revolt (1972)

Screenplay: Paul Morrissey. Director of photography: Paul Morrissey.

CAST: Candy Darling, Jackie Curtis, Holly Woodlawn.

### Flesh for Frankenstein (1974, a.k.a. *Andy Warhol's Frankenstein*)

Screenplay: Paul Morrissey. Director of photography: Luigi Kuveiller.

CAST: Joe Dallesandro, Monique Van Vooren, Udo Keir, Dalila Di Lazzaro, Srdjan Zelenovic.

### Blood for Dracula (1974, a.k.a. *Andy Warhol's Dracula)*

Screenplay: Paul Morrissey. Director of photography: Luigi Kuveiller.

CAST: Joe Dallesandro, Udo Keir, Vittorio De Sica, Maxime McKendry, Roman Polanski, Arno Juerging.

### The Hound of the Baskervilles (1977)

Screenplay: Peter Cook, Dudley Moore, and Paul Morrissey, based on the novel by Arthur Conan Doyle. Directors of photography: Dick Busch, John Wilcox.

CAST: Peter Cook, Dudley Moore, Denholm Elliott, Joan Greenwood, Terry-Thomas, Max Wall, Irene Handl, Kenneth Williams, Hugh Griffith, Prunella Scales, Spike Milligan, Penelope Keith.

### Madame Wang's (1981)

Screenplay: Paul Morrissey. Director of photography: Juan Drago.

CAST: Patrick Schoene, Christina Indri, Paul Ambrose, Jack Simmons, William Eggar, Ronald Levin, Susan Blond, John Emerson.

**Forty Deuce** (1982)
Screenplay: Alan Bowne, based on his play. Directors of photography: François Reichenbach, Stefan Zapasnik, and Steven Fierberg.
CAST: Orson Bean, Kevin Bacon, Mark Keyloun, Harris Laskaway, Tommy Citera, John Anthony, Carol Jean Lewis, Esai Morales.

**Beethoven's Nephew** (1984)
Screenplay: Paul Morrissey and Mathieu Carrière, based on a novel by Luigi Magnani. Director of photography: Hanus Polak.
CAST: Wolfgang Reichmann, Dietmar Prinz, Jane Birkin, Nathalie Baye, Mathieu Carrière, Ulrich Beer.

**Mixed Blood** (1985)
Screenplay: Paul Morrissey and Alan Bowne. Director of photography: Stefan Zapasnik.
CAST: Marilia Pera, Richard Ulacia, Linda Kerridge, Geraldine Smith, Angel David, Ulrich Beer, Rodney Harvey.

**Spike of Bensonhurst** (1988)
Screenplay: Paul Morrissey and Alan Bowne. Director of photography: Steven Fierberg.
CAST: Sasha Mitchell, Ernest Borgnine, Anne DeSalvo, Sylvia Miles, Geraldine Smith, Maria Pitillo, Talisa Soto, Rick Aviles, Antonio Rey, Justin Lazard, Rodney Harvey.

### CHRISTOPHER MÜNCH

**Goldenoise** (1985, uncompleted)
Screenplay: Christopher Münch. Directors of photography: Christopher Münch, William H. Neal.

CAST: Clement Von Franckenstein, Joan Day Dykman, Scott Sacks, David Paul Jensen, Albert Lord, Mary Kahl, Michael Hewitson, Tom Challis.

**In Laura's Garden** (1987)
Screenplay: Christopher Münch. Director of photography: Christopher Münch.
CAST: Tom Challis, Lynn-Holly Johnson, Scott Valentine, Nina Ninette Perilise, Richard Brandes, Jessica St. John, Michael Hewitson, Lucile Bissiri, Joan Day Dykman.

**The Hours and Times** (1991)
Screenplay: Christopher Münch. Director of photography: Christopher Münch.
CAST: David Angus, Ian Hart, Stephanie Pack, Robin McDonald, Sergio Moreno, Unity Grimwood.

### VICTOR NUÑEZ

**Gal Young 'Un** (1980)
Screenplay: Victor Nuñez. Director of photography: Victor Nuñez.
CAST: Dana Preu, David Peck, J. Smith, Gene Densmore, Jenny Stringfellow, Tim McCormick.

**A Flash of Green** (1984)
Screenplay: Victor Nuñez, based on the book by John D. MacDonald. Directors of photography: Victor Nuñez, Gus Holzer.
CAST: Ed Harris, Blair Brown, Richard Jordan, George Coe, Joan Goodfellow, Jean De Baer, Helen Stenborg, William Mooney, Isa Thomas, Bob Murch, John Glover, Joan MacIntosh, Bob Harris, Nancy Griggs, Linda Lee Larsen, Michael Doyle, Joe Carioth, Maggie Beistle, Maggie Klekas, Gregory Jones, Brad Wallace.

**Ruby in Paradise** (1993)
Screenplay: Victor Nuñez. Director of photography: Alex Vlacos.
CAST: Ashley Judd, Todd Field, Bentley Mitchum, Allison Dean, Dorothy Lyman, Betsy Douds, Felicia Hernandez, Divya Satia, Bobby Barnes.

## JOHN O'BRIEN

**The Big Dis** (1989)
Codirected with Gordon Eriksen. Screenplay: Gordon Eriksen and John O'Brien. Director of photography: John O'Brien.
CAST: James Haig, Kevin Haig.

**Vermont Is for Lovers** (1992)
Story: John O'Brien. Screenplay: "Cast improvisation." Director of photography: John O'Brien.
CAST: George Thrush, Marya Cohn, Ann O'Brien, Euclid Farnham, Jeremiah and Dan Mullen, Edgar Dodge, George and Alan Lyford, Robert Button, Joe and Fred Tuttle, Gladys Noyes, and 41 other Vermonters.

## SEAN PENN

**The Indian Runner** (1991)
Screenplay: Sean Penn. Director of photography: Anthony B. Richmond.
CAST: David Morse, Viggo Mortensen, Valeria Golino, Patricia Arquette, Charles Bronson, Sandy Dennis, Dennis Hopper, Jordan Rhodes, Enzo Rossi, Harry Crews, Eileen Ryan.

## NORMAN RENÉ

**Longtime Companion** (1990)
Screenplay: Craig Lucas. Director of photography: Tony Jannelli.
CAST: Bruce Davison, Campbell Scott, Stephen Caffrey, Mark Lamos, Patrick Cassidy, Mary-Louise Parker, John Dossett, Brian Cousins, Dermot Mulroney, Brad O'Hara, Michael Schoeffling.

**Prelude to a Kiss** (1992)
Screenplay: Craig Lucas, based on his play. Director of photography: Stefan Czapsky.
CAST: Alec Baldwin, Meg Ryan, Kathy Bates, Ned Beatty, Patty Duke, Stanley Tucci, Sydney Walker, Rocky Carroll, Debra Monk, Ray Gill.

## MATTY RICH

**Straight Out of Brooklyn** (1991)
Screenplay: Matty Rich. Director of photography: John Rosnell.
CAST: George T. Odom, Ann D. Sanders, Lawrence Gilliard, Jr., Reana E. Drummond, Barbara Sanon, Mark Malone, Matty Rich.

## TIM ROBBINS

**Bob Roberts** (1992)
Screenplay: Tim Robbins. Director of photography: Jean Lepine.
CAST: Tim Robbins, Giancarlo Esposito, Ray Wise, Brian Murray, Gore Vidal, Rebecca Jenkins, Harry J. Lennix, John Ot-

tavino, Kelly Willis, Susan Sarandon, James Spader, Alan Rickman, Fred Ward, Peter Gallagher, Helen Hunt, Anita Gillette, Jack Black.

## MARC ROCCO

### Scenes from the Goldmine (1987)

Screenplay: John Norvet, Danny Eisenberg, and Marc Rocco. Director of photography: Cliff Ralke.

CAST: Catherine Mary Stewart, Cameron Dye, Steve Railsback, Joe Pantoliano, Lesley-Anne Down.

### Dream a Little Dream (1989)

Screenplay: Daniel Jay Franklin, D. E. Eisenberg, and Marc Rocco. Director of photography: King Baggot.

CAST: Jason Robards, Jr., Corey Feldman, Meredith Salenger, Piper Laurie, Harry Dean Stanton, William McNamara, Corey Haim, Susan Blakely.

### Where the Day Takes You (1992)

Screenplay: Michael Hitchcock, Kurt Voss, and Mark Rocco. Director of photography: King Baggot.

CAST: Sean Astin, Lara Flynn Boyle, Peter Dobson, Balthazar Getty, Ricki Lake, James LeGros, Dermot Mulroney, Will Smith, Kyle MacLachlan, Adam Baldwin, Rachel Ticotin, Laura San Giacomo, Alyssa Milano, Christian Slater.

## ALEXANDRE ROCKWELL

### Lenz (1981)

Screenplay: Alexandre Rockwell, based on the work by Georg Buchner. Directors of photography: Eugene Lynch and Alexandre Rockwell.

CAST: William Frederick Maher, Alexandre Rockwell, Kim Mariet Radonovich.

**Hero** (1983)
Screenplay: Alexandre Rockwell. Directors of photography: Robert Yeoman and Alexandre Rockwell.
CAST: Paul Rockwell, Kim Flowers, Mika Yamada, Cody Maher, Willie "Bluehouse" Johnson.

**Sons** (1989)
Screenplay: Alexandre Rockwell and Brandon Cole. Director of photography: Stefan Czapsky.
CAST: William Forsythe, D. B. Sweeney, Robert Miranda, Samuel Fuller, Stephane Audran, Judith Godreche, Bernard Fresson, Jennifer Beals, Shirley Stoler, William Hickey.

**In the Soup** (1992)
Screenplay: Alexandre Rockwell and Tim Kissel. Director of photography: Phil Parmet.
CAST: Steve Buscemi, Seymour Cassel, Jennifer Beals, Pat Moya, Will Paton, Sully Boyer, Steven Randazzo, Francesco Messina, Jim Jarmusch, Carol Kane, Stanley Tucci, Rockets Redglare, Elizabeth Bracco, Debi Mazar, Ruth Maleczech.

## ROBERT RODRIGUEZ

**El Mariachi** (1993)
Screenplay: Carlos Gallardo and Robert Rodriguez. Director of photography: Robert Rodriguez.
CAST: Carlos Gallardo, Consuelo Gómez, Peter Marquardt, Reinol Martinez.

## NANCY SAVOCA

**True Love** (1989)
Screenplay: Nancy Savoca and Richard Guay. Director of photography: Lisa Rinzler.
CAST: Annabella Sciorra, Ron Eldard, Aida Turturro, Roger Rignack, Star Jasper, Michael J. Wolfe, Kelly Cinnante.

**Dogfight** (1991)
Screenplay: Bob Comfort. Director of photography: Bobby Bukowski.
CAST: River Phoenix, Lili Taylor, Richard Panebianco, Mitchell Whitfield, Anthony Clark, Holly Near, E. G. Daily, Brendan Fraser.

## JOHN SAYLES

**Return of the Secaucus Seven** (1980)
Screenplay: John Sayles. Director of photography: Austin De Besche.
CAST: Bruce MacDonald, Maggie Renzi, Adam Lefevre, Maggie Cousineau, Gordon Clapp, Jean Passanante, Karen Trott, Mark Arnott, David Strathairn, John Sayles, Marisa Smith.

**Lianna** (1983)
Screenplay: John Sayles. Director of photography: Austin De Besche.
CAST: Linda Griffiths, Jane Hallaren, Jon DeVries, Jo Henderson, Jessica Wight MacDonald, Jesse Solomon, Maggie Renzi, John Sayles, Chris Elliott.

**Baby, It's You** (1983)
Screenplay: John Sayles, based on a story by Amy Robinson. Director of photography: Michael Ballhaus.

CAST: Rosanna Arquette, Vincent Spano, Joanna Merlin, Jack Davidson, Nick Ferrari, Dolores Messina, Leora Dana, Sam McMurray, Tracy Pollan, Matthew Modine, Robert Downey, Jr., Fisher Stevens.

### The Brother from Another Planet (1984)
Screenplay: John Sayles. Director of photography: Ernest R. Dickerson.

CAST: Joe Morton, Darryl Edwards, Steve James, Leonard Jackson, Bill Cobbs, David Strathairn, John Sayles, Fisher Stevens, Josh Mostel, Maggie Renzi, Tom Wright, Rosette Le Noire, Ren Woods, Reggie Rock Bythewood.

### Matewan (1987)
Screenplay: John Sayles. Director of photography: Haskell Wexler.

CAST: James Earl Jones, Chris Cooper, Will Oldham, Jace Alexander, Ken Jenkins, Bob Gunton, Gary McCleery, Kevin Tighe, Gordon Clapp, Mary McDonnell, Josh Mostel, Joe Grifasi, Maggie Renzi, David Strathairn, John Sayles.

### Eight Men Out (1988)
Screenplay: John Sayles, based on the book by Eliot Asinof. Director of photography: Robert Richardson.

CAST: John Cusack, Clifton James, Michael Lerner, Christopher Lloyd, John Mahoney, Charlie Sheen, David Strathairn, D. B. Sweeney, Gordon Clapp, Don Harvey, Michael Rooker, Perry Lang, James Read, Bill Irwin, Kevin Tighe, Studs Terkel, John Anderson, Richard Edson, Maggie Renzi, John Sayles.

### City of Hope (1991)
Screenplay: John Sayles. Director of photography: Robert Richardson.

CAST: Vincent Spano, Tony Lo Bianco, Joe Morton, John Sayles, Angela Bassett, David Strathairn, Maggie Renzi, Anthony John Denison, Kevin Tighe, Barbara Williams, Chris Cooper, Jace Alexander, Todd Graff, Frankie Faison, Gloria Foster, Tom Wright, Michael Mantell, Josh Mostel, Joe Grifasi, Rose Gregorio, Louis Zorich, Gina Gershon, Lawrence Tierney, Maeve Kinkead, Bill Raymond, Ray Aranha.

**Passion Fish** (1992)
Screenplay: John Sayles. Director of photography: Roger Deakins.
CAST: Mary McDonnell, Alfre Woodard, David Strathairn, Vondie Curtis-Hall, Angela Bassett, Michael Mantell, Tom Wright, Maggie Renzi, John Henry Redwood, Mary Portser, Nora Dunn, Jennifer Gardner, Sheila Kelley, Shauntisa Willis, John Henry Redwood.

## JOHN SINGLETON

**Boyz N the Hood** (1991)
Screenplay: John Singleton. Director of photography: Charles Mills.
CAST: Larry Fishburne, Ice Cube, Cuba Gooding, Jr., Nia Long, Morris Chestnut, Tyra Ferrell, Angela Bassett, John Singleton, Whitman Mayo, Baha Jackson.

**Poetic Justice** (1993)
Screenplay: John Singleton. Director of photography: Peter Lyons Collister.
CAST: Janet Jackson, Tupac Shakur, Tyra Ferrell, Regina King, Joe Torry, Roger Guenveur Smith, Maya Angelou, Q-Tip, Tone Loc, Miki Howard, Keith Washington, Mikki Val, Dina D., Baha Jackson.

## STEVEN SODERBERGH

**Sex, Lies and Videotape** (1989)
Screenplay: Steven Soderbergh. Director of photography: Walt Lloyd.
CAST: James Spader, Andie MacDowell, Peter Gallagher, Laura San Giacomo, Steven Brill.

**Kafka** (1991)
Screenplay: Lem Dobbs. Director of photography: Walt Lloyd.
CAST: Jeremy Irons, Theresa Russell, Joel Grey, Ian Holm, Jeroen Krabbe, Armin Mueller-Stahl, Alec Guinness.

**King of the Hill** (1993)
Screenplay: Steven Soderbergh, based on the book by A. E. Hotchner. Director of photography: Elliot Davis.
CAST: Jesse Bradford, Jeroen Krabbé, Lisa Eichhorn, Joe Crest, Geraldine Fitzgerald, Spalding Gray, Elizabeth McGovern, Karen Allen, Adrien Brody, Cameron Boyd.


## MICHAEL STEINBERG

**The Waterdance** (1992)
Codirected with Neal Jimenez. See under Jimenez.

**Bodies, Rest & Motion** (1993)
Screenplay: Roger Hedden, based on his play. Director of photography: Bernd Heinl.
CAST: Bridget Fonda, Eric Stoltz, Tim Roth, Phoebe Cates, Scott Johnson, Scott Frederick, Peter Fonda, Sidney Dawson, Jon Proudstar, Amaryllis Borrego, Alicia Witt, Rich Wheeler.

## WHIT STILLMAN

**Metropolitan** (1990)
Screenplay: Whit Stillman. Director of photography: John Thomas.

CAST: Carolyn Farina, Edward Clements, Taylor Nichols, Christopher Eigeman, Allison Rutledge-Parisi, Dylan Hundley, Isabel Gillies, Bryan Leder, Will Kempe, Elizabeth Thompson.

## QUENTIN TARANTINO

**Reservoir Dogs** (1992)
Screenplay: Quentin Tarantino. Director of photography: Andrzej Sekula.

CAST: Harvey Keitel, Tim Roth, Michael Madsen, Chris Penn, Steve Buscemi, Lawrence Tierney, Randy Brooks, Kirk Baltz, Eddie Bunker, Quentin Tarantino, Lawrence Bender, Steven Wright.

## JOHN TURTURRO

**Mac** (1993)
Screenplay: John Turturro and Brandon Cole. Director of photography: Ron Furtunato.

CAST: John Turturro, Michael Badalucco, Carl Capotorto, Katherine Borowitz, Ellen Barkin, John Amos.

## GUS VAN SANT

**Mala Noche** (1985)
Screenplay: Gus Van Sant, from the story by Walt Curtis. Director of photography: John Campbell. Additional photography: Eric Alan Edwards.

CAST: Tim Streeter, Doug Cooeyate, Ray Monge, Nyla McCarthy, Sam Downey, Bob Pitchlynn, Eric Pedersen, Marty Christiansen, Bad George Connor, Don Chambers, Kenny Presler, Walt Curtis, Matt Cooeyate.

**Drugstore Cowboy** (1989)
Screenplay: Gus Van Sant and Daniel Yost, from the novel by James Fogle. Director of photography: Robert Yeoman.
CAST: Matt Dillon, Kelly Lynch, James LeGros, Heather Graham, Max Perlich, James Remar, Beah Richards, William S. Burroughs, Grace Zabriskie, Ray Monge, Doug Cooeyate.

**My Own Private Idaho** (1991)
Screenplay: Gus Van Sant. Directors of photography: Eric Alan Edwards, John Campbell.
CAST: River Phoenix, Keanu Reeves, James Russo, William Richert, Rodney Harvey, Chiara Caselli, Michael Parker, Vana O'Brien, Jessie Thomas, Flea, Tom Troupe, Udo Keir, Sally Curtice, Oliver Kirk, Robert Lee Pitchlynn, Mickey Cottrell, Wade Evans, Matt Ebert, Scott Patrick Green, Ana Cavinato.

## JOSEPH B. VASQUEZ

**Street Story** (1988)
Screenplay: Joseph B. Vasquez. Director of photography: Joseph B. Vasquez.
CAST: Angelo Lopez, Cookie, Lydia Ramirez, Melvin Muza.

**The Bronx War** (1989)
Screenplay: Joseph B. Vasquez. Director of photography: Gordon Minard.
CAST: Fabio Urena, Charmaine Cruz, André Brown, Joseph, Frances Colon, Marlene Forte, Miguel Sierra, Kim West.

**Hangin' with the Homeboys** (1991)
Screenplay: Joseph B. Vasquez. Director of photography: Anghel Decca.
CAST: Doug E. Doug, Mario Joyner, John Leguizamo, Nestor Serrano.

## JOHN WATERS

**Eat Your Makeup** (1968)
Screenplay: John Waters. Director of photography: John Waters.
CAST: Maelcum Soul, David Lochary, Marina Melin, Divine, Mary Vivian Pearce, Mona Montgomery.

**Mondo Trasho** (1969)
Screenplay: John Waters. Director of photography: John Waters.
CAST: Mary Vivian Pearce, Divine, David Lochary, Mink Stole.

**Multiple Maniacs** (1970)
Screenplay: John Waters. Director of photography: John Waters.
CAST: Divine, David Lochary, Mary Vivian Pearce, Mink Stole, Edith Massey.

**Pink Flamingos** (1972)
Screenplay: John Waters. Director of photography: John Waters.
CAST: Divine, David Lochary, Mary Vivian Pearce, Mink Stole, Danny Mills, Edith Massey.

**Female Trouble** (1974)
Screenplay: John Waters. Director of photography: John Waters.

CAST: Divine, David Lochary, Mary Vivian Pearce, Mink Stole, Danny Mills, Edith Massey.

**Desperate Living** (1977)
Screenplay: John Waters. Director of photography: John Waters.
CAST: Liz Renay, Mink Stole, Susan Lowe, Edith Massey, Mary Vivian Pearce, Jean Hill.

**Polyester** (1981)
Screenplay: John Waters. Director of photography: David Insley.
CAST: Divine, Tab Hunter, Edith Massey, Stiv Bators, David Samson, Mary Garlington, Ken King, Mink Stole, Joni-Ruth White.

**Hairspray** (1988)
Screenplay: John Waters. Director of photography: David Insley.
CAST: Sonny Bono, Ruth Brown, Colleen Fitzpatrick, Divine, Michael St. Gerard, Deborah Harry, Ricki Lake, Leslie Ann Powers, Jerry Stiller, Shawn Thompson, Ric Ocasek, Pia Zadora, John Waters.

**Cry-Baby** (1990)
Screenplay: John Waters. Director of photography: David Insley.
CAST: Johnny Depp, Amy Locane, Susan Tyrrell, Iggy Pop, Ricki Lake, Traci Lords, Kim McGuire, Stephen Mailer, Darren Burrows, Polly Bergen, Patricia Hearst, David Nelson, Troy Donahue, Mink Stole, Joe Dallesandro, Joey Heatherton, Willem Dafoe.

# Index

## ABOUT THE AUTHOR

DONALD LYONS is a regular contributor to *Film Comment* magazine. He is also the theatre critic for *The New Criterion* and a contributor to *The American Spectator* and to the book review pages of *The Wall Street Journal*. He has also written for *Commentary*. Mr. Lyons lives in New York City.